Social Work Theories in Action

of related interest

Settlements, Social Change and Community Action
Good Neighbours
Edited by Ruth Gilchrist and Tony Jeffs
ISBN 1 85302 764 2

Learining to Practise Social Work
International Approaches
Edited by Steven M. Shardlow and Mark Doel
ISBN 1 85302 763 4

Spirituality and Social Care
Contributing to Personal and Community Well-being
Edited by Mary Nash and Bruce Stewart
ISBN 1 84310 024 X

Integrating Theory and Practice in Social Work Education
Florence Watson, Helen Burrows and Chris Player
With contributions from Lorraine Agu, Simon Shreeve and Lee Durrant
ISBN 1 85302 981 5

The Child's World
Assessing Children in Need
Edited by Jan Horwath
ISBN 1 85302 957 2

Supporting Parents
Messages from Research
David Quinton
Foreword by the Right Honourable Margaret Hodge, Minister for Children, Young People and Families
ISBN 1 84310 210 2

The Working of Social Work
Edited by Juliet Cheetham and Mansoor A.F. Kazi
ISBN 1 85302 498 8

Social Work Management and Practice
Systems Principles
Second Edition
Andy Bilson and Sue Ross
ISBN 1 85302 388 4

Social Work, Immigration and Asylum
Debates, Dilemmas and Ethical Issues for Social Work and Social Care Practice
Edited by Debra Hayes and Beth Humphries
Foreword by Steve Cohen
ISBN 1 84310 194 7

Handbook of Theory for Practice Teachers in Social Work
Edited by Joyce Lishman
ISBN 1 85302 098 2

Social Work Theories in Action

*Edited by Mary Nash, Robyn Munford
and Kieran O'Donoghue*

Foreword by Jim Ife

Jessica Kingsley Publishers
London and Philadelphia

First published in 2005
by Jessica Kingsley Publishers
116 Pentonville Road
London N1 9JB, UK
and
400 Market Street, Suite 400
Philadelphia, PA 19106, USA

www.jkp.com

Copyright © Jessica Kingsley Publishers 2005
Foreword copyright © Jim Ife 2005

Library of Congress Cataloging in Publication Data
Social work theories in action / edited by Mary Nash, Robyn Munford, and Kieran O'Donoghue ; foreword by Jim Ife.
p. cm.
Includes bibliographical references and index.
ISBN-13: 978-1-84310-249-6 (pbk.)
ISBN-10: 1-84310-249-8 (pbk.)
1. Social service—Australia. 2. Social service—New Zealand. 3. Social work with minorities—Australia. 4. Social work with minorities—New Zealand. I. Nash, Mary, 1946- II. Munford, Robyn. III. O'Donoghue, Kieran.
HV473.S634 2005
361.3'0994—dc22

2004030909

British Library Cataloguing in Publication Data
A CIP catalogue record for this book is available from the British Library

ISBN-13: 978 1 84310 249 6
ISBN-10: 1 84310 249 8

Printed and Bound in Great Britain by
Athenaeum Press, Gateshead, Tyne and Wear

Contents

Dedications and Acknowledgements

To my family, with love, wonder and admiration for who and what you all are.

To those who taught me social work: academics, clients, students and members of the Aotearoa/New Zealand Association of Social Workers. The work of the contributors and the publishing team is also acknowledged with gratitude.

Mary Nash

I dedicate this book to my family, to those who have gone before and who have influenced the way I see the world and to those who are here today and share both the happy and sad times. Thank you to my parents who have shown me what it means to care for others. To my partner, Garth, and to my sons, Matt and Josh, thank you for keeping me real and reminding me to celebrate the many ordinary, but special moments in our busy days. A special thank you goes to Miha who has been in our life for many years and who has taught me about strengths-based practice and never giving up no matter how hard the journey. Thank you to two special colleagues – to Jackie my research partner, thank you for the fun and inspiration. Janet, thanks go to you for the support on a daily level and for making work fun. And to my co-editors – it has been a joy working with you and I look forward to the next project. Thank you.

Robyn Munford

To Rosemary, Richard, Rebekah and Dorothy and in memory of 'Auckland Granddad'.

I wish to acknowledge the work of the contributors and the publishing team.

Kieran O'Donoghue

Foreword

There is no one right way to do social work. That is the clear message after many years of research, theory, conceptualization and debate. For a long time, social work was caught in the trap of the modernist search for certainty, that there must be one right answer, one best way to do it, or one unified grand 'theory of everything'. Different theories would compete with each other for supremacy. The search for this holy grail has now been recognized as futile. Social work is a human activity, about people working with people. Both the people who do the working (the social workers) and the people with whom they work display the human frailties, contradictions, weaknesses and imperfections that are a part of the human condition; they do not fit a single stereotype, and steadfastly refuse to fit neatly into any of the categories that theoreticians, policy makers and managers try to create for them. In this messy, uncertain and contradictory world, social workers will not all be the same, nor will they all work in the same way, and this is both appropriate and necessary. Diversity of approaches among social workers is more likely to lead to a profession that is able to be responsive to a range of people, and a range of problems.

Moving beyond the idea that there is one right way to do social work, however, does not imply that it is a case of 'anything goes'. There is still good practice and bad practice, or more appropriately, good practices and bad practices. Getting away from the need for the one right answer should not be taken as an excuse for the kind of atheoretical practice that can be characterized as 'if it feels good, do it'. Such practice may indeed feel good, and may at the same time do great harm. There remains a need to understand what makes for good practice in any one circumstance, and for any one social worker. There are competing theories, competing claims for how to do 'good' social work, and the ones that really count are based on a mix of good conceptualizing, research, and practice wisdom. There may not be a single 'right' way to do it, but this does not mean there are no right ways at all; rather there are a number of 'right ways', ways that will be right for particular workers, in particular contexts.

Moving away from the binary thinking implied in the term 'competing' theories, we must also note that the existence of more than one theory, set of theories, model or practice framework does not mean that they are necessarily in opposition. While they may emphasize different aspects of knowledge and action, they can also complement and enrich each other. Theories are neither completely independent of each other (as eclecticism might suggest), nor are they fully integrated (this would take us back to the grand 'theory of everything'). Rather, they are somewhere in between, both reinforcing and enriching each other, while at the same time drawing the practitioner in different directions, leading to different questions being asked and different actions initiated.

This dynamic equilibrium among different theoretical perspectives is the domain of this book, through the idea of integrated social work as outlined in the Introduction. The contributors to the book present four different perspectives/theories on social work: ecosystems, community work, strengths-based and attachment theories. These are not the only theories used in social work, but they have all been important in informing social work theory, practice and research in recent years, and are central to social work as it is practised in Aotearoa/New Zealand, Australia, and a number of other countries. It is essential for social workers, in the contemporary context, to have some grounding of each of these four, even though each individual social worker, in constructing their own practice within their own context, will draw differentially from all four, and indeed from other sources as well.

How, then, does a social worker find her/his way among these different theories and approaches? The simple eclectic answer, that 'it depends on the situation', though obviously true, is insufficient. There need to be some criteria for that selection, some underlying principles about the nature and purpose of social work, that will allow a social worker to make appropriate choices in any practice context. There are several such principles that emerge from the different sections of this book, and it is worth identifying them, as they provide some common themes that weave across the perspectives discussed in the various chapters.

One important element is that of reflective practice. Whatever the theory or model, the social worker has a strong responsibility always to engage in critical and informed reflection on the context, the issues, the people involved, and on her/his own practice. Social work practice is never easy; it requires practitioners who are not so sure of themselves that they are supremely confident, but rather practitioners who are always questioning, wondering, seeking alternatives, and engaging in critical evaluation of themselves, their practice, and the practice environment. Critically reflective practice is a key element of all four approaches discussed in this book, and is a common factor in all the practice examples. Critically reflective practice requires that a social worker be aware not only of the immediate circumstances of an individual, family, group or community, but also of the wider social and political context within which they are located. Structures and discourses of disadvantage, dominant ideologies, and political reality all impact on a social worker's practice.

This critical reflection, however, is not undertaken in a neutral, or value-free way. The rejection of one 'right way' to do social work does not imply the rejection of a value base for social work practice. Social workers are not only aware of dominant structures and discourses of disadvantage, but they are motivated to change them to bring about a more just, fair society, in which the people they represent will have adequate opportunities to realize their full potential, and will have their rights protected and respected. Such a value position has been important throughout the history of social work, and has been articulated in different ways – the inherent worth of each person, social justice, equity, and, more recently, human rights. The recent interest in human rights as a grounding for social work practice reflects a wider community interest in the importance of human rights in the contemporary world. From a human rights perspective, social workers play a crucial role in ensuring that the rights of the people with whom they work are both protected and realized, including rights to an adequate income, to housing, to education, to health care, to be treated with dignity and respect, to personal security, to freedom from intimidation, to cultural heritage, and to self-determination. Seeing such entitlements as rights, rather than privileges to be earned or needs to be met, strengthens the claims of the people concerned, and the claims of social workers who are advocating on their behalf. Social workers, in this sense, become human rights workers, and social work can find its moral basis and legitimacy in the various human rights declarations and conventions that now hold an important place in national and international law. Such a commitment to human rights underpins all the chapters in this book. Although social workers may need to puzzle about different theoretical positions and appropriate practice actions, their underlying value position is clear.

Another common theme underlying this book is that of the experience of colonization and the importance of post-colonial understandings of practice, cultural heritage, and diversity. As the experience of the authors is largely located in Aotearoa/New Zealand, it is natural that this should be the post-colonial context within which these issues are explored. The experience of colonization, however, and the oppressive power of colonialism, are not confined to Aotearoa/New Zealand, but are experienced throughout the world. Whenever one person or group seeks to impose their worldview on others, and to devalue the worldview of those others, we find the experience of colonization. This imposition of world-views may take the form of cultural domination as experienced by indigenous peoples in many countries. But colonizing world-views can also be imposed in the name of 'democracy', or of 'development', defined inevitably from within a Western perspective, with often disastrous consequences all too evident in the contemporary world. They can be imposed in the name of religion, they can be imposed through patriarchy, or they can be class-based, where ruling-class or middle-class culture is defined as the norm and working-class culture is devalued. In each case, the message is that 'it is for your own benefit', and if the intended recipients react negatively to this, the response is usually to impose the dominant world-view all the more strongly, if necessary by coercion. Colonization is not confined to history; it is happening today in different forms, and people are suffering as a consequence.

The struggles of indigenous peoples against colonization, and their attempts to challenge the ideology of colonialism, provide valuable lessons for social workers in many different settings, and can be used as a source of wisdom and expertise about other struggles for liberation and genuine self-determination. For this reason it is important that all social workers, in whatever cultural context they are practising, listen to the voices of indigenous people, and learn from their experiences. The chapters in this book reflect a serious and genuine move on the part of indigenous and non-indigenous social workers to dialogue and move forward in developing culturally sensitive, appropriate and affirming forms of practice, which take full account of the experiences of colonization. Social workers in Aotearoa/New Zealand have moved further in this regard than their colleagues in other countries, and as a reader who is not from Aotearoa/New Zealand, to me these discussions have a resonance and an application which moves beyond the specifics of the Maori/Pakeha context, and from which social workers in other cultural contexts have much to learn.

Another theme which is a constant throughout this book is the need for contextual grounding. Social work tends not to work very well when it relies on abstract or universalized theories that take little or no account of the local and which are supposed to apply to all people, everywhere (usually this means they have been developed in a dominant culture and are being imposed on the rest of the world as a form of cultural imperialism). While universalized theories can have some useful things to say, it is essential that social work be adequately grounded in the local experience: local culture(s), local knowledge(s), local practices, local values, local language(s) and local institutions. The acknowledgement and utilization of such 'wisdom from below' is essential to good social work practice and effective outcomes for those whom social work claims to represent. The theories described in this book, if they are to be helpful in social work, must be related to the local context, and must be open to such local wisdom and understanding. If they privilege professional wisdom over the wisdom of the people with whom social workers are working, they will not be in the spirit of social work, which is based on a more dialogical approach. The social worker brings certain understandings and expertise to the domain of practice, but so do the people with whom the worker is working, and neither should be privileged or devalued. Rather, it is from a genuine dialogue that each can learn from the other's wisdom, and the two can then move forward together in a mutual programme of action. The ultimate test of the theories in this book is whether they can be used in this way, not to exclude or marginalize through professional domination, but to empower and to make such dialogical practice a reality. This is the challenge presented to the reader; and each reader will respond in a unique way, shaped by her/his own worldview, personal attributes, skills, understanding and wisdom.

Professor Jim Ife
Centre for Human Rights Education
Curtin University of Technology
Perth, Western Australia

Introduction: Integrating Theory and Practice

Mary Nash, Kieran O'Donoghue, Robyn Munford

An integrated framework for practice situating the practitioner and client in a working relationship at a central point where theory and action meet is the key concept of this book. Integrated practice is a term with a history. It provides social and community workers with a sound holistic practice base. The integrated framework is one in which theory informs social work practice, which then in turn informs theory in a dialogical relationship. Our theoretical 'map' situates social work theory in action within an ecological perspective with community development, strengths-based and attachment theory as explanatory theories and practice models (see Figure 0.1).

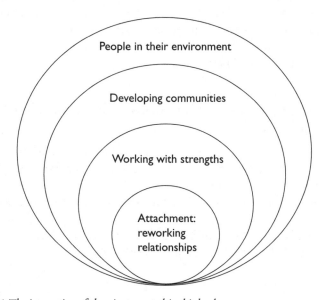

Figure 0.1 The integration of theories presented in this book

This chapter discusses the development of foundational concepts and frameworks in social work, as taught and practised in Aotearoa/New Zealand and Australia where most of the authors of this volume are based and draws connections throughout to international social work practice. It introduces the concept of an integrated framework for practice, as it has been taught and used by practitioners. It concludes with an overview of the book that is designed to critically present four key theoretical approaches currently being used by social and community workers, together with examples of their application in social and community work practice. The four theoretical approaches presented are: ecological systems, community development, strengths-based approaches and attachment theories.

If social work is seen as a process of planned change that requires intervention in the personal, familial and societal spheres of a person's life (Hancock, 1994; Middleman and Goldberg 1974; Reynolds 1942), then it follows that the role of social work practice will change and adapt to meet new needs and take account of new information and approaches to practice. Social work theory is likewise developing and, in our view, being re-worked to take account of emerging ideas as well as state and agency responses to personal and social problems.

There are ever-changing alliances between those with an interest in the social services, namely government ministers with responsibility for welfare-related portfolios, social service agencies, their employees and social work practitioners, professional social service associations and users of the social services and their advocates. Alliances take shape in response to social attitudes and economic opportunities and international influences reflecting the global environment. If one recognizes these factors, it becomes easier to understand the development of professional social work through changes in the provision of social work education, systems of accreditation, practice standards and models of intervention.

International and local influences on development of social work in practice

Students preparing themselves for social work in the twenty-first century will increasingly need a global perspective and should be prepared to widen the horizons of their learning in recognition of our global environment. International influences have always affected the development of social work (Healy 2001), hence the tradition of introducing students to the roles of Charity Organization Societies and the Settlement movement that also illustrate the social control/social change spectrum of social work activity.

International influences

The Charity Organization Societies and the Settlement Houses originated in England in response to poverty, distress and inequality. They were expressions of philanthropy and idealism, and in different ways embodied key aspects of social work.

Charity Organization Societies

The Charity Organization Societies developed in Britain and North America in response to the need to co-ordinate the plethora of philanthropic agencies in the nineteenth century which sprang up in response to the appalling social consequences of the industrial revolution. They sought to rationalize the distribution of charitable resources, both material and human, so that charitable assistance could be distributed scientifically and fairly, according to need, to deserving individuals and families. They worked in accord with the establishment and in enabling agencies to join forces, they were able to monitor who was using their services and why. They also began to provide training for their workers, frequently in association with Settlement Houses.

Mary Richmond, author of *Social Diagnosis* (1917) and *What is Social Case Work?* (1922) was an early influence on the direction of the social work profession. It is interesting to look at her process for defining social casework. She argued that: 'There was real teaching in the world long before there was a science or art of teaching; there was social case work long before social workers began, not so many years ago, to formulate a few of its principles and methods' (1922, p.5). She drew up a framework: 'Insights and Acts'.

- *Insights*

    o   Insights into individuality and personal characteristics.

    o   Insights into the resources, dangers and influence of the social environment.

- *Acts*

    o   Direct action of mind upon mind.

    o   Indirect action through the social environment.

(Richmond 1922, p.101)

Perhaps this schema can be usefully translated into contemporary language as individual and family assessment, recognition of environmental context and its implications for the service user, direct intervention with individuals and families, and social change work, involving community development. This is still the standard range of recognized social work practice, the continuum along which we function. What makes social work identifiable is that it operates on all four levels at once.

The Settlement Movement

The Settlement Movement is situated at the other end of the spectrum from the Charitable Organization Societies. In other words, it sits more comfortably with self-help, political and community action than with specialist casework. A contemporary description of a settlement explains that it was:

> simply a means by which men and women may share themselves with their neighbours; a club house in an industrial district, where condition of membership is the performance of a citizen's duty; a house among the poor, where residents may make friends with the poor. (Gilchrist and Jeffs, 2001 p.10)

The settlement houses were community-based centres that provided resources for working-class people who wanted to further their education. Many had had to leave school early in order to earn their living. Typical courses included the arts and sciences, while the study of social problems and their remedies was also encouraged. Many of those involved in settlement houses such as Toynbee Hall in London, were deeply involved in local government and philanthropy and regularly provided placements for social work students.

What Mary Richmond was to social casework, Mary Ward in England and Jane Addams in America, were to the Settlement Movement (Gilchrist and Jeffs, 2001). Jane Addams visited the oldest settlement house, Toynbee Hall in London, and then founded Hull House in Chicago where they assisted people with employment, and provided courses in music, languages, arts and crafts. Settlement houses were part of the movement for social change to bring about equality and a more just society for all. All countries will have pioneers like Mary Richmond and Jane Addams and we encourage students of social work to find out who were the key players in the social work history of their countries and local contexts.

Early social work courses began with limited resources and students would learn about public health, sociology, philosophy and economics and matters considered relevant such as health, housing, management and social administration. They learned the principles and practice of social casework and they went on to carry out placements in the community and in welfare agencies. As psychoanalytic theory and its implications for casework became recognized in the 1920s, the individual therapeutic aspects of social casework gained acceptance and were assured their place in the schools of social work. At the same time, social reform workers responded to the dire consequences of the Depression years of the 1930s. One can discern a clear progression in the social work curriculum from apprenticeship learning, to scientific and rational instruction followed by a psychoanalytic and bio-psychosocial theories.

By the 1960s, humanist ideas were established and behavioural psychology was gaining ascendance. Later, in the 1970s, there was an international re-emergence of civil rights and community development movements. At the same time, social work responded to the question of effectiveness in practice with the publication of research of brief effective interventions and the development of task-centred practice (Reid 1978; Reid and Epstein 1972). These developments contributed to the conceptualization of the 'scientific practitioner' or 'practitioner-scientist' and the empirical practice stream within social work theory that has subsequently evolved into what is termed evidence-based practice (Fischer 1981; Rein and White 1981; Reid 2002; Rosen 2003).

By the 1980s, task-centred, problem-solving and systems theory were firmly ensconced in the social work curriculum and client-centred social work, empowerment theories and critiques of traditional social work had gained momentum. Community and voluntary agencies provided their own training in group and community work to meet the needs of radical and feminist workers. Action-reflection and conscientization had been recognized as significant for social and community workers, and by the end of the twentieth century social work theory had matured and developed a variety of significant theoretical perspectives. A generalist-eclectic approach (Lehmann and Coady 2001) offers a convincing account of this generic approach, which has the advantage of recognizing the place and value of many social work theoretical approaches and models, to be used as appropriate. Drawing on the latest in social work, the authors present strengths-based, constructivist and solution-focused social work, building on the foundations from which these models have come, and allowing space for the future.

Today, demographic and social change mean that the environment we work in will be different from that in which we were educated and trained (Statham 1994). The social contract has been renegotiated with resultant 'alterations in the balance of responsibilities carried by the state, the family and local communities' (Statham 1994, p.1).

The role of the state is a matter of constant political negotiation, a balancing act between safeguarding or smothering the rights of citizens, encouraging self-reliance without reneging on security and protection for the vulnerable. For some, the state provides the means whereby society can function with co-operation between stakeholders. For others, the state represents the interests of whoever controls the means of production and its role in the preservation of peace in a conflictual arena. Either way, the state in Aotearoa/New Zealand has customarily been seen as responsible for providing, at the very least, a residual welfare system, without which it would be unable to obtain sufficient political consensus for government. The more residual state social services become, the more social work is challenged with regard to its social justice stance and the more pressure may be placed on social work educators to concentrate on teaching technical skills rather than critical and theoretical material.

The Aotearoa/New Zealand context

Since the 1980s, both the recognition and acceptance of the significance of Maori culture and politics for social work practice, and the reorganization of state and community provision for social welfare, have radically changed the course of social work practice and, therefore, education and training for practice in Aotearoa/New Zealand. Fashions and priorities in social work never completely disappear, and they make the study of social work education interesting. We need to be aware of our histories and what they tell us about where we are heading. McCreary listed some key factors that have played their part in the shaping of the social work curriculum, and these are still pertinent today. These include: the role of the universities, which have traditionally had difficulty accommodating a practical subject like social work, the shaping and evolution of the social services, government policies for welfare, the growth of a professional approach to social work together with the formation of the Aotearoa and New Zealand Association of Social Workers (ANZASW), training packages, and changes in Aotearoa/New Zealand society as well as international social changes (1971b, p.43). Social work needs to take into account the challenges that come from within and outside the profession, and the development of social work practice in Aotearoa/New Zealand has been particularly challenged to understand the central role of indigenous frameworks for practice. (A glossary of Maori and Pacific words is provided on p.261.)

Students who anticipate that there will be contradictions and expect to find conflictual relations in the world of social work are believed to be more likely to cope constructively with the fact that what they have learnt about sound social work practice on their courses is challenged by agency protocol, cultures and practices (Harré Hindmarsh 1992). The development of critical reflective analysis highlights the role that power plays in social work. Being prepared for these conflicts enables the practitioner to confront the tensions between social work as a change agent and as an agent of control. For example, Te Tiriti o Waitangi (1840) and Puao-Te-Ata-Tu (1986) are two documents with special significance for New Zealanders. The first is the treaty between tangata whenua (indigenous people of Aotearoa New Zealand) and the English Crown that, in return for the Crown's guarantee of protection of indigenous customary rights and taonga (treasures), gave the Crown governing rights over Aotearoa New Zealand and Maori equal rights as citizens. The second was a government report into racism in the erstwhile Department of Social Welfare; it challenged social workers and Aotearoa New Zealand institutions to examine themselves for institutional, cultural and personal racism. This report caused a paradigm shift in social work thinking in Aotearoa New Zealand, as a result of which our use of theoretical social work material from overseas is now critically interrogated for its cultural relevance and safety. The ANZASW has reorganized itself in order to work in such a way as to honour Te Tiriti O Waitangi and its practice standards reflect this objective. Ruwhiu (2001, p.105) summarizes the effect of these developments when he states that:

> Having a very clear understanding of New Zealand's historical development and the place of Te Tiriti o Waitangi in formatting race relations has gone a long way towards dealing with those concerns expressed, usually by students who are ill-informed, uninformed, or new to the profession and the academic rigours of social work studies and practices.

Furthermore, two Maori women, reflecting on their bicultural practice experience recently observed:

> As Maori practitioners who have worked in mental health we have seen the value and effectiveness of working within the two worlds (Maori and Western). Although the differences are many the goal is wellness and therefore the task and/or challenge is to utilize the tools within Western and Tangata Whenua paradigms that are appropriate for Maori. The challenge for practitioners is to provide appropriate interventions that meet the cultural and clinical needs of Maori. Our beliefs and traditions offer an alternative to Western-based methods, and incorporate cultural practices which are often more familiar and sometimes more accepted by Maori. (Webster and Bosmann-Watene 2003, p.10)

The next section looks at the place of postmodernism and critical approaches in social work theory. This section will also introduce the integrated framework for practice which we see as a useful guiding framework for understanding the nature of social work practice, the phases in relationship building between clients and social workers and the strategies they use to identify how issues can be addressed and changes achieved.

Postmodernism and its influences

Over the last ten years, postmodern ideas have gained currency in social work literature as well as in the social sciences. An entry point for these ideas on social work practice came through solution focused, narrative therapy and strengths-based practice approaches. These practice approaches promote collaboration and partnership between service user and agency and active participation in the process of social work practice.

In social work practice, a modernist practice emphasized the expertise and knowledge of the social worker who would deductively apply a recognized assessment/diagnosis and intervention/treatment theory in their work with clients (Reid 1996; Trotter 1999). Parton and O'Byrne (2000) describe modernism as characterized by its belief in unalterable truth, the pursuit of objective unbiased knowing, the certainty or ability to generalize from knowledge, and the provision of expert status to the holder of the knowledge. Postmodernism, on the other hand, is described as including many perspectives and truths, contextually based knowledge (shaped by the social, cultural, ideological, political and historical setting), subjectivity, and uncertainty. Moreover, it views people as co-creators of knowledge and interpreters of meaning who exercise self-agency (Parton and O'Byrne 2000; O'Donoghue 2003). The starting point in practice from a postmodern position is the particular situation and context within which social work is practised. It is from this location that theorizing occurs and those involved are critical of the positions from which they have interpreted the event.

Another way of describing the approach is that the cloth of practice is cut to fit the setting and the people involved, by the people involved, who are mindful of the influence that their designing perspectives have in framing up the shape of the cloth. With the traditional modernist approach, the people and the setting were fitted into an already cut cloth of a practice theory and model designed from a pre-existing pattern and applied by the practitioner. Essentially, the paradigm shift from modernist practice to postmodern practice is a shift in emphasis from the deductive application of theory to practice in a process of hypothesis generation and confirmation or disconfirmation, to an inductive theorizing in which theory develops from the practice. In other words, it is a shift from applying general approaches to particular situations, to the approach emerging from the dialogue between the persons, situations and context. The differences between the modernist and postmodernist positions are also found in their responses to the question of 'What is social work theory?'

The modernist view argues that theory provides general propositions concerning the real world whose truth can be supported by evidence obtained through scientific method. According to Payne (1997), this approach considers theory to be an objective, general, and valid truth that has been proved by testing to a level of confidence (based on statistical probability). It is also very precise about its use of terms and distinguishes between theory, models and perspectives (Payne 1997).

The postmodern view is more inclusive in its definition of theory, which is not limited to an explanatory function but which also includes models and perspectives as theory. In the postmodern sense, theory is understood as one or more of the following:

- provable explanations as to why something happens (*explanatory theory*)

- organized descriptions of an activity in a structured form (*models*)

- ways of conceptualizing the world or a particular subject (*perspectives*).

This worldview sees theory as a social construction or narrative that is related to circumstance and context (Saleebey 2001). Theory is understood to be embedded within a historical, social, and cultural context that emphasizes particular ideologies, values, beliefs, cultural conventions and worldviews. In recognizing this and taking an inclusive perspective, the postmodern view of theory accepts theoretical pluralism and does not place one theory or a particular group of theories over another. In other words, all knowledge counts. This means that local and culturally specific theories are as valid and significant as empirically tested theories. This valuing of a wide theoretical knowledge base is reinforced in the following statement from commentary on a definition of social work

> Social work bases its methodology on a systematic body of evidence-based knowledge derived from research and practice evaluation, including local and indigenous knowledge specific to its context. It recognises the complexity of interactions between human beings and their environment, and the capacity of people both to be affected by and to alter the multiple influences upon them including bio-psychosocial factors. The social work profession draws on theories of human development and behaviour and social systems to analyse complex situations and to facilitate individual, organisational, social and cultural changes. (International Federation of Social Workers 2000)

In Aotearoa New Zealand, the recognition and valuing of local and indigenous knowledge is evident in the promotion and support of Tangata Whenua theories in the ANZASW Bicultural Code of Practice (1993) and the publication of *Te Komako* issues of *Social Work Review,* authored by Tangata Whenua social workers. Likewise, the local knowledge and theories of people from Pacific Island nations is affirmed in the publication of the *Tu Mau* issue of *Social Work Review,* authored by social workers from Pacific Island nations.

The postmodern definition recognizes that definitions of theory are of our own making, and that in defining theory we are making statements concerning whose knowledge and theory counts. These statements are generally embedded in and representative of a particular historical, cultural and social discourse, which operates from a particular value and assumption base that often gives preference to a dominant discourse. The postmodern definition of theory asserts that all theory stories are equally valid in their own context and promotes theoretical pluralism.

So, if theory is made by us – who are we? And how do we make theory? Briefly, in response to these questions, 'we' are those involved in social work and 'we' make theory through the process of social construction, which means that theories of social work practice are products of the political, social and cultural contexts in which they are developed and used (O'Donoghue 2003; Payne 1997; Rein and White 1981). In all cases, social work theory in practice includes distinct patterns of behaviour, a range of conceptual ideas, and expectations, as well as specific cultural norms derived from the social context. In the postmodern paradigm, social work theory develops from within social work from its reflexive interaction with social work practice (O'Donoghue 2003). Social work theories are also open systems that develop, change, grow and adapt from interaction with both the practice setting and the social context in which practice takes place (Reid 2002; Turner 1996). They are constantly changing in response to practice and current social situations and problems, social work practitioners' and services, interests and concerns, as well as the histories of theoretical traditions, profession and social services. By its very nature, the postmodernist view will argue that social work theory is not universal, rather it is an agreed perspective that is accepted within a social group as a reasonable representation of the terrain that it covers (Payne 1997; Turner 1996).

Introduction to the integrated framework for practice

The integrated framework for practice referred to in this book is a heuristic device intended to assist practitioners to think critically about the knowledge base that informs their knowing, decision-making and action in social and community work practice. It aims to promote informed and intentional social work practice and is a means through which the practitioner can describe, explain, scrutinize, evaluate and justify their assessment of and intervention with clients. The framework orientates practitioners to critically reflect on themselves as social workers whose vision and imagination is influenced by the set of lenses they use to make sense of the situation, problems presented and the social work task. It is through this set of lenses that they develop the interpretive understanding that influences how they perceive, relate to and with the person of the client in the reality of social work practice. In other words, integrated practice provides a frame for organizing and conceptualizing social work practice events, as well as inviting the practitioner to engage in an ongoing process of action-reflection through which they evaluate what informs and influences them as a social worker engaged in practice. It recognizes that there is no standard approach to social work practice and avoids imposing one by accepting that different practitioners begin from varying philosophical positions and, likewise, will choose to emphasize particular theoretical orientations and models (Prasad 1993).

The chapters that follow present a conceptualization of the integrated practice framework that is informed by the perspectives, theories and models presented in each of the four sections. The perspectives, theories and models we have selected are those that have currency in both Aotearoa New Zealand and internationally, and when combined address the multi-levelled nature of social work practice. They also emphasize: a) the reciprocal influence that environment and persons have on each other (ecological systems metaphor); b) a collectivist approach to the analysis of structures, developing network and becoming empowered within a locality (community development); c) a method by which individuals' strengths, capabilities, and resilience may be mobilized and supported by both natural networks and service-based resources (strengths approaches); and d) a map for understanding the significance of relationships, emotions and history and their ongoing influence upon human development, as well as an explanation of how to help clients rework their relationships (attachment theory).

Overview of chapters

The book is divided into four key parts as described below. Each part has a lead chapter that provides an introduction to the theory or framework explored in the following chapters. Each part ends with a chapter that develops the inte-grated framework for practice.

Part I: People in their environments

This part begins with a chapter by Kieran O'Donoghue and Jane Maidment, which provides an overview of the ecological approach to social work practice. It identifies a number of key concepts that provide a foundation for what is to follow in subsequent chapters in this part. The second chapter, written by Christa Fouché, uses an ecological approach to explore social work practice in the context of HIV/Aids. Fouché provides a comprehensive discussion on how global events impact on communities and how social work practice is intri-cately linked to policies and decisions at the micro-level. Carole Adamson, in the third chapter of this section, uses an ecological approach to make sense of the experience of trauma in mental health settings and, as with the other chapters, demonstrates the strong links between the micro and macro levels. The final chapter is in the form of a conversation between Mathew Keen and Kieran O'Donoghue. They continue the theme of mental health, and demon-strate the key elements in using an ecological framework to develop an inte-grated social work approach for mental health settings.

Part II: Developing communities

The second part of the book focuses on community development approaches. In the first chapter, Robyn Munford and Wheturangi Walsh Tapiata present a framework for community development practice and identify a number of key principles. Many of these principles can be seen in practice in the second chapter by Rachael Selby, who looks at a Maori model of community work, based on Ngati Raukawa protocols. Tracie Mafile'o, in the next chapter, takes a particular perspective on community development and shares her story about the way that Tongan community development practice functions. Her discussion has relevance for understanding the challenges faced by cultural groups as they try to mediate dominant discourses and practices. Mary Nash finishes this part with reflections based on recent research, on how community development approaches can be used in supporting migrant populations.

Part III: Working with strengths

The third part of the book moves to focus on a particular way of working in social and community work and develops the ideas around strengths-based approaches. This part begins with a chapter by Robyn Munford and Jackie Sanders, and identifies how this approach has much to offer in work alongside families. Based on research on families and parenting, the authors identify a number of key elements of strengths approaches. The chapter by Rodger Jack focuses on how strengths-based approaches can be used in statutory settings. As with the other chapters in this part fresh insights into the efficacy of strengths approaches are offered. This part concludes with a chapter by Chris Thomas and Sharlene Davis, who have worked together to provide a framework for strengths-based supervision that incorporates the generic and indigenous aspects of strengths approaches.

Part IV: Attachment: reworking relationships

The final part of the book provides a discussion on attachment and reworking relationships. We have included a part on attachment based on current practice and research, because we believe that working through issues of grief, abandonment and lack of attachment remains central to the social work task. This is especially so when we look at the number of troubled youth around the globe and the number of displaced persons. Sue Watson presents the essential concepts of attachment theory and these are developed further by Nicola Atwool who, like Sue, clearly demonstrates how attachment is a central component of successful and healthy relationships. This theme continues in the chapter by Nikki Evans and Marie Connolly. As with the previous two chapters in this part useful insights about how attachment difficulties can be addressed are clearly presented.

The four parts and their chapters have been positioned so as to fit within an ecological framework that informs our thinking in social and community work. We have begun with a macro perspective, and moved to the community level, and then to working with strengths, whether of groups, families or individuals, and finished by placing our thoughts clearly with the experience of individuals and how individuals develop strong and resilient selves.

References

Fischer, J. (1981) 'The social work revolution.' *Social Work 26*, 3, 199–207.

Gilchrist, R. and Jeffs, T. (eds) (2001) *Settlements, Social Change and Community Action.* London, Philadelphia: Jessica Kingsley Publishers.

Hancock, M. (1994) 'A conversation with Merv Hancock.' In R. Munford and M. Nash (eds) *Social Work in Action.* Palmerston North, New Zealand: Dunmore Press.

Harré Hindmarsh, J. (1996) *Social Work Oppositions.* Aldershot: Avebury.

Healy, L. (2001) *International Social Work.* New York, Oxford: Oxford University Press.

International Federation of Social Workers (2000) 'Definition of social work.' http://www.ifsw.org/Publications/4.6.pub.html, accessed 6 October 2001.

Lehmann, P. and Coady, N. (2001) *Theoretical Perspectives for Direct Social Work Practice.* New York: Springer Publishing.

McCreary, J. R. (1971b) 'The school of social science: Part two – the minions.' *The New Zealand Social Worker 7*, 2, 41–50.

Middleman, R. and Goldberg, G. (1974) *Social Service Delivery: A Structural Approach to Social Work Practice.* New York: Columbia University Press.

Ministerial Advisory Committee on a Maori Perspective for the Department of Social Welfare. (1986) *Puao-te-ata-tu.* Wellington: Department of Social Welfare.

New Zealand Association of Social Workers (1993). *Code of Ethics.* Palmerston North: Wandering Quill Communications.

O'Donoghue, K. (2003) *Restorying Social Work Supervision.* Palmerston North: Dunmore Press.

Parton, N. and O'Byrne, J. (2000) *Constructive Social Work: Towards a New Practice.* Basingstoke: MacMillan.

Payne, M. (1997) *Modern Social Work Theory,* 2nd edn. London: Macmillan.

Prasad, R. (ed) (1993) *Book of Readings: 79651 Integrated Practice in Welfare and Development.* Palmerston North: Massey University.

Reid, W. and Epstein, L. (1972) *Task-centered Casework.* New York: Columbia University Press.

Reid, W. (1978) *The Task-centered System.* New York: Columbia University Press.

Reid, W. (1996) 'Task-Centered Social Work.' In F. Turner (ed) *Social Work Treatment,* 4th edn. New York: Free Press.

Reid, W. (2002) 'Knowledge for direct social work practice: An analysis of trends.' *Social Service Review 76*, 1, 6–33.

Rein, M. and White, S. (1981) 'Knowledge for practice.' *Social Service Review 55*, 1, 1–41.

Reynolds, B. (Classic Edition, 1985) *Learning and Teaching in the Practice of Social Work.* National Association of Social Workers. New York: Russell and Russell (1942).

Richmond, M. (1917) *Social Diagnosis.* New York: Russell Sage Foundation.

Richmond, M. (1922) *What is Social Case Work?* New York: Russell Sage Foundation.

Rosen, A. (2003) 'Evidence-based social work practice: Challenges and promise.' *Social Work Research 27*, 4, 197–208.

Ruwhiu, L. (2001) 'Bicultural issues in Aotearoa/New Zealand.' In M. Connolly (ed) *New Zealand Social Work.* Auckland: Oxford University Press.

Saleebey, D. (2001) *Human Behavior and Social Environments: A Biopsychosocial Approach.* New York: Columbia University Press.

Statham, D. (1994) *Social Work Education for Uncertainty. Keynote speech.* Amsterdam: 27th Congress, International Association of Schools of Social Work.

Trotter, C. (1999) *Working with Involuntary Clients.* St Leonards: Allen and Unwin.

Turner, F. (1996) *Social Work Treatment,* 4th edn. New York: Free Press.

Webster, J. and Bosmann-Watene, G. (2003) 'Walking in two worlds: A critique of the diagnostic and statistical manual of mental disorders from a perspective of Te Ao Maori.' *Te Komako, Social Work Review,* 8–11.

Part I

People in their Environments

Introduction

The focus upon the interrelationship between people and their environments has been a distinctive feature of social work since it emerged in the late nineteenth century (Kemp, Whittaker and Tracy 1997). The ecological systems theoretical tradition has, over the past 30 years, become the main theoretical metaphor for understanding context and the relationship between people and their situation. It is the perspectival theory in the integrated practice framework. This part contains four chapters that present an overview to ecological systems theories in action.

It begins with a chapter by Kieran O'Donoghue and Jane Maidment that critically reviews ecological systems theory. This review traces the evolution and development of the ecological systems tradition, outlines the key theoretical concepts, and discusses the strengths and limitations of ecological systems theories in social work in Aotearoa New Zealand and Australia.

The three chapters that follow apply ecological systems theories to specific practice settings, namely HIV practice, trauma and an acute inpatient mental health ward. Christa Fouché's chapter applies ecological systems theory as an analytical framework for conceptualizing HIV practice within the South African context. The argument presented by her multi-level analysis is that an ecological assessment of the HIV situation in South Africa reveals that changes in the South African situation will occur only by altering the environments in which the virus, and the human carriers of this virus, live. The next chapter, written by Carole Adamson, applies an ecological perspective to trauma theory and practice and emphasizes the significance of context in both social workers' and supervisors' responses to traumatic events. The last chapter in this part is presented in the form of a conversation between Mathew Keen and Kieran O'Donoghue on the topic of integrated practice in mental health social work. The areas covered include the authors' views concerning integrated practice and its place in the ecological systems tradition, its application in the inpatient mental health setting and with the indigenous and settler populations living in Aotearoa New Zealand.

Reference

Kemp, S., Whittaker, J. and Tracy, E. (1997) *Person-Environment Practice: The Social Ecology of Interpersonal Helping.* New York: Adeline de Gruyter.

Chapter 1

The Ecological Systems Metaphor in Australasia

Kieran O'Donoghue and Jane Maidment

This chapter provides a critical review of the ecological systems metaphor as understood and utilized in Australasia. This will be achieved through an overview of the evolution and development of the ecological systems tradition, and consideration of its location as a metatheory within social work thought. The guiding concepts of ecological systems theory will also be outlined, together with a critique that pays particular attention to the Aotearoa New Zealand and Australian contexts. This chapter concludes with a summary, which reviews the main points and directs the reader's attention towards the subsequent chapters that demonstrate ecological systems theory in practice.

Introduction

Throughout its history, social work has maintained a dual focus upon both people and their environments (Mattaini and Meyer 2002; O'Donoghue 2003). Ecological systems theory is widely accepted as a metaphor that assists social workers to maintain this dual focus (Greif 1986; Rothery 2001; Wakefield 1996a). It has developed into a theoretical tradition that is predominately described as a perspective or metatheory (Mattaini and Meyer 2002; Rothery 2001). Coady (2001, p.29) describes a metatheory as an abstract theory that is highly explanatory and minimally prescriptive. As a metatheory, ecological systems theory is considered to provide a foundational big picture perspective used in combination with other more specific mid-range theories that give a more specific understanding of human behaviour, as well as techniques that facilitate change (Mattaini and Meyer 2002).

Evolution and development

The evolution of both systems theory and ecological theory in social work has resulted in the development of a significant tradition within the general social work theory and practice literature (Andreae 1996; Mattaini and Meyer 2002; Reid 2002; Rothery 2001; Wakefield 1996b). This tradition includes theories ranging from those which are systems focused, to those that are ecologically based. In between are the theories that unify both ecological and systems theories. This review of the evolution and development of the ecological systems tradition will discuss the development of systems theory first, then ecological theory and will conclude with the ecological systems perspectives, which combine both theories.

Systems theory

The emergence of systems and ecological theory occurred in the 1970s (Gitterman and Germain 1976; Pincus and Minahan 1973; Siporin 1975; Vickery 1974). Social work theoreticians from North America and Great Britain were developing new ways to explain the connections between the personal and environmental aspects of practice, as well as finding a unifying framework of practice for the social work profession (Reid 2002).

Systems theory was promoted as a foundational framework for social work practice. Pincus and Minahan's book (1973), described by Payne (1997, pp.139–141) as being widely used and influential, was one of the early attempts at applying ideas and concepts from systems theory to general social work practice. Their approach included:

1. the recognition of the influence of systems in the life of people

2. the identification of three kinds of systems that contribute to people's wellbeing, namely informal or natural systems (family, friends, neighbours colleagues), formal systems (community organizations, unions, professional associations) and societal systems (government departments, hospitals and schools)

3. the conceptualization of the four basic systems in social work practice (change agent, client, target and action systems)

4. clearly identified stages and methods of systemic practice.

Vickery (1974), in the first British article that applied systems theory to social work practice, developed the application of systems theory with individuals and families by examining the interactions between client-system and environmental-system and the role of input, feedback, transformation and output with regards to change in both systems.

Early conceptualizations of systemic practice were criticized due to the 'level of abstraction, the range of competing perspectives within systems theory and the mechanistic, nonhuman nature of much of its language' (Kemp *et al.* 1997, p.41). A further limitation levelled at general systems theory was its lack of prescription of interventive strategies for the social worker.

Another influence in the development of systems theory was family systems theory, through the family therapy movement (Agass and Preston-Shoot 1990; Andreae 1996; Reid 2002; Wood 1997, 2001). Family theorists adapted systems theory to develop family systems theory, which uses concepts such as circular causality, homeostasis, subsystems, triangulation, structures, and boundaries to explain family functioning (Dallos and Draper 2000; Reid 2002).

Turning to current systems thinking, one finds that the theory continues to evolve and develop. Key areas of development have emerged from the study of cybernetics as well biotechnology. Mattaini and Meyer (2002, p.7) argue that the following ideas reflect the latest developments in systems thinking:

- a shift to viewing networks of transactional relationships, rather than objects, as the basic elements of reality

- the central importance of self-organization in those networks, and

- the crucial place of diversity in those self-organizing systems.

Ecological theory

There are three phases of development in the social work ecological literature. The first identifies concepts from ecology as a metaphor that assists social workers to conceptualize the transactions between the person and their environment (Gitterman 1996a, 1996b; Gitterman and Germain 1976). The second involves the combination of the ecological perspective with systems theory to create a comprehensive, unifying framework or paradigm for social work practice. The third involves the development of a social ecological theory and signals a divergence from systems theory (Ungar 2002). This section will focus on the first and third phases. The second phase will be discussed in the ecological systems section.

When the ecological perspective emerged in the 1970s, it was described as a form of general systems theory that was less abstract and was based upon an 'evolutionary adaptive view of human beings (and all organisms) in continuous transactions with the environment' (Germain 1979, p.7). The perspective used the ecological metaphor as the lens for viewing and conceptualizing the exchanges between people and their environments (Gitterman 1996b). The purpose of the ecological perspective was to help the social worker customize their intervention to the person, the environment or the interaction between the two. In doing this, the aim was to facilitate the restoration of the adaptive balance between persons and environment by reducing stress, enhancing coping mechanisms or establishing stability (Germain and Gitterman 1980; Gitterman 1996b; Gitterman and Germain 1976). Central to the development of the ecological perspective in social work has been the 'Life Model'.

The Life Model aims to improve the 'level of fit between people's perceived needs, capacities, and aspirations and their environmental supports and resources' (Gitterman 1996b, p.395). It utilizes a mutual assessment process involving both practitioner and client and aims to: improve the client's ability to manage life stresses; influence the responsiveness of the social and physical environment to the client; and improve the quality of person and environment interactions and relationships.

The interventive methods and modalities of the Life Model, according to Gitterman (1996b, p.403), emphasize an 'integrated perspective on practice', that is modelled on life, with three phases: initial, ongoing and ending. Gitterman (1996b, p.404) also makes the point that it is 'not prescriptive' and relies on an integration of professional skills with the humanity of the practitioner. Or, in other words, it also depends upon an adaptive balance and level of fit between the person of the practitioner, their professional role as social worker and the environment of social work practice in the society in which they are located.

Before discussing approaches that combine both ecological and systems theory, three recent developments in the field of social ecological theory will be overviewed. The first is that of Kemp et al. (1997, pp.2–3), whose person–envinonment practice (PEP) is an emergent social ecological model of interpersonal helping that is time limited and aims to achieve the following:

1. an improvement in the client's sense of mastery in managing stressful life situations, environmental challenges, and utilization of environmental resources

2. an active multidimensional (involving the perceived, physical, social/interactional, institutional/organizational, social/political/cultural dimensions) assessment, engagement and intervention in the environment, with particular emphasis on the mobilization of the personal social network

3. the linking of individual concerns in ways that promote social empowerment though collective action.

The second development is Besthorn's (2001) 'Deep-Ecological Social Work', which challenges social workers to recover the elements of spirituality and the natural environment and incorporate them into a deep-ecological social work practice that that is attuned to both spirituality and nature. There are two main dimensions to Besthorn's (2001) deep-ecology: the first is ecological awareness, the second, political involvement in ecological issues. The third development is Ungar's (2002, pp.484–97) proposal of a new ecology based on the adoption of the following eight principles as a means of deconstructing 'the relative power of competing discourses among privileged professional service providers and the marginalized groups they serve' (p.493):

1. the intrinsic value of individuals

2. diversity and diverse solutions

3. structured alliances between communities and service

4. management by community stakeholders not bureaucracies

5. divestment of resources to the communities being served

6. public policy that expands communities' capacity and sustains members' functioning and wellbeing

7. enlightened social and economic development based on benchmarking what is good for individuals and communities

8. an ethical obligation to foster change.

This new ecology appears to mark an attempt to progress the ecological perspective through integration with feminist, critical and postmodern practice discourses.

These three recent developments appear to remain at the edge of the ecological systems tradition, with the core of ecological systems paradigm being occupied by approaches that unify ecological and systems theories.

Ecological systems theory

The synthesis or merging of ecological and systems theory emerged from two pathways. The first was in response to the criticisms of systems theory. The second, was the pursuit of a unifying conceptual framework for practice. In this part, Siporin's (1975) and Bronfenbrenner's (1979) ecological systems theories will be discussed as examples of theories that add ecology to a systems theory base. Following this, Meyer's (1983) ecosystems theory will be reviewed as an example of both the combination of ecological and systems theory, as well as an attempt to provide a unifying conceptual theory for social work practice.

Siporin (1975), in adding ecological theory to systems theory, recognized that, despite their 'separate histories and distinctive features', general systems, social systems and ecological theories had sufficient commonalties to be used together under the title of 'ecological-systems theory' (Siporin 1975, p.107). Moreover, in his situational analysis and situational intervention he considered both the micro and macro-systems (Siporin 1975, p.123).

Our second example is Bronfenbrenner's (1979) ecological theory of human development, which held that the interaction between the developing person and the environment was pivotal and recognized that the developing person was an active participant who changes, restructures, and finds a mutual accommodation with their environment. In this theory, the environment involved a variety of settings with a range of interconnections that extended from the direct setting to larger social settings. For Bronfenbrenner (1979) the ecology of human development was based in a concentric arrangement of systems, which he categorized as the microsystem, mesosystem, exosystem and macrosystem. The microsystem is the smallest and most direct system that a person directly experiences (e.g. household, classroom or office). The links between two or more microsystems (e.g. the links between home and school or home and work) are described as the mesosystem. The stronger and more diverse the links are between microsystems, the greater positive influence the mesosystem has upon the developing person. Forces external to the developing person are accounted for by the concept of the exosystem, which involves one or more settings that do not involve the developing person as a direct partici-pant, but nonetheless have influence upon the developing person (e.g. a spouse's workplace or a sibling's school). The macrosystem encapsulates the wider social policy and socio-cultural setting and includes the ideological, cus-tomary and legal norms. It influences all the other levels of the environment. According to Garbarino (1982), there are socio-cultural risks and opportuni-ties present at each of the four levels. By risk, he means a threat posed by the way the world beyond the developing person is organized, which may have a negative influence on their development (e.g. parents using and dealing drugs in the home). On the other hand, he describes the concept of opportunity as a person–environment interaction that aligns with the needs and abilities of the developing person (e.g. the child of the parents described previously, being supported by a sports coach to trial for a representative or professional team).

Meyer's (1979, 1983) ecosystems perspective, which emerged out of a search for a coherent unifying theory for social work, rather than an attempt to enrich systems theory is our third example (Greif 1986; Kemp *et al.* 1997; Mattaini and Meyer 2002; Meyer 1979, 1983; Wakefield 1996a, 1996b). This perspective was developed to enable casework to be conceptualized in a way that balanced the relationship between persons and environments. It joins both ecological and systems concepts without a hierarchy between the two and applies both sets of ideas to the casework situation. In doing this, the ecosys-tems perspective has claimed the ecomap as its pictorial tool that facilitates its application in practice (Hartman 1978; Mattaini and Meyer 2002). As a per-spective, the ecosystems framework is purely explanatory and does not pre-scribe how and where to intervene, rather, it provides guidance in regard to what to look at when assessing a case (Mattaini and Meyer 2002). It provides a foundation for eclectic practice through its accommodation of models of practice and specific therapies (Rothery 2001).

Local Literature in Australasia

During the past three decades ecological systems theories in their various forms have become widespread and influential in Western social work practice (Reid 2002; Rothery 2001). Locally, in Aotearoa/New Zealand and Australia, there is a small literature base that describes the use and influence of this theory. In Aotearoa/New Zealand, Bronfenbrenner's (1979) ecological systems theory appears to be the most widely recorded (Adamson 1999; 2001a, 2001b; Ellis 1994; Prasad 1986, 1988). This can be attributed to the influence and development of the 'integrated practice framework' taught on the social work programme at Massey University (Keen 2001; pp.40–44). This framework is predicated upon Bronfenbrenner's ecological systems theory, which is used as the foundation for the multi-level analysis phase (Prasad 1986, 1988, 1993). Recently, Adamson (1999, 2001a, 2001b) has applied Bronfenbrenner's (1979) ecological systems theory in the fields of trauma, supervision and evidence-based practice in mental health. A range of examples of other Aotearoa/New Zealand literature which sits within the ecological systems tradition was located by the authors; this list includes:

- Amor (2002) and Jaquiery *et al.*'s (2002) references to ecological theory as part of their reflections on their personal practice theory in their respective fields of Maori mental health and social work in schools

- Ellis (1994), which is concerned with social work in voluntary welfare agencies

- McKenzie-Bridle's (1997) application of an ecological model of human development in the setting of child, youth and family

- O'Donoghue's (2003, p.92–108) reliance upon the 'persons and their environments' paradigm of social work practice as one of the foundations for his contextual framework for social work supervision, and

- Sarjeant's (2002, p.168) reference to her use of 'an ecological chart' in her reflection upon her practice in a Christian child and family support service.

With regard to the Australian social work literature, we searched the *Australian Social Work* journal from 1978 to 2002, as well as a number of recent social work texts (Elliott *et al.* 2000; Fook 1993, 2002; Ife 1995, 1996, 2001; O'Connor *et al.* 1998; Pease and Fook 1999; Trotter 1999). The journal search located only two articles that had a specific reference to the ecological systems theory tradition. The first article, that of Grinnell *et al.* (1982), was concerned with environmental modification, identifies that this subject has received little attention and also argues for environmental modification to be a core practice activity through reference to ecological theory. The second article, Wood (1997), makes a passing comment that the ecosystem perspective has been 'popular among social work schools in Australia since the early 1980s' (Wood 1997, p.4). The search of recent Australian social work texts revealed that the social work theoretical perspectives emphasized were community development, critical and postmodern theories, and problem-solving approaches (Elliott *et al.* 2000; Fook 1993, 2002; Ife 1995, 1996; 2001; O'Connor, *et al.* 1998; Pease and Fook 1999; Trotter 1999). From the local literature reviewed, it appears that the conceptualization and use of the ecological systems metaphor in Australasia has been shaped by its Western origins. The development and adaptations made to the ecological systems tradition as a result of its engagement with the indigenous and settler cultures of both Aotearoa/New Zealand and Australia appears to be at an emergent stage.

Key ecological systems concepts

In this section, key ecological and systems theory concepts will be outlined. The ecological concepts of level of fit and the environment will be discussed first, followed by a brief overview of the systems theory concepts of reciprocal influence, circularity, structure and unpredictability. The concept of the ecomap will also be discussed through reference to an illustrative case study.

Ecological concepts

Ecology is described as concerned with the interrelationship and adaptation of organisms with each other and with their surroundings, be they organic or inorganic (Mattaini and Meyer 2002; Ungar 2002). Central to this interrelationship and adaptation is the concept of *level of fit*, which concerns the degree of balance and reciprocity between the person's needs, capacities and aspirations and the resources and expectations accessible and available in their environment (Gitterman 1996a). According to Gitterman (1996b), when the degree of balance and reciprocity between these two aspects is positive, the *level of fit* achieves the condition of *adaptedness*, in which the exchanges or interactions between them is likely to facilitate the actualization of both human and environmental development. However, when the personal and environmental exchanges are not positive they are described as *dysfunctional* and have the potential to inhibit, frustrate, damage and oppress both human and environmental potential (Gitterman 1996b). When people perceive an imbalance between the demands of their environment and their ability to mobilize resources to manage such demands, the result is stress. According to Gitterman (1996b, p.391), stress can only be relieved by improving: a) the level of person and environment fit through change in the person's perception or behaviour, or b) the environment's response to the person, or c) the quality of exchanges between both person and environment.

The second key ecological concept is that of the *environment*. The environment is a multidimensional entity, which contains physical, social and cultural aspects (Germain 1979; Kemp *et al.* 1997). It contains dynamic and interactive features that are mediated through place, time and space, as well as human beings' perceptions, structures, relationships and meaning-making activities. According to Kemp *et al.* (1997, p.85), the levels of the environment include the following:

- the perceived environment, that is, the environment as constructed in individual and collective systems of meaning and belief

- the physical environment, both natural and built

- the social/interactional environment, comprised largely of human relationships at various levels of intimacy, and including family, group and neighbourhood networks and collectivities

- the institutional and organizational environment

- the cultural and socio-political environment.

The ecological concepts of *habitat* and *niche* are important terms for understanding the impact of the environment on people. A person's habitat is the location where a person is found and will involve all of the levels of the environment described above, but particularized to their locale. A person's niche, on the other hand, involves the person's place and status within the habitat. According to Rapp (1998), a niche can be either entrapping or enabling. An entrapping niche is one in which people are marginalized, with minimal available resources or support and little prospect of social mobility and/or belonging. An enabling niche is the opposite of an entrapping niche and is one that provides resources and support that enable social mobility, social belonging and social connectivity (Rapp 1998).

Systems concepts

As mentioned above, the systems concepts of reciprocal influence, circular causality, structure and unpredictability will be briefly outlined in this section. The first concept, reciprocal influence, refers to the idea that all parts of a system share an influence upon each other. A fairly common example of reciprocal influence comes to our attention when people leave a system (e.g. Sue's leaving Matt in our case study below reciprocally influences relationships and functioning across the various systems). The second concept is circular causality, which sees an effect or outcome influencing its own cause (Ridley 2003). This differs from linear causality in which an effect or outcome is caused by something specific. An illustration of the difference between circular and linear causality can be drawn from our case study below, where an example of linear causality would be to argue that Matt has a situational depression caused solely by the ending of his relationship with Sue. Whereas, if we considered Matt's mood state using circular causality, we may see it as both influencing and being influenced by the following:

- the situation of his unemployment

- the stresses encountered with Centrelink concerning his benefit and financial situation

- his relationships with Sue and other family members

- the stresses of becoming a new parent and involvement with the Department of Human Services.

Structure is our third key concept and involves the system's patterns of organization, which guide and maintain its functioning. Within each system there are subsystems, and every individual system is also part of a bigger system or suprasystem (Agass and Preston-Shoot 1990). Individual systems and subsystems are differentiated by *boundaries*, non-physical dividers that separate one system from another. Boundaries vary in type and in the amount of information they receive and transmit. Generally, problems occur in systems when the boundaries are either too open or too closed and the structure is either too rigid or too flexible (Rothery 2001). *Unpredictability* is our fourth key systems theory concept and this is based upon the circular and reciprocal nature of systems in which everything effects everything else in a system. The terms *equifinality* and *multifinality* describe the nature of this unpredictability well. Equifinality means that similar or the same ends are achieved from different starting points, whereas multifinality means that similar or the same starting points result in multiple and differing outcomes. What these terms and the concept of unpredictability reveal is that the system's response to the social worker's intervention influences the outcome, and because of the complex nature of systems and (human persons) they do not act predictably (Rothery 2001).

The ecomap

The ecomap, developed by Hartman (1978), is the most commonly used and longstanding visual tool used by social workers to find their way through the complexity of person and environment information. It is a diagrammatic illustration of where the client locates him- or herself in relation to the surrounding systems, and shows the nature of those relationships using a legend of symbols denoting differing types of connections between the systems. Drawing an ecomap can be a useful way for the practitioner and client together to gain an appreciation of where the major stressors and supports exist in the client's life. It is possible to condense a great range of complex information succinctly in diagrammatic form. In this way, developing an ecomap can be used as part of the assessment process, to be referred back to over time, reviewed, and used as a means for evaluating ongoing relationships, social supports, stressors, and changes in the level of fit between the client and their environment. Once clients have become accustomed to illustrating relationships using ecomaps, it is not uncommon for them to invent their own signs, images and symbols to describe these, which serves further to personalize and enrich the depth of information conveyed in these diagrams. Figure 1.1 shows an eco-map for the brief case study outlined below.

> Matt (19) comes to the community mental health team for assessment, having been referred by his GP. In the referral letter, the GP notes that Matt has just recently returned to live with his parents after breaking up with his girlfriend, Sue (17). Together, Matt and Sue have a daughter, Zoe, who is just a few months old.

Near the end of the first discussion with Matt, the practitioner begins to draw an ecomap of people and institutions that currently impact on Matt's life (see Figure 1.1).

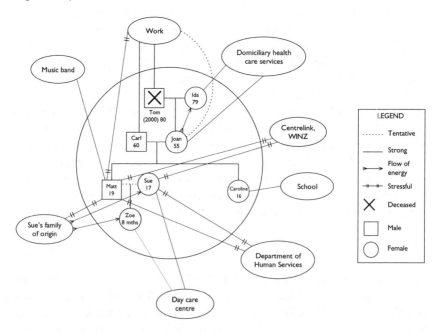

Figure 1.1 Ecomap of Matt's current life

In the centre of the ecomap is a small genogram of Matt's immediate family. Both of Matt's parents, Carl and Joan, work in paid employment. Carl enjoys his work and does not see himself retiring for some time. Joan works 'on call' at a hospital canteen, work she has done for a long time. She does not particularly enjoy the job, but continues to help 'save for retirement'. Joan's mother, Ida, has moderate dementia, and although she still lives at home, needs a lot of input from Joan and community services. Both Joan and Carl have a strong work ethic and are displeased that Matt has just lost his job due to a prank at work that compromised health and safety regulations. Matt has broken up with his partner, Sue, during the last month. He has a poor relationship with Sue's parents, and now has infrequent contact with his daughter, Zoe. Both Matt and Sue have had conflicted contact with Centrelink (Work and Income [WINZ] or Social Security Department), with disputes over benefit eligibility. They have also had some difficult contact with the Department of Human Services (Department of Child, Youth and Family or Department of Child Protective Services) when a neighbour reported a dispute at their flat shortly after the birth of Zoe. During this contact, the worker from the Department organized for Zoe to attend day care a couple of times a week. Sue has now established some good links with the staff at the centre.

From the discussion and development of the ecomap with Matt it becomes clear that his only really supportive and positive relationships at the moment are connected with the band he plays in on Friday and Saturday nights. He feels his parents favour his sister, whom he describes as 'goody two-shoes' and who excels at school work. He misses Sue and Zoe, has a sense of failure about losing his job, is angry with his father for 'going on' about work, and has little to do with his mother who is juggling the care of Ida (her mother) with her own part-time work. The ecomap provides Matt and the social worker with some clues about where to begin with intervention.

Critique of ecological systems approach

The following section provides a critique of an ecological systems approach contextualized within an Aotearoa/New Zealand and Australian locale. This critique will pay particular attention to a range of defining features that greatly influence the person-in-environment transactions, some of which these two countries share, and others that are unique to each country.

Mixed perceptions of an ecosystemic paradigm

One of the major strengths of using an ecological systems perspective to understand client issues is that it incorporates an analysis of both formal and informal networks around the client, including relationships with individuals, groups, family, community and the environment as a whole. In this way, it is a perspective that can help the worker and client gain an appreciation of the multiple factors that contribute to, or inhibit client wellbeing. The examination of boundaries between the client system and others enables a fluid interpretation in terms of what constitutes healthy relationships and boundary setting within differing cultural contexts.

On a more contentious note, the degree to which an ecological systems approach does or does not acknowledge the notions of power, oppression and marginalization is the subject of enduring debate (Ungar 2002; Greif 2003). Since both Australia and New Zealand share a history punctuated by indigenous dispossession and alienation from the land, compromised indigenous human rights, and poor statistics for wellbeing amongst indigenous populations, questions of authority and self-determination are important. Early users of systems theory focused on the notions of relationship, 'goodness of fit' and successful *adaptation* of the individual within the environment (Ungar 2002). These early interpretations of systems and an ecological perspective have been criticised for being dominated by a narrow focus on psycho-social imperatives. However, more recent applications of these ideas have emphasized the integral connectedness between client spirituality and notions of wellbeing, acknowledging economic and political determinants (Anglem and Maidment 2004). In this way, emerging models of practice derived from an ecological systems analysis overtly recognize the unique and differing cultural interpretations of how the person-in-environment transactions might justifiably occur.

Further evidence of this evolving politicization of ecological systems analysis can be found in literature in which the notion of 'environment' is redefined in ways that explicitly acknowledge the social, political and economic determinants of powerlessness in individual daily living arrangements and institutional structures (Woo Sik Chung and Pardeck 1997). Thus, while the perspective can be interpreted as being apolitical, in that it does not specifically promote a particular ideological position to address structural change, it includes a framework that can be used to identify where change processes at micro, meso and macro levels of intervention need to occur.

For indigenous populations in both countries the relationship with the natural environment is powerfully linked to questions of personal identity, spiritual strength and ongoing survival (Hunter 2000; Patterson 1999; Ruwhiu 2001). An ecological systems understanding of functioning, which integrates environmental perspectives, is therefore particularly relevant for work with these populations. Nevertheless, it is an approach that has also been criticized as being hard to test empirically, and overly inclusive (Payne 1997; Wakefield 1996a, 1996b). Both of these 'limitations', however, come from a non-indigenous position. This position privileges positivist inquiry, fails to acknowledge the importance of broad kinship networks, and overlooks the integral relationship indigenous populations have with the land and other natural habitats such as flora, fauna and the waterways.

The ecological systems framework has been further criticized for providing no guidance to practitioners in terms of suggesting what methods to use, or when and how to intervene with the client-system (Mancoske, cited in Payne 1998; Wakefield 1996a). This is a fair criticism, as it is not a prescriptive model of practice, and as such does not provide a concise 'recipe' for client intervention in the way that task-centred social work or brief solution-focused therapy does so well. Nevertheless, it is a perspective that can be used by practitioners and clients to analyze and understand the complex network of relationships and systems that influence the client's world. In this way, the framework provides the means to trace and map the major sources of client tension and support, using visual cues such as the ecomap. This process promotes joint client and worker understanding of the issues at hand, and assists with the engagement and rapport building so necessary in the initial stages of contact.

One of the more unique features of an ecological systems perspective is that it can illustrate and take account of the non linear passage of time and interactions between different parts of the system in a way that other perspectives do not. This is particularly important in relation to working with indigenous communities, where temporal considerations cannot be limited to a linear understanding based on the notion of cause and effect. In the *Dreaming*, 'from any particular point in time, the past may be the future and the future may be the present. Time does not extend back through a series of pasts' (Hume 2003, p.38).

As outlined above, an ecological systems approach to working with clients has both its strengths and weaknesses. In selecting what theoretical principles to use to guide practice, the important considerations for the worker must centre on how the client might best be able to move forward in a positive direction, the nature of the presenting issues, and what framework might address these in the most constructive way. An ecological systems analysis can be used on its own, or in conjunction with other perspectives to inform this process.

Conclusion

The ecological systems metaphor is used in Australasia to conceptualize the relationship and interactions between persons and their environments and as metatheory for social work practice. It usage reflects its northern hemisphere origins and 30 years of evolution and development into a theoretical tradition, which spans approaches that emphasize the systems dimensions and those that emphasize the ecological dimensions. Sitting between these two dimensions are approaches that synthesize both in a non-hierarchical manner. There is an emergent ecological systems literature in Australasia, which appears to reflect a limited engagement between this theoretical tradition and indigenous andsettler cultures. This is, arguably, reflective of the ongoing challenge both countries face as they attempt to move beyond the colonizing discourse (O'Donoghue 2003). The strengths of this perspective are its capacity to assist practitioners to assess the interactions between clients and their environment and its use as an organizing framework in the development of personal practice theories. In the chapters that follow, the application of the ecological systems theories will be discussed in the areas of HIV practice, trauma and acute mental health.

Questions for reflection

1. What are key features of the ecological systems theory?

2. In what ways do you believe the development of the ecological systems approach has or has not reflected the changing socio-political norms over the last three decades?

3. An ecological systems approach has been criticized for not overtly addressing issues of dominance, power and oppression in practice. How might you use it to address these factors in your own work?

4. Consider how you might apply an ecological systems metaphor to guide a research process. What would the implications be in terms of the research design, methodology and process of conducting the research with stakeholders?

References

Adamson, C. (1999) 'Towards a social work knowledge base for traumatic events.' *Social Work Review XI*, 1, 29–34.

Adamson, C. (2001a) 'The role of supervision in the management of critical incidents and traumatic events.' In L. Beddoe and J. Worrall (eds) *Supervision Conference: From Rhetoric to Reality. Keynote Address and Selected Papers*, Auckland: Auckland College of Education.

Adamson, C. (2001b) 'Social work and the call for evidence-based practice in mental health: Where do we stand?' *Social Work Review XIII*, 2, 8–12.

Agass, D. and Preston-Shoot, M. (1990) 'Defining the theory: A systems approach.', In D. Agass and M. Preston-Shoot (eds) *Making Sense of Social Work*. London: MacMillan.

Amor, V. (2002) 'Reflections on working in a Kaupapa Maori mental health service.' In R. Truell and L. Nowland (eds) *Reflections on Current Social Work Practice*. Palmerston North: Dunmore Press.

Andreae, D. (1996) 'Systems theory and social work treatment.' In F. Turner (ed) *Social Work Treatment*, 4th edn. New York: Free Press.

Anglem, J. and Maidment, J. (2004) 'Introduction to assessment.' In J. Maidment and R. Egan (eds) *Practice Skills in Social Work and Welfare*. Allen and Unwin: Sydney.

Besthorn, F. (2001) 'Towards a deep-ecological social work: Its environment, spiritual and political dimensions'. http://www.washburn.edu/ecosocialwork/prspctvs.html [accessed 7 October 2001].

Bronfenbrenner, U. (1979) *The Ecology of Human Development Experiments by Nature and Design*. Cambridge, Mass: Harvard University Press.

Coady, N. (2001) 'An overview of theory for direct practice and an artistic, intuitive-inductive approach to practice.' In P. Lehmann and N. Coady (eds) *Theoretical Perspectives for Direct Social Work Practice: A Generalist-Eclectic Approach*. New York: Springer Publishing.

Dallos, R. and Draper, R. (2000) *An Introduction to Family Therapy: Systemic Theory and Practice*. Buckingham: Open University Press.

Elliott, B., Mulroney, L. and O'Neil, D. (2000) *Promoting Family Change: The Optimism Factor*. St. Leonards, N.S.W: Allen and Unwin.

Ellis, G. (1994) 'Social work in voluntary welfare agencies.' In R. Munford and M. Nash (eds) *Social Work in Action*. Palmerston North: Dunmore Press.

Fook, J. (1993) *Radical Casework: A Theory of Practice*. North Sydney: Allen and Unwin.

Fook, J. (2002) *Social Work: Critical Theory and Practice*. London: Sage.

Garbarino, J. (1992) *Children and Families in the Social Environment*, 2nd edn. New York: Aldine De Gruyter.

Germain, C. (1979) 'Introduction: ecology and social Work.' In C. Germain (ed) *Social Work Practice: People and Environments*. New York: Columbia University Press.

Germain, C. and Gitterman, A. (1980) *The Life Model of Social Work Practice*. New York: Columbia University Press.

Gitterman, A. and Germain, C. (1976) 'Social work practice: A life model.' *Social Service Review 50*, December, 601–610.

Gitterman, A. (1996a) 'Ecological perspective: Response to Jerry Wakefield.' *Social Service Review 70*, 3, 472–476.

Gitterman, A. (1996b) 'Life model theory and social work treatment.' In F. Turner (ed) *Social Work Treatment*, 4th edn. New York: Free Press.

Greif, G. (1986) 'The ecosystems perspective "Meets the Press".' *Social Work 31*, 3, 225–226.

Greif, G. (2003) 'In response to Michael Ungar's "A deeper, more social ecological social work practice" debate with Authors.' *Social Service Review 77*, 2, 306–311.

Grinnell, R., Bostwick, G. and Kyte, N. (1982) 'Modifying the environment.' *Australian Social Work 35*, 4, 11–14.

Hartman, A. (1978) 'Diagrammatic assessment of family relationships.' *Social Casework 59*, 465–476.

Hume, L. (2003) *Ancestral Power. The Dreaming, Consciousness and Aboriginal Australians*. Melbourne: Melbourne University Press.

Hunter, B. (2000) 'Looking after country – the ACF indigenous Program takes shape.' *Habitat Australia 28*, 4, 23.

Ife, J. (1995) *Community Development: Creating Community Alternatives – Vision, Analysis and Practice*. Melbourne: Longman.

Ife, J. (1996) *Rethinking Social Work: Towards Critical Thinking*. Melbourne: Longman.

Ife, J. (2001) *Human Rights and Social Work: Towards Rights-based Practice*. Melbourne: Cambridge University Press.

Jaquiery, N., Baskerville, M. and Selby, R. (2002) 'Social work in schools (SWIS).' In R. Truell and L. Nowland (eds) *Reflections on Current Social Work Practice*. Palmerston North: Dunmore Press.

Keen, B. (2001) '"Queer Practice" A consideration of some psychiatric/mental health social work practitioners' constructions of gay male sexualities.' Palmerston North: Massey University.

Kemp, S, Whittaker, J. and Tracy, E. (1997) *Person-Environment Practice: The Social Ecology of Interpersonal Helping*. New York: Adeline de Gruyter.

Mattaini, M. and Meyer, C. (2002) 'The ecosystems perspective: Implications for practice.' In M. Mattaini, C. Lowery and C. Meyer (eds) *The Foundations of Social Work Practice*, 3rd edn. Washington DC: NASW Press.

McKenzie-Bridle, P. (1997) 'Another way of seeing.' *Social Work Now 7*, August 1997, 21–24.

Meyer, C. (1979) 'What directions for direct practice?' *Social Work 24*, July 1979, 267–272.

Meyer, C. (ed) (1983) *Clinical Social Work in the Eco-systems Perspective*. New York: Columbia University Press.

O'Connor, I., Wilson, J. and Setterlund, D. (1998) *Social Work and Welfare Practice*, 3rd edn. Melbourne: Longman.

O'Donoghue, K. (2003) *Restorying Social Work Supervision*. Palmerston North: Dunmore Press.

Patterson, J. (1999) 'Respecting nature: the Maori way.' *The Ecologist 29*, 1, 33–39.

Payne, M. (1997) *Modern Social Work Theory*, 2nd edn. London: Macmillan.

Pease, B. and Fook, J. (eds) (1999) *Transforming Social Work Practice: Postmodern Critical Perspectives*. St Leonards, NSW: Allen and Unwin.

Pincus, A. and Minahan A. (1973) *Social Work Practice: Model and Method*. Illinois: Peacock.

Prasad, R. (1986) *Transitions in Foster Care – The Development of Training Programs for Foster Care Workers*. Palmerston North: Massey University.

Prasad, R. (1988) *Towards A Theoretical Framework in Foster Care: A Framework for the Management of and Research into Transitions in Foster Care*. King George, Virgina: American Foster Care Resources.

Prasad, R. (ed) (1993) *Book of Readings: 79651 Integrated Practice in Welfare and Development*. Palmerston North: Massey University.

Rapp, C. (1998) *The Strengths Model: Case Management with People Suffering from Severe and Persistent Mental Illness*. New York: Oxford University Press.

Reid, W. (2002) 'Knowledge for direct social work practice: An analysis of trends.' *Social Service Review 76*, 1, 6–33.

Ridley, M. (2003) *Nature via Nurture: Genes, Experience and What Makes Us Human*. London: Fourth Estate.

Rothery, M. (2001) 'Ecological systems theory.' In P. Lehmann and N. Coady (eds) *Theoretical Perspectives for Direct Social Work Practice: A Generalist-Eclectic Approach*. New York: Springer Publishing.

Ruwhiu, L. (2001) 'Bicultural issues in Aotearoa/New Zealand.' In M. Connolly (ed) *New Zealand Social Work*. Auckland: Oxford University Press.

Saleebey, D. (1992) 'Biology's challenge to social work: Embodying the person-in environment perspective. *Social Work 37*, 2, 112–118.

Sarjeant, V. (2002) 'Social work in a Christian context.' In R. Truell and L. Nowland (eds) *Reflections on Current Social Work Practice*. Palmerston North: Dunmore Press.

Siporin, M. (1975) *Introduction to Social Work Practice*. New York: MacMillan.

Trotter, C. (1999) *Working with Involuntary Clients*. St Leonards, NSW: Allen and Unwin.

Ungar, M. (2002) 'A deeper, more social, ecological social work practice.' *Social Service Review 76*, 3, 480–97.

Vickery. A. (1974) 'A systems approach to social work intervention: Its uses for work with individuals and families.' *British Journal of Social Work, 4*, 4, 389–404.

Wakefield, J. (1996a) 'Does social work need the eco-systems perspective? Part 1. Is the perspective clinically useful?' *Social Service Review 70*, 1, 1–32.

multi-systems level analysis as identified by Bronfenbrenner (1989) and Hefferman, Shuttlesworth and Ambrosino (1988) to guide the discussion on ecological understanding of HIV practice in South Africa:

- the macrosystem, which consists of the broader social context and a range of community organizations and institutions as well as geographic, cultural, political and economic environments and related global issues

- the exosystem, which encompasses the processes and relationships occurring between two or more systems not including the individual person but including an agency assessment

- the mesosystem, which encompasses the processes and relationships occurring between two or more systems including the individual person and indicates the social support for the individual, such as the family, school, church and peers

- the microsystem, which comprises the person as an individual organism and his/her face-to-face relations in the immediate setting.

The social work context in South Africa

Before the multi-systems level of the ecological perspective can be sensibly applied to HIV practice in South Africa, it is necessary to highlight some aspects of the South African situation impacting on an ecological understanding of HIV practice. It is important to note that this discussion is highly relevant in an international context and has relevance for many countries in similar situations.

South Africa is currently emerging from many years of minority rule where the practice of apartheid has left huge discrepancies between groups of people – largely divided along colour lines and rural and urban lines – in relation to employment opportunities, income, education and provision of social services. With the introduction of a new welfare dispensation under the newly elected government, a White Paper for Social Development (1997) was instituted. This document provides the policy framework for social welfare in South Africa and adopts the internationally accepted developmental approach to social welfare.

The stated aim of this document is to build an 'integrated social welfare system...which is... equitable, sustainable, accessible, people-centred and developmental...' (White Paper for Social Development 1997, p.8). It also acknowledges past discrepancies by stating that: 'Past welfare policies and programmes were inequitable, inappropriate and ineffective in addressing poverty, basic human needs and the social development priorities of all people...' (White Paper for Social Development 1997, p.4). Social workers dealing with the problems surrounding HIV/AIDS in South Africa are therefore called upon to do so within this developmental paradigm. The term 'empowerment' is often used within this developmental paradigm and it is most apt when attempting the significant challenge that HIV presents in South Africa.

Moreover, the process of urbanization continues unabated, with increasing numbers of people leaving rural areas for cities where they search for work and hope to find a better quality of life for themselves and their families. According to a 2003 UNAIDS report, South Africa has an urbanization rate of 49 per cent. This has resulted in growing numbers of squatter settlements filling vacant land on the periphery of South African cities, inception of pavement communities in city centres and large numbers of street children trying to survive on city streets (Gray 1998). Accommodating the 11 official languages and numerous different cultural and ethnic groups in this mix makes it clear that creativity and innovation is expected from social workers addressing the HIV/AIDS challenges of South Africa in the context of a unique time and place in history.

Demographic information

The global HIV/AIDS epidemic killed more than 3 million people in 2003, and an estimated 5 million acquired the human immunodeficiency virus (HIV), bringing to 40 million the number of people living with the virus around the world (UNAIDS 2003). More than two-thirds of those infected reside in sub-Saharan African nations (UNAIDS 2000). Although it is difficult to know the true prevalence, the situation is regarded as extremely serious. In recent reports, South Africa is claimed to have one of the fastest growing HIV-1 epidemics in the world (Morris et al. 1997) and more HIV positive citizens than any other country: 5.3 million out of a population of 45 million (The Economist 2003). In June 2000, people infected with HIV were estimated at 4.2 million (UNAIDS 2000).

Pregnant women are considered to be one of the more reliable indicators of general prevalence. The prevalence among pregnant women in the sub-Saharan region is as high as 40 per cent in some cities (Holden 1996). In South Africa, 1 per cent of pregnant women attending ante-natal services in the public sector in 1990 was HIV positive, while in 1999 this figure had risen to 22.4 per cent (SA Department of Health 2000). In 12 years, therefore, HIV prevalence rose from less than 1 per cent to more than 20 per cent (UNAIDS 2003). This figure may actually underestimate prevalence, because it does not account for women who do not use ante-natal services nor for those who use ante-natal services outside of the public sector. It is further estimated that 15,000 South Africans are infected daily and that one in eight adults (15–49 years of age) is infected with HIV in South Africa (SA Department of Health 2000). Adolescent girls are considered the most vulnerable population with an infection rate five times that of boys. Mother-to-child transmission is believed to account for up to 20 per cent of the new infections or 50,000 infected newborns in 1996 (McIntyre 1996). In areas where most women breast-feed infants, this rate is expected to climb above 25 per cent (McIntyre 1996). Finally, an estimated 420,000 orphans (either the mother or both parents have died) are living in South Africa (UNAIDS 2000), with some expecting that figure to increase to one million orphans in the next five years (Geduld 1999).

Under-reporting is, however, a huge factor in the statistics available on HIV/AIDS in South Africa. This is due to a number of reasons: lack of commitment and time on the part of health workers; an absence of appropriate infrastructure and the tendency of patients, health workers and physicians to avoid the diagnosis of AIDS.

The population at risk

Due to the heterogeneous nature of a country of extreme contrasts, it is enormously difficult to assess and predict the impact of AIDS for the population as a whole and hence there has been some tendency to over-generalize. Some vulnerable groups are even more severely affected, as implied by the statistics. Just as there is a difference in the prevalence and spread of the virus between AIDS in the first world and AIDS in third world countries, distinctions need to be made between AIDS in wealthy, urban, Westernised areas of South Africa and the poorer, rural and traditional areas of the country. South African society is made up of many cultures and the population at risk differs not only from that of other countries, but the population at risk in the country varies from area to area. Generally speaking, however, there is a unique pattern of HIV/AIDS in South Africa (similar to the rest of southern Africa) according to Walker and Gilbert (2001), which has the following main features:

- it is mainly heterosexual
- the rates of infection in the general population are very high
- the percentage of HIV-positive women is greater than men
- the age of onset is very young.

With an estimated 18 million South Africans being under the age of 20 (accounting for approximately 44% of the total population), young people are considered a particularly vulnerable group. With women also being disproportionately affected by HIV/AIDS, young females are of particular concern. Bearing in mind that HIV is transmitted by unsafe sex (amongst other ways) and that sex and sexuality is integral to the self-assertion of this particular vulnerable group, one can predict that unless something is done, a staggering number of South African females younger than 20 years of age could die of AIDS-related causes in the next eight to ten years at the current rate of infection. The impact of HIV/AIDS on the health sector is already noticeable. The percentage of hospital beds occupied due to AIDS ranges from 26 per cent to 70 per cent for adults and from 26 per cent to 30 per cent for children (UNAIDS 2003). With this as background, an ecological assessment of HIV practice in South Africa can be attempted.

The multi-systems levels of the ecological perspective in understanding HIV practice in South Africa

Imagine a disease that is spread through sex, that has no symptoms and may take a decade to show itself: a disease which initially seemed to 'prefer' marginalized and oppressed people, homosexuals and blacks, before moving into the whole population. Think of a virus that attacks the very cells that should order its destruction, which multiply, mutate and destroy, until many years later the host will die a cruel and wasting death (Crewe 1992, p.2).

It seems hard to believe and even more difficult to accept that, despite a decade of knowledge about and involvement with this phenomenon, the origin and treatment is still unknown, most fundamental facts remain misunderstood, people are still dying in huge numbers and the epidemic continues to spiral out of control. It is therefore not surprising that discussions about HIV and AIDS are clouded by conspiracy, prejudice, fear or disbelief and that the reaction to this is discrimination, blame and lack of responsibility.

When trying to make sense of this from publications and attendance at various conferences and public forums, it seems as though the entire subject is shaped by an agenda that is as medically misinformed, as it is socially misleading and politically motivated. But this phenomenon still captures the attention of academics, politicians, social scientists, businessmen and the general public at large, due to its massive social and economic consequences. It has become the most studied disease in history and has spawned a host of journals, books, newsletters and conferences across a great many disciplines. One can therefore safely state that HIV/AIDS is a disease of the broad social context and society, as much as a virus spread by individuals; a disease that impacts on relationships as much as on the individual's ability to function as a human being. What better justification does one need to explore understanding of this phenomenon from a multi-systems level?

The macrosystem

An important feature of HIV/AIDS in South Africa is the politicized and controversial response of the present government to this epidemic. The spread of HIV/AIDS in South Africa has been mostly unhindered and governmental intervention in South Africa has had very little impact on the course of the epidemic. According to Webb (1997), of all the countries in the southern

African region, the response of the South African government to HIV/AIDS has been the one most characterized by denial, ministerial wrangling and the misallocation of resources. It has thereby created a debate fuelled by media hysteria and shaded by political colourings. Despite South Africa having the fastest growing AIDS epidemic in the world and more HIV positive people than in any other country, the government's response has been slow, stumbling and at times counterproductive (Skordis and Nattrass 2001).

The importance of social workers exercising competence from a critical social work perspective to address these issues should not be underestimated. According to Allan, Pease and Briskman (2003, p.71), this refers to 'the requirement to work in ways that link the personal and the political to ensure that people's immediate material needs are addressed and that also consider the need for longer-term social change'.

Preventative policy-making in South Africa lags far behind other African countries, which have made successful inroads in stemming the AIDS pandemic (see e.g. Piot 1998). Former President Nelson Mandela did not include any mention of AIDS in national speeches until 1999. When Thabo Mbeki succeeded Nelson Mandela as President, he introduced the 'African Renaissance' – striving to find African solutions to African problems. In the process, however, he denounced anti-retroviral treatments: the use of three different types of drugs taken in combination and shown to be highly effective in slowing HIV progression. He also discouraged the use of AZT because of unknown side effects (Sithole 1999), although these drugs offer a quality and quantity of life (impossible a few years ago) to those who decide to pursue the medical treatment despite a number of difficulties. Finally, Mbeki even questioned the link between HIV and AIDS (Power 2003). This stance not only bewildered people outside of South Africa, but also alienated many of his supporters at home. In discouraging the use of treatment, Mbeki contributed to many more deaths and in questioning the cause of AIDS, he created a confusion that effectively helped to undo much of the success preventative work had already achieved.

The South African government unveiled a well-funded and long-term plan for treating sick citizens with anti-retroviral drugs in November 2003 (*The Economist* 2003). Whether they will competently implement this plan (since they have failed to deliver on earlier promises) and whether it will prove to be 'too little too late', only time will tell.

The cultural context of HIV in South Africa is another important element in the macro environment to take into consideration. Every culture includes belief systems that help its members predict, diagnose, prevent and treat many health problems. Most commonly, African cultures look to ethno-medical practitioners, referred to as traditional healers or herbalists, for health care. Traditional healers play a particularly important role in South African townships, where one Western-trained doctor may be responsible for nearly 7,000 people (Couper 1997). A study on the link between belief systems and AIDS (Riffe and Fouché 2001) highlighted the fact that young people might have all the scientific knowledge to take the necessary precautions against HIV infection, but that cultural norms and beliefs often lead them to act very differently. Within a heterosexual relationship, women often express their powerlessness to convince their partners to wear condoms and their inability to ensure faithfulness. Interwoven with the cultural context are the wider social issues of stigma, discrimination and attitudes of disgust, blame and fear based on cultural views of right and wrong and what is acceptable and unacceptable.

On an economic level, the option to pursue treatment for AIDS such as AZT and anti-retroviral agents are available to only the wealthiest South Africans, as these drugs are not available as generics as is often the case in other countries. Consequently, most people infected with AIDS die within ten years of contracting the virus, while in countries such as the USA, AIDS is seen as a chronic, but manageable condition. It was understood, however, that the South African government would not subsidize anti-retroviral treatment until drug companies dropped their prices or their patents. Many lobbying groups, such as the Treatment Action Campaign (TAC) highlighted the need for cheaper drugs. After years of fighting and legal action, five major pharmaceutical companies have announced discounts on anti-retroviral drugs, effectively making it possible for the government to provide these drugs to HIV-positive mothers and babies via primary health care provision. Anti-retroviral treatment would then also have been available to individuals who wanted to exercise the choice of using these drugs. However, at this point, the South African government had staked its reputation on the belief that anti-retroviral drugs had serious side effects and that therefore the government would not make them available. Once again, HIV-related deaths have increased and HIV infection soared.

It is clear from the above discussion that a number of elements in the macro environment will have to be addressed for the effective prevention of HIV infection in South Africa and the elements addressed here are by no means comprehensive. Other global issues such as poverty, unemployment, the socio-cultural position of women in society, domestic violence and breakdown in traditional family structures have not been discussed, but all add in some macro way to the challenge of HIV in South Africa. The social/community worker should at times choose to intervene at this level.

The exosystem

The processes and relationships occurring between systems in South Africa impacting on the HIV epidemic is the next level to be assessed from the ecological perspective. As would be clear from the discussion about macro issues, relationships between the government and other systems such as pharmaceutical companies and action groups have not been very positive. Moreover, relationships between other systems in the country are also working towards prevention or, in some instances, inadvertently towards the spread of HIV/ AIDS. In addition to the overall lack of resources in social provision in South Africa, people living in impoverished areas often experience limited access to social services and medical resources. In terms of HIV-related needs, poor individuals and communities are deprived not only of preventative educational opportunities, but they also lack access to information on best treatment practices, medicines and support.

It is widely acknowledged that social care of the terminally ill aims to maximize the quality of the patient's remaining life. This often implies support for existing family and care involving a huge multi-disciplinary effort (Cowles 2003). Social workers – already overworked and underpaid – need specialized knowledge concerning the medical and social implications of HIV/AIDS, updated information about and access to appropriate resources and, in particular, effective supervision in a very emotional and highly demanding field. Those who have the luxury to equip themselves in this way are offered huge salaries by private medical providers and offer their services as private practitioners – once again excluding the poorest of the poor from much needed support.

Support services are then often replaced by community interventions, as often happens in other African countries (Subedi and Gallagher 1996): personal growth services, AIDS support organisations, home-care programmes and family AIDS caring trusts. The assistance of local helpers and volunteers, in combination with professional helping strategies, are invaluable in delivering these services. Community interventions are sometimes targeted at the infected in an attempt to bridge the gap between the Western hospital-based approach to disease and the community-based African approach, but sometimes include interventions for prevention and intervention for those caring for the ill. These are often the only available resource where Western methods are unavailable, inaccessible or inappropriate and include the actions of traditional healers, self-help initiatives, income generating projects and participation in setting up of services. Many of these initiatives are either privately funded, operated by NGOs, or established as extensions of religious organizations' activities. They contribute enormously to the efforts and success stories of delivering HIV and AIDS-related services in South Africa.

The circumstances as outlined above compound the problems of identifying and treating people living with AIDS and those dying of HIV-related illnesses. The scarcity of HIV counselling, HIV testing and condoms in communities where there is an increase in prostitution, domestic violence and rape, often explains why those infected are unaware of their HIV status and may unknowingly transmit the virus to many others. Success stories that follow from effective community interventions are unfortunately also not disclosed and documented, and as such, these exosystem factors are both a cause of concern and a focus for assessment and intervention.

The mesosystem

Meso level factors of HIV/AIDS from an ecological perspective lead us to assess social support for both the HIV-positive individual or person with AIDS and the significant others in the lives of these people.

Being diagnosed with HIV often highlights for the first time associated behaviours such as homosexuality, drug dependency, sexual activity in children, adolescent pregnancy, or sex outside of marriage. HIV infection therefore alters the relationship the individual has with a number of significant other people in his or her life, which can be detrimental at a time of such crisis. Due to the stigma attached to a positive HIV diagnosis, relationships with support structures such as the church, school, peers and family are also seriously affected.

A number of factors determine an individual's ability to recover or adapt after a crisis (often referred to as *resilience*). These so-called 'resiliency factors' are identified by Norman (2000, p.4) as being personally or interpersonally related. One of these factors, as also emphasized by Muir (1991), draws on evidence that individuals with strong social ties are more likely to alter behaviours than those with weaker social connections, and that the behaviour and attitudes of family and friends have a powerful effect on the behaviour of individuals. Many social work interventions on the meso level, therefore, are aimed at helping the family members of the infected individual find and enhance linkages ('improve the fit') between the family and its environments or facilitate the sharing between group members. Being closely involved with a social network of family members, friends, colleagues, neighbours, members of social clubs or church groups, among others, contributes to a sense of support not only in times of joy, but also in times of trouble (Norman 2000).

Social support for young persons bereaved by AIDS is one of the huge challenges social workers in South Africa face. Children who experience the loss of a loved one through AIDS often have to cope not only with being orphaned, but also with multiple deaths in the family, the secrecy, stigma and misconceptions still attached to the disease, as well as extreme poverty. Often, young people drop out of school to look after ailing or surviving relatives, while others may leave work – sometimes as sole provider for a family – to take up the role as caregiver. In a country where access to benefits is very limited, this obviously does not contribute positively to the situation. There are never enough professionals to sustain the kind of help these young people need, but limited community interventions aimed at providing bereavement counselling as well as physical, emotional, educational and spiritual support are a much needed resource for these children and young people.

The microsystem

When social workers deal with the individual as the client-system – be it the infected person or the person living with (or without) an infected significant other – one has to face the hard realities of HIV infection and dying from AIDS. In ecological terms, the 'person as an individual organism' becomes a stark reality in this field.

HIV interventions have operated on the assumption that conveying knowledge and information about HIV/AIDS is central to the development of appropriate and effective preventative measures. Individual responsibility remains a major focus of reducing the risk of transmission and the concept of 'behaviour change' is still often used as a focus of HIV prevention efforts. Infection with HIV eventually causes immune suppression, resulting in an increased susceptibility to a spectrum of illnesses. People do not die from HIV itself, but from a variety of opportunistic infections or from the wasting syndrome (AIDS), caused by the retro-virus. The disease is transmitted by sexual contact, by infected blood or blood products (including practices associated with intravenous drug use), and from mother to baby. No other human interpersonal behaviours transmit the virus. People who are HIV-positive carry the virus, can transmit the infection and are vulnerable to HIV-related diseases.

However, programmes that provide only education about HIV/AIDS prevention have shown little promise in changing the behaviours that put individuals at risk. MacNair-Semands and Simono (1996) contend that the key to risk reduction lies in the person's perceived susceptibility to contracting the virus, while Feldman et al. (1997) assert that coping resources and changing values and norms are key. Obviously, the real answer to HIV prevention lies in a combination of these viewpoints and an integrated ecological understanding of the situation. But on a micro-level, individuals must first understand the facts about HIV transmission and prevention in order to identify behaviours that may put them at risk. It is amazing how many people are aware of the acronyms 'HIV' and 'AIDS', but do not know what they stand for, and how many are not aware of the distinction between HIV and AIDS and often use the terms interchangeably.

Young people must perceive that they are at risk of contracting the virus before they can challenge cultural values and norms – so that when they perceive that they are at risk, they can take steps to modify their behaviours. Once individuals understand that they may contract the disease, they will be more likely to personalize the risk. Only at this point will social workers be able to intervene at a micro-level to empower individuals to take the necessary steps to reduce their risks. As Subedi and Gallagher (1996) assert, AIDS is transmitted as a result of behaviour at an interpersonal level, and as such, intervention efforts must not ignore the potential of approaches that seek a better understanding of the interaction and negotiation that takes place with regard to sex.

In terms of alleviating individual distress, social workers collaborate with clients to decide on a number of issues. Stanley (2000) and Furley (2000) highlight the following:

- disclosure – not only about whether they should disclose, but also when and to whom

- drug treatment – again not only in terms of whether it is applicable, but also the emotional disruption linked to its use and the intense side effects ranging from nausea and vomiting, to a total loss of taste and even impotence

- work or career planning and even future life planning – due to the unpredictability of living with HIV

- other psycho-social issues – not least of which, the decision whether to have an HIV test in the first instance.

Another element in the microsystem to take into account in HIV practice is the caring professional or social worker as individual. As Furley (2000) states, social workers need a skill level and comfort with issues concerning sexuality, dying, death and bereavement, sexual and physical abuse, and HIV-related information. Where the main focus of assessment and intervention is on death and bereavement, burn-out amongst professionals can be expected to be very high. Furthermore, this is a field that challenges one's own beliefs and worldviews. According to Woods (1998), professionals working in this field may be aware of HIV and AIDS long before they are required to deal with it professionally. Consequently, they may approach issues with a wide range of attitudes, opinions and personal experiences. These individuals may also have a cultural or religious lifestyle that makes it difficult for them to accommodate lifestyles that are perceived to lead to infection. They may find it difficult to talk about issues often regarded as social taboos or they may even be concerned about being exposed to infection themselves. As outlined above, it is clear that the microsystem in HIV practice surrounds different people with a wide range of related psychosocial issues.

Conclusion

Taking into account the unique South African context in terms of its apartheid history, diverse geography, extreme mix of first world urban infrastructures and third world rural characteristics, a culturally diverse population as well as the characteristics of the population at risk, the overwhelming challenge of AIDS becomes apparent. Assessing this from an ecological point of view, it becomes clear that we can alter the status of HIV infection in South Africa only by altering the environments in which the virus and the human carriers of this virus operate. 'Dealing with HIV infection means dealing with the complexities of the environments that surrounds us' (Muir 1991, p.172). The ruling government, policy makers, professionals and the public at large must understand the ecological perspective when formulating public information, launching prevention campaigns, working with client groups and sharing community life. All must comprehend that no one intervention is going to combat the spread of HIV or cure AIDS. Rather, this situation will require systemic changes to belief systems, motivations and behaviours with a focus on individuals, communities and the macro political and societal environment. Behaviour change models encouraging safer sex practice need to be supported and sustained by appropriate resources and changes at a structural level, but eventually society as a whole needs to be mobilized to develop responses to HIV infection.

If we recognize that HIV infection can be understood and prevented then, provided we use this phenomenon to rethink, rework and revise the ecological framework of our lives, HIV infection in South Africa can be adequately dealt with. It makes the quote by the USA satirist James Thurber (1894–1961) so relevant: 'Let us not look back in anger, nor forward in fear, but around us in awareness'.

Questions for reflection

1. How does the ecological perspective help identify the context for understanding HIV practice?

2. Do you consider the ecological systems approach as used in this chapter adequately deals with issues of dominance, power and oppression in practice?

3. How could you use the multi-level systems analysis described in this chapter in your own social work practice?

References

Allan, J., Pease. B. and Briskman, L. (2003) *Critical Social Work: An Introduction to Theories and Practices.* NSW, Australia: Allen and Unwin.

Bronfenbrenner, U. (1989) 'Ecological systems theory.' *Annals of Child Development 6,* 187–249.

Couper, I. (1997) 'The future of rural medicine in South Africa.' *South African Medical Journal 87,* 3, 290–292.

Cowles, L.A.F. (2003) *Social Work in the Health Field – A Care Perspective.* New York: Haworth Press.

Crewe, M. (1992) *AIDS in South Africa – The Myth and The Reality.* London: Penguin.

Feldman, D.A., O'Hara, P., Baboo, K.S., Chitalu, N.W. and Lu, Y. (1997) 'HIV prevention among Zambian adolescents: Developing a value utilization/norm change model.' *Social Science and Medicine 44,* 4, 455–468.

Furley, R. (2000) 'HIV and AIDS – Current issues for the social work role.' *Social Work Review 12* , 3, 26–28.

Geduld, S. (1999) 'South African AIDS orphans may number 1 million in 5 years.' *Reuters Health Information.* http://www.ama-assn.org/special/hiv/newsline/reuters/ 11187169.htm.

Germain, C.B. (ed) (1979) *Social Work Practice: People and Environments. New York: Columbia University Press.*

Germain, C.B. and Gitterman, A. (1980) *The Life Model of Social Work Practice.* New York: Columbia University Press.

Gray, M. (ed) (1998) *Developmental Social Work in South Africa – Theory and Practice.* Cape Town: David Philip Publishers.

Greene, R.R. (1999) *Human Behaviour Theory and Social Work Practice,* 2nd edn. New York: Walter de Gruyter.

Greene, R.R. and Watkins, M. (eds) (1998) *Serving Diverse Constituencies – Applying the Ecological Perspective.* New York: Aldine de Gruyter.

Hefferman, J., Shuttlesworth, G. and Ambrosino, R. (1988) *Social Work and Social Welfare.* St Paul: West Publishers.

Holden, C. (1996) 'Scourge of Africa.' *Science 274,* 8, 923.

Kalichman, S.C., Carey, M.P. and Johnson, T. (1996) 'Prevention of sexually transmitted HIV infection: A meta-analytic review of the behavioral outcome literature.' *Annals of Behavioral Medicine 18,* 1, 6–15.

MacNair-Semands, R.R. and Simono, R.B. (1996) 'College student risk behaviours: Implications for the HIV-AIDS pandemic.' *Journal of College Student Development 37,* 5, 574–582.

Marshall, E., Roberts, T.L., Barton, W., Stephany, C. and Lighty, B. (1998) 'Ecological approach to families living with HIV disease.' In R.R. Greene and M. Watkins (eds) *Serving Diverse Constituencies – Applying the Ecological Perspective.* New York: Aldine de Gruyter.

McIntyre, J. (1996) 'HIV/AIDS in South Africa – a relentless progression?' *South African Medical Journal 86,* 1, 27–28.

Morris, L., Van der Ryst, E., Gray, C. and Williamson, C. (1997) 'Should South Africa be preparing for HIV-1 vaccine efficacy trials?' *South Africa Medical Journal 87,* 3, 285–290.

Muir, M.A. (1991) *The Environmental Contexts of AIDS.* London: Praeger.

Norman, E. (ed) (2000) *Resiliency Enhancement: Putting the Strengths Perspective into Social Work Practice.* New York: Columbia University Press.

Payne, M. (1997) *Modern Social Work Theory,* 2nd edn. Illinois: Lyceum Books.

Piot, P. (1998) 'UNAIDS executive director warns of unprecedented emergency in South Africa.' http://www.unaids.org/unaids/press/sadec98e.html

Power, S. (2003) 'The AIDS rebel.' *The New Yorker.* 19 May, 2003, 54–67.

Powers, G.T. (1999) 'The search for social work coherence: The ecological perspective.' In R.R. Greene (ed) *Human Behaviour Theory and Social Work Practice,* 2nd edn. New York: Walter de Gruyter.

Riffe, H. and Fouché, C. (2001) 'Indigenous belief systems and AIDS in South Africa: The missing link between knowledge and behaviour change.' *Social Work Researcher-Practitioner 13,* 2, 1–19.

Sithole, E. (1999) 'South African goverment's opposition to AZT criticized.' *Reuter's Health Information* http://www.ama–assn.org/special/hiv/newsline/reuters/ 11167149.htm

Skordis, J. and Nattrass, N. (2001) 'What is affordable? The political economy of policy on the transmission of HIV/AIDS passed from mother to child.' Paper presented at an international 'AIDS in Context' conference: University of the Witwatersrand, Johannesburg, April 2001.

South African Department of Health (2000) *10th National Antenatal Survey, 1999.* Pretoria: Government Printers.

South African Department of Welfare and Population Development (1997) *White Paper for Social Welfare.* Pretoria: Government Printers.

Stanley, T. (2000) 'HIV positive living: Managing the social tensions.' *Social Work Review 12,* 3, 29–31.

Subedi, J. and Gallagher, E.B. (1996) *Society, Health and Disease: Transcultural Perspectives.* New Jersey: Prentice Hall.

The Economist (2003) 'AIDS: Help at last.' *The Economist 369,* 8352, 11.

Thurber, J. (1894–1961) http://www.quotationspage.com/quotes/James_Thurber, accessed 10 May 2004.

UNAIDS (2000) *Report on the Global HIV/AIDS Epidemic.* June 2000. Geneva: WHO.

UNAIDS (2003) *AIDS Epidemic Update 2003.* Geneva: WHO.

Walker, L. and Gilbert, L. (2001) 'Women pay the price: HIV/AIDS and social inequalities.' *SA Labour Bulletin 25,* 1, 76–82.

Webb, D. (1997) *HIV and AIDS in Africa.* London: Pluto Press.

Woods, R. (1998) 'Responding to HIV and AIDS: A challenge for social workers in South Africa.' In M. Gray *Developmental Social Work in South Africa – Theory and Practice.* Johannesburg: David Philip Publishers.

Further reading

Germain, C.B. (ed.) (1979) *Social Work Practice: People and Environments.* New York: Columbia University Press.

Germain, C.B. and Gitterman, A. (1980) *The Life Model of Social Work Practice.* New York: Columbia University Press.

Greene, R.R. and Watkins, M. (eds) (1998) *Serving Diverse Constituencies – Applying the Ecological Perspective.* New York: Aldine de Gruyter.

Kalichman, S.C., Carey, M.P. and Johnson, T. (1996) 'Prevention of sexually transmitted HIV infection: A meta-analytic review of the behavioral outcome literature.' *Annals of Behavioral Medicine 18,* 1, 6–15.

MacNair-Semands, R.R. and Simono, R.B. (1996) 'College student risk behaviours: Implications for the HIV-AIDS pandemic.' *Journal of College Student Development 37,* 5, 574–582.

Marshall, E., Roberts, T.L., Barton, W., Stephany, C. and Lighty, B. (1998) 'Ecological approach to families living with HIV disease.' In R.R. Greene and M. Watkins (eds) *Serving Diverse Constituencies – Applying the Ecological Perspective.* New York: Aldine de Gruyter.

Payne, M. (1997) *Modern Social Work Theory,* 2nd edn. Illinois: Lyceum Books.

Powers, G.T. (1999) 'The search for social work coherence: The ecological perspective.' In R.R. Greene *Human Behaviour Theory and Social Work Practice,* 2nd edn New York: Walter de Gruyter.

Walker, L. and Gilbert, L. (2001) 'Women pay the price: HIV/AIDS and social inequalities.' *SA Labour Bulletin 25,* 1, 76–82.

Chapter 3

Complexity and Context: An Ecological Understanding of Trauma Practice

Carole Adamson

The theoretical terrain in which social workers encounter the impact of trauma is governed by a complex array of knowledge, much of which is familiar and well received by a social work perspective, and other parts of which sit less comfortably within our holistic approach. This chapter sets out to explore an ecological understanding of trauma theory and practice, and in so doing, highlights some current knowledge of trauma and issues for social work practice in Aotearoa New Zealand.

Ecology and social work: theoretical perspectives

Social work theory and practice in Aotearoa New Zealand is governed by the implicit knowledge of interconnections between events, processes and human experience. The contribution of systems approaches to social work, arising first within the paradigm shift in Western epistemology in the 1970s, is in the recognition of holism and non-lineal explanations of causality (Auerswald 1968; Germain 1980, 1991; Meyer 1976). An awareness of non-lineal and complex relationships sits comfortably within both indigenous and Western epistemologies (see, for instance Durie 2001, 2003; IFSW/IASSW 2001), and has been conceptualized within social work as an ecological approach. The essence of this approach is the application of a matrix of knowledge spanning the ontological (the personal histories and experiences of one person) to the macro (the values and core identities that underpin our cultural and collective locations), and the interaction and mutual influences that result.[1]

Ecological theory is sometimes construed simply as a systems perspective, utilizing the metaphors of biology to describe the complex processes of change, interaction and homeostasis that we, as living beings, behaviourally demonstrate (for example, Leon 1999). As such, it can be seen as a theoretical response to the structural and psychodynamic influences that lie at the basis of many explanations of human experience and which have determined much of the shape of early social work theory.

A more sophisticated ecological perspective within critical social work borrows from current understandings of constructivist, chaos and autopoietic theories,[2] and it is this framework of understanding that I intend to employ in the following discussion about ecological approaches to trauma practice in social work. What might be termed 'quantum' social work means that whilst our professional activity can be stripped down to its component parts – individual, family, group or community – it must also be viewed as being concerned with the dynamic relationships between these parts, relationships that will appear different according to where we stand. From this stance, an ecological perspective is not merely a systems approach, but is a framework that holds various sets of knowledge together, and which simultaneously offers different sets of information and understanding about a situation (see, for instance, Jack 2000; Parton 2000; Thyer 2002). Social work, in its commitment to both personal and political change, is required to handle multiple sets of knowledge simultaneously (Connolly 2001). It takes a relational and transtheoretical approach that can establish non-lineal causality in a given situation, and as such is a discipline that is particularly suited to working within the area of trauma.

The overwhelming imperative from this ecological framework is a validation of many sets of knowledge from different sources. It requires that these knowledge bases interact and communicate with each other to determine the priorities for any given intervention, and that the variously informed interventions interact with each other. Nowhere is this clearer than in the area of social work practice and trauma.

Trauma knowledge for social work: the importance of context

Trauma shapes much of social work. From statutory child protection, elder care and mental health services, through domestic violence and refugee services, to community development and social work within indigenous social structures such as whanau, hapu and iwi,[3] traumatic experience is embedded in our work. There is no discrete 'field of practice' for trauma; rather, it spans many diverse fields.

The scientific contribution

In contrast to the ecological perspective of social work, the current construction of trauma theory and knowledge is lodged predominantly within a biomedical perspective. The capture of the human experience of trauma within a scientific paradigm is reflective of the influence that medicine and neurobiology had over Western knowledge over much of the twentieth century. It has produced a detailed and growing understanding of the physiological characteristics of trauma that gives such extreme stress some qualitatively different characteristics from that of other stressful experiences. Classification of the symptoms of traumatization is made within the psychiatric terminology of the Diagnostic and Statistical Manual of the American Psychiatric Association, the DSM (for instance, the 1994 edition and its revision in 2000). A medical diagnosis of post-traumatic stress disorder (PTSD) or acute stress disorder (ASD) provides access and gate keeping in relation to financial compensation and therapeutic services.

DSM descriptions of the diagnoses of PTSD and ASD reveal the significance of markers such as dissociation, avoidance, arousal and intrusion.[4] Knowledge about the physiology of brain response to trauma underpins much of our knowledge for intervention in areas such as child and sexual abuse (see, for instance, Perry and Pate 1994; van der Kolk 1996a; Rothschild 2000).

The emphasis on the findings of positivist science is invaluable to the understanding of the needs of tangata whaiora[5]/consumers/clients within social work practice. Few if any social work courses contain this level of detail. A knowledge of the biological impact of trauma, or at least an alliance with those who do know, is thus an imperative for multi-disciplinary and transtheoretical perspectives.

The social and intellectual dominance of scientific knowledge has, however, had some disadvantages for work with the traumatized, in that it has constructed a short-sighted focus on the physical and behavioural aspects of traumatization and has underplayed the role that the environmental context has in both creating the trauma, and in our response to recovery from trauma. An ecological understanding suggests that the dynamic interaction between different levels of experience will influence any outcome of intervention.

The influence of the environment: the role of the stressor

The inclusion of the 'stressor' within the diagnoses of PTSD and ASD was a milestone in psychiatry, and one of fundamental importance. No other psychiatric diagnosis acknowledges the power of the environment in such an integral manner. It suggests an intellectual and epistemological acceptance of the interconnectedness between people and their environment, and provides a practice imperative for social work in the area of trauma.

Recognition that the environment has a crucial bearing on determining traumatization and healing allows us to chart the path of the impact of trauma beyond the physiological and into behavioural, social and existential realms. This opens up the opportunity to incorporate into our trauma knowledge such theoretical contributions as attachment theory (for example, Bowlby 1982; McFarlane and van der Kolk 1996), humanistic and relational psychology (Bracken and Thomas 2003; Janoff-Bulman 1992), and the vast areas of human rights, indigenous struggles and decolonization processes (Becker 1995; Davies 2001; van Dijk and Igreja 1999; Sachdev 2001). Not all of these theoretical contributions are presented as located within the knowledge base of trauma, but all offer informed discussion as to how the impact of traumatic experience may pan out in human experience. The challenge to social work practitioners is to use their knowledge of human experience gained from education and experience and to integrate this with appreciation of the immediate, long-term and generational impact of trauma.

Issues of complexity

Scientific constructions of trauma, however, tend to rely upon a single or readily identifiable event. DSM diagnoses, thus far, struggle with notions of complexity such as the effects of multiple or cumulative abuse, or the long-term developmental impact of trauma on the growing person. Legal interpretations of harm, for instance, have only in the last decade begun to acknowledge the power of cumulative stress, and the environment's responsibility in harming and healing. The Health and Safety in Employment Amendment Act (2002) in Aotearoa New Zealand now reflects this; the Accident Compensation legislation (the New Zealand legislative framework that supports victims of accidents and injury within both work and personal environments) is yet to change to reflect this paradigm shift. Compensation entitlement for cumulative or vicarious injury is restricted and difficult to access.

Psychiatric classification that recognizes complex traumatization may be developed within the next decade or so in an attempt to recognize complexity. Readers may be aware that the European-based psychiatric classification system, the International Classification of Diseases (ICD) now recognizes the developmental impact of prolonged or multiple abuse (World Health Organisation 1992).[6] The relationship between traumatic experience and the development of other mental disorders and social problems is now opening up the boundaries of the scientific descriptions of trauma. Research into the transgenerational impact of trauma, originally fuelled by the Nazi Holocaust, is now focused upon the impact of both open conflict and colonization processes (Adamson et al. 2003; Davies 2001; Duran et al. 1998; Turia 2000).

An ecological understanding of trauma practice has, underpinning its effectiveness, the knowledge of how holistic trauma's impact can be. What begins as a unique individual or community response to experience may be laid down over time as a series of behavioural and social responses, created by traumatic experience but now masked by other descriptive labels of violence, addiction, loss of values and beliefs, and depression etc. (Janoff-Bulman 1992; van der Kolk 1996b). Herman's and Bloom's reviews of the relational and social destruction caused by traumatic experience, from military to domestic violence settings, suggest that recognition of the physiological and behavioural effects is often subsumed within bigger picture patterns that can become entrenched into the communication patterns of families, communities and nations (Bloom 1997; Bloom and Reichert 1998; Herman 1992). Bentovim talks in terms of 'trauma-organized' behaviour, and Bloom refers to trauma-organized societies (Bentovim 1992; Bloom and Reichert 1998).

The ecological imperative in our response to trauma

The recognition of traumatic impact beyond the personal and individual clearly becomes less easy, the further away from the immediate victim of trauma and the signal event or events that one works. A scientific focus on the neurobiology of trauma, and interventions that focus upon the psychological aftermath, e.g. cognitive behavioural therapy (CBT), or the much used but still empirically contested eye movement desensitization and reprocessing (EMDR) (Shapiro 1995), will address some of the concerns of those who are primary victims. Their wider social, cultural and spiritual needs (addressing the impact of social isolation, the severing of relationships with wider family, community, culture and existence) are less easily addressed. Nor are the strengths of these wider ecological levels or ecosystems recognized. It is a scientific bias that assumes that if the physiology and psychology of trauma are addressed, other disruptions to 'normal' life will fall away. This belief flies in the face of evidence that trauma can have long-term impact both by the creation of defensive behavioural patterns, distorted communication styles and alterations to belief systems, for both the initial people affected, their family members and those with whom they successively interact.

Three frameworks of understanding suggest that an ecological approach can assist in trauma practice. Contrary to the assumption that intervention with trauma should always start with healing the trauma, attention to the environmental context is in many cases as, or more, appropriate.

The contribution of social work

The first of these perspectives is social work itself. We practise in the dynamic environment of systems relationships. For instance, we include networking, resource identification and acquisition, and case management amongst our skills. Very few practitioners focus upon one theoretical orientation to the exclusion of others, and so our validation of a consumer's narrative may also be informed by knowledge of the structural implications of poverty and policy. Our understanding of disenfranchisement as a result of colonization may also be informed by Western theories of addiction or mental health. There is an oft-heard sigh of 'I told you so' that social workers emit periodically at multi-disciplinary meetings, when members of other professions pronounce their discovery that an ecological strategy appears to be the best way forward. For social work there is no paradigm shift necessary (Rapp and Hanson 1988). By outlining our practice as ecologically based, we can provide many examples of the importance of physical health, housing, income, social support and cultural identity to any intervention.

In specific relation to trauma practice, once recognition is made that trauma has played a role in domestic violence, addiction or mental health, for instance, the social work imperative is to provide multi-systemic, or multi-level intervention. Take the scenario of a young child exposed to high levels of violence within the home. From a positivist perspective, she may be psychologically traumatized, experiencing symptoms of dissociation, high levels of arousal and avoidance, and may go on in later life to be vulnerable to relational problems, addictions and other behavioural manifestations of distress. From a psycho-dynamic perspective, the child's attachments may become negative or ambiva-lent, and from a systems perspective, the domestic isolation of an abusive family environment erodes her resilience and increases the likelihood of further abuse. Constructivist interpretations might focus on the meaning of the experience as a key to locating strengths and opportunities for change. Structural, feminist and post-colonial explanations may focus upon the resources, oppressions and wider forces within which this family is located.

Which perspective holds the key to the interventions that social work may make? Perhaps no single perspective contains the sole answer. Social work aimed at reducing the traumatic impact on that child, family, community and society will be informed by a variety of theoretical explanations and interven-tions. What holds these together and creates a sense of cohesion in our inter-ventions is an ecological framework. This determines that where perhaps a positivist knowledge base is employed in the first instance (such as attention to the physical and psychological impact of abuse), this will be tempered and balanced over time with approaches informed by attachment theory (enabling a focus, for example, on non-trauma focused relationships and the development of a positive sense of self). Systemic and structural interventions, including critical social work, also gain validity here. They can focus on the bigger picture change in values and social conditions that may reduce the strains upon indi-vidual families and reduce the likelihood of further violence. Strengths per-spectives, forged in part out of constructivist understanding, may govern the individual and community response to healing.

Tangata whenua knowledge

Part of the process of decolonization internationally has been the increasing prominence and application of existing indigenous frameworks of knowledge. Commonalities between Western models of holistic practice and indigenous constructions of health and wellbeing can be established through mutual exploration of holism and interconnection within an ecological framework. It is significant that indigenous models have gained greater recognition within Western practice awareness since the paradigm shift that has moved Western understanding from a reliance on positivism.

Frameworks within Aotearoa New Zealand such as te whare tapa wha[7] lay out the implicit and inseparable relationship between components of our identity and resonate with indigenous and holistic social work practice both in this country and internationally (Durie 2001). This model is used to develop assessment and intervention models both in practice and in evaluation (Harrop *et al.* 2000; Kingi and Durie 2000). In te whare tapa wha, for instance, no one component of experience is privileged over another, and the four components are themselves underpinned by knowledge about whenua, that is, the identity that comes from land, belonging and security. In this approach, human rights issues have as much legitimacy as psychological processes, and may offer the key to successful community-level intervention.

Tangata whenua knowledge of colonization and its effects can contribute strategically to an understanding of the long-term impact of trauma on a culture and on identity. Key debates around areas as diverse as child abuse (for instance, Turia 2000) and ownership of the foreshore and seabed[8] implicitly contain awareness of the collective and cross-generational impact of drastic change, violence and deprivation, and can usefully dialogue with what is known about the long-term effects of trauma.

A social work perspective on trauma practice within Aotearoa New Zealand has therefore both an obligation and an opportunity to work within such holistic frameworks. Western ecological perspectives and indigenous approaches, both Maori and Pacific Island, can jointly work to construct sound guidelines for trauma practice.

Trauma models: 'safety first'

Despite the dominance of scientific models of trauma practice, it is noteworthy that most of the leaders in the trauma research and practice fields articulate a holistic approach to practice. Some envisage the growing understanding of trauma as a force that will lead practice out of the scientific paradigm:

> It may be that traumatology will lead the mind sciences out of their limited linear scientific vision, into their more natural home in non-linear paradigms, which are indeed the home of modern physics and mathematics...

> Traumatology, like physics, will be an ever more unifying and whole science. It will become the first science to truly subsume biological, psychological and social arenas, and include knowledge of processes of human harmony and disruptions, charted from molecular to spiritual dimensions. (Valent 1999, p.4)

Writers such as van der Kolk, McFarlane, Herman and Bloom urge activity on human rights and political levels simultaneously with therapeutic work with traumatized individuals.[9]

Whilst these writers advocate multi-systemic approaches to trauma practice, there is a set of governing principles for practice that emerge as crucial for effective social work intervention in the area. Readers may be familiar with the Western humanistic framework of Maslow's hierarchy of needs, taught in many social work and human development courses (Maslow 1998). His work is dated and very Western in philosophical orientation, placing an individual's self actualization at the pinnacle of human endeavour, a goal that may not sit comfortably within collective approaches in indigenous and some Western societies. Its strength lies, however, in the practical imperative that the establishment of safety through housing, elimination of violence, and provision of income and sustenance underpins successful development of social and cultural interactions.

The 'safety first' guideline has been developed by Herman and forms the basis of a code of practice for social work in the area of trauma (Herman 1992). Resonating with the stage or phase approach of many in the field (for example, Chu 1998, Herman proposes that work with the traumatized will go through three stages of development: safety, remembrance and mourning, and reconnection. The underpinning rationale for a staged process of recovery is that active trauma work (remembrance, for instance) will be undermined if safety issues such as absence of violence, work on addictions and so on, has not been accomplished. For many, the work on safety may last for years.

Social work has a pivotal role here. Our understanding of the importance of context, of building social support, resource bases and networking, suggests that any intervention that focuses explicitly on trauma memories and post-traumatic impact must be based soundly on the establishment of supportive environments and therapeutic safety.

Social work practice and the impact of trauma

The final section of this chapter addresses the impact of trauma on social work, and establishes key practice principles that govern our response to this. There is first a focus upon an ecological interpretation of staff support, addressing supervision and critical incident response. The section concludes with an acknowledgement of the role and nature of evaluation, with a focus on the current debate concerning psychological debriefing. All three areas suggest ecological principles affirming that both the immediate physical and psychological impact, and the longer-term social, cultural and spiritual resonance be addressed.

Principles for supervision

Work in the trauma zone can have an immediate impact where, for instance, a mental health consumer suicides, or a child is killed. The cumulative toll of working with those whose lives have been traumatized may interweave with our personal histories to create a matrix of vulnerability, and may impact upon social work practice to the extent that defensive and dangerous patterns emerge. A social worker may begin to avoid naming or working in areas that trigger memories, high degrees of anxiety, conflict or role confusion, or which appear existentially insoluble. Symptoms of avoidance, intrusion and high arousal mimic the direct effects of traumatization and are every bit as powerful an influence on practice.

The supervisor must work within the ecological dynamic of the worker's personal attributes, the understanding of the potential impact of single events and of cumulative exposure, and the relational qualities of the supervision itself (Brown 1996; Yassen 1995). The supervisory skill will also need to recognize that supervision itself is not a container for all impacts of trauma on the worker, that an individual may require greater access to supports, or more intensive or personalized approaches than agency supervision can provide. Supervisors within and external to organizations will also need to be able to recognize where individual and organizational culpabilities overlap, and to have systems approaches to tackling defensive agency practices, such as knee jerk reactions to risk, or 'pass the parcel/client' (Morrison 1993).

ECOLOGICAL PRACTICE PRINCIPLES FOR SUPERVISION

- The social work supervisor must be prepared for the impact of traumatization on his or her self.

- Social work supervision must be alert to both immediate and cumulative effects of trauma.

- The supervisory focus on integrating the personal and the professional needs to recognize that the client's experience of trauma may resonate with a social worker's own experiences.

- Supervision may create an initial container of safety for identification of these vulnerabilities.

- Supervision in itself may not be large enough a container of safety for the impact of trauma on the social worker.

- The supervisor needs to be vigilant for indications of dangerous practice created by traumatization, and be prepared to take action in relation to this.

- The content of supervision, and supervisors themselves, must be linked to larger processes and structures that will ensure that the context of trauma is understood and addressed. This may take forms such as onward referral, critical incident support, systemic change and professional development.

Principles for critical incident support

As a response to potentially traumatic incidents in the workplace, psychological debriefing such as critical incident stress debriefing (CISD) has been incorporated into many organizational environments in which social workers are located (for instance, Agnew et al. 1998). The development of CISD, and the more comprehensive process of critical incident stress management (CISM) in which it should be ecologically embedded, has occurred alongside practice, organizational and legislative changes that recognize that some work roles and tasks are intrinsically stressful.[10] Forms of debriefing have been introduced as a means of being seen to respond to staff support needs after crisis.

Current critiques of CISD[11] suggest that some basic flaws with its wholesale adoption would have been avoided with a greater ecological understanding of its context. Criticism is often that as a one-off intervention, CISD does not achieve its goal of reducing traumatization in workers, and may well cause iatrogenic damage (Kenardy 2000). From an ecological perspective, any staff support system will need to be cognizant of the immediate needs of both teams and the individuals within them, and of the longer-term effects of traumatization. Defusing and debriefing processes may address some of the immediate safety needs (as outlined in Herman's three stage model for instance), but if the working environment continues to offer potential re-traumatization without stress reduction, support mechanisms may be undermined or disempowered. The longitudinal impact of trauma may be neglected in favour of discharging immediate organizational responsibilities. Current research evidence suggests that the contextual environment of the workplace is an equal if not greater influence on organizational wellbeing (and therefore, most likely, on practice) than the traumatic nature of the work encountered (Huddleston 2002). Ecologically speaking, CISD without a CISM package tailored to the work environment is not sound practice.

ECOLOGICAL PRACTICE PRINCIPLES FOR CRITICAL INCIDENT SUPPORT

- Any initiative such as psychological debriefing or CISD needs to be embedded within a broader delivery of staff support services that can respond to both acute and cumulative, short and long-term impacts of trauma.

- Debriefing initiatives should reflect best practice identification of the effects of cumulative, acute and traumatic stress.

- Debriefing initiatives should ecologically reflect the nature of the work environment and should not be utilized merely as a means of discharging organizational responsibility.

- Reviews of psychological debriefings should address the potential for the organizational environment to re-traumatize the social worker.

Ecological principles for evaluation

The combination of medical models of best practice and the outcomes-driven managerial structures of many social work organizations may work together to create a single focus for evaluation of social work intervention. Evidence-based practice tends to give primacy to scientific methodologies of research that are epistemologically and culturally located within lineal and positivist traditions. Many of the critiques of CISD, for instance, focus on single events and single issues (such as reduction of trauma symptomatology). They tend to under-emphasize the impact of an event on later experience and practice, on a community or wider team, or on the relationship between complex sequences of events. Management structures and social work statistical processes may underplay the complexity of interventions required, and may favour discrete and clearly measurable responses over multi-level (and often multi-agency) interventions.

For the girl traumatized through domestic violence, a successful outcome may be measured in many complex ways, the matrix for which can be suggested by an ecological framework. Ecological interpretation of research data, and the construction of sound social work evaluation measures, requires the development of holistic research and evaluation methodology. This should incorporate both the scientific attention to, for example, trauma symptoms, and responsiveness to social and cultural interpretations of outcome.

PRACTICE PRINCIPLES FOR EVALUATION

- Ecologically informed social work evaluation should take into account the issues of complexity that surround the impact of trauma on both client and worker.

- Issues of complexity in evaluation entail consideration both of the nature of the trauma itself, and the ecological location of its impact.

Conclusion

Both the profession of social work and the growth in knowledge of trauma, its impact and our response, have developed within the age of positivism and an epistemological focus on the individual and the single traumatic event. As Western knowledge has matured into holism and has begun to develop relationships of understanding with indigenous perspectives, an ecological understanding of trauma has emerged. To understand trauma, knowledge across traditional disciplines is required. A social work knowledge base and research methodology is therefore legitimized and an alliance between the positivist strengths of neurobiology and medicine with the systemic, structural and interpretive viewpoints is forged and maintained. An ecological framework for practice, a framework that incorporates both scientific knowledge and the integrative skills of holism, provides a key role for social work.

Questions for reflection

1. What contribution does the ecological perspective outlined in this chapter make to trauma knowledge and social work practice?

2. In what ways do you believe that the development of the ecological imperative in response to trauma has or has not reflected changes in mental health policy and practice over the past three decades?

3. How could this chapter assist you to develop a culturally competent approach to working with trauma?

4. Consider how you might apply the supervision and practice principles in your social work practice?

Notes

1 For examples of the application of ecological theory to social work issues and practice, see Belsky (1980); Bronfenbrenner (1979); Edelson and Tolman (1992); Garbarino (1990); Germain (1980, 1991); Jack (2000); Meyer (1995).

2 The essence of these perspectives is a fundamental acknowledgment that the perceptions of a situation by one person, family or community may differ from that of others by virtue of their different locations in time and space, and that their reality is the basis for both their actions and interventions by others (Cooper 2001; Maturana and Varela 1980).

3 Social work in Aotearoa New Zealand works within a recognition of indigenous social organization; these terms approximate Western understandings of, respectively, extended family, groups of interrelated families connected to an original ancestor, and tribes. These form the basis of interaction and decision-making within Maori society.

4 For a reader-friendly description of these diagnostic symptoms I would suggest Herman (1992), and for a description of each diagnostic symptom, the DSM itself (American Psychiatric Association 1994).

5 The adoption of this term, literally meaning 'people working towards health', suggests a philosophical approach congruent with strengths practice in social work.

6 This nosological system, however, is not in use in Aotearoa New Zealand except for statistical gathering by the Ministry of Health. We will have to wait for the next edition of the DSM (DSM-V). In the meantime, various prototypes of the classification of complex traumatization are available. Readers are referred to Herman (1992) and van der Kolk (1996b), and for discussion about these prototypes, Jongedijk *et al.* (1995) and Valent (1999).

7 Symbolizing the necessary four cornerstones of a house, the elements of health in this model are portrayed as te taha hinengaro (mental processes), te taha tinana (physical processes), te taha whanau (family and social processes) and te taha wairua (spiritual processes). Whole health and wellbeing is to be achieved by maintaining a balance in each of these areas.

8 This current social and political debate in Aotearoa New Zealand concerns the tension between customary usage of, and responsibility for, the beaches and waterways of the country, and the colonially entrenched assumption that Crown ownership ensures rights of access and use for all.

9 For an introduction to these issues, I have already cited work by Herman (1992) and by Bloom and colleagues (1997, 1998). Van der Kolk and McFarlane write extensively, both separately and together: see, for instance, McFarlane and van der Kolk (1996).

10 Occupational Safety and Health within Aotearoa New Zealand recognizes that social work in statutory child protection, for instance, falls into this category: see their website www.osh.govt.nz for some very sound material and guidelines on the management of incidents and cumulative stress.

11 A thorough review of psychological debriefing is provided by the British Psychological Society (Professional Practice Board Working Party 2002).

References

Adamson, C.E., Ruwhiu, L.A. and Walsh-Tapiata, W. (2003) 'The Trauma Paradigm and the generational impact of colonization.' *European Psychotherapy 4* (special edition), 283.

Agnew, R., Dawson, M. and Elliott, C. (1998) 'Dealing with the Aftermath: Why debriefing is critical.' *Social Work Now 10*, August, 6–11.

American Psychiatric Association (1994) *Diagnostic and Statistical Manual of Mental Disorders*, 4th edn. Washington DC: American Psychiatric Association.

American Psychiatric Association (2000) *Diagnostic and Statistical Manual of Mental Disorders*, 4th edn, text revision. Washington DC: American Psychiatric Association.

Auerswald, E.H. (1968) 'Interdisciplinary versus ecological approach'. *Family Process 7*, 202–15.

Becker, D. (1995) 'The deficiency of the concept of posttraumatic stress disorder when dealing with victims of human rights violations'. In R.J. Kleber, C.R. Figley, and B.P.R. Gersons (eds) *Beyond Trauma: Cultural and Societal Dynamics*. New York: Plenum Press.

Belsky, J. (1980) 'Child maltreatment: An ecological integration.' *American Psychologist 35*, 4, 320–35.

Bentovim, A. (1992) *Trauma Organized Systems*. London: Karnac Books.

Bloom, S. (1997) *Creating Sanctuary: Toward the Evolution of Sane Societies*. New York: Routledge.

Bloom, S.L. and Reichert, M. (1998) *Bearing Witness: Violence and Collective Responsibility*. Binghamton, NY: Haworth Press.

Bowlby, J. (1982) *Attachment*. New York: Basic Books.

Bracken, P. and Thomas, P. (2003) 'Time to move beyond the mind–body split.' *British Medical Journal 325*, 21–28 December, 1433–4.

Bronfenbrenner, U. (1979) *The Ecology of Human Development*. Cambridge, MA: Harvard University Press.

Brown, A. and Bourne, I. (1996) *The Social Work Supervisor*. Buckingham: Open University Press.

Chu, J. (1998) *Rebuilding Shattered Lives: The Responsible Treatment of Post-traumatic and Dissociative Disorders*. New York: John Wiley.

Connolly, M. (2001) 'The art and science of social work.' In M. Connolly (ed) *Social Work in New Zealand*. Auckland: Oxford University Press.

Cooper, B. (2001) 'Constructivism in social work: Towards a participative practice viability.' *British Journal of Social Work 31*, 721–737.

Davies, D.R. (2001) 'Within and without (the story of the Welsh): The impact of cultural factors on mental health in the present day in Wales.' In D. L. Bhugra R. (ed) *Colonialism and Psychiatry*. Oxford: Oxford University Press.

Duran, E., Duran, B., Braveheart-Jordan, M. and Yellowhorse-Davis, S. (1998) 'Healing the American Indian soul wound.' In Y. Danieli (ed) *International Handbook of Multigenerational Legacies of Trauma*. New York: Plenum Press.

Durie, M. (2001) *Mauri Ora: The Dynamics of Maori Health*. Auckland: Oxford University Press.

Durie, M. (2003) 'The health of indigenous peoples.' *British Medical Journal 326*, 8 March, 510–1.

Edelson, J.L. and Tolman, R.M. (1992) *Interventions for Men who Batter: An Ecological Approach*. London: Sage.

Garbarino, J. (1990) 'The ecology of early risk.' In S.J. Meisels and J.P. Shontoff (eds) *Handbook of Early Childhood Interventions*. Cambridge: Cambridge University Press.

Germain, C.B. (1980) 'Social work identity, competence, and autonomy: The ecological perspective.' *Social Work in Health Care 6*, 1, 1–10.

Germain, C.B. (1991) *Human Behaviour in the Social Environment: An Ecological View*. New York: Columbia University Press.

Harrop, R., Prasad, P. and Ison, L. (2000) 'A Maori social work model of trauma intervention in an acute hospital setting.' *ACISA Forum 4*, 4, 14–26.

Herman, J. (1992) *Trauma and Recovery*. New York: Basic Books.

Huddleston, L.M. (2002) 'The impact of traumatic and organizational stressors on New Zealand police recruits: A longitudinal investigation of psychological health and posttraumatic growth outcomes.' *Department of Psychology*. Palmerston North: Massey University.

IFSW/IASSW (2001) *Historic Agreement on International Definition of Social Work.* Berne/Southampton: International Federation of Social Workers/International Association of Schools of Social Work.

Jack, G. (2000) 'Ecological influences on parenting and child development.' *British Journal of Social Work 30,* 6, 703–20.

Janoff-Bulman, R. (1992) *Shattered Assumptions: Towards a New Psychology of Trauma.* New York: Free Press.

Jongedijk, R.A., Carlier, I.V.E., Schreuder, B.J.N. and Gersons, B.P.R. (1995) 'Is there a place for the Complex Post-traumatic Stress Disorder?' *Tijdschrift voor Psychiatrie 37,* 1, 287–302.

Kenardy, J. (2000) 'The current status of psychological debriefing.' *British Medical Journal 321,* 28 October, 1032–3.

Kingi, T. and Durie, M. (2000) 'Hua Oranga: A Maori measure of mental health outcome.' In *Mental Health Outcomes Research in Aotearoa: Mental Health Research and Development Strategy.* Wellington: Health Research Council.

Leon, A.M. (1999) 'Family support model: Integrating service delivery in the 21st century.' *Families in Society 80,* 14–24.

Maslow, A.H. (1998) *Toward a Psychology of Being.* New York: John Wiley.

Maturana, H. and Varela, F. (1980) *Autopoiesis and Cognition.* Dordrecht: Reidel.

McFarlane, A.C. and van der Kolk, B.A. (1996) 'Trauma and its challenge to society.' In B.A. van der Kolk, A.C. McFarlane and L. Weisaeth (eds) *Traumatic Stress: The Effects of Overwhelming Experience on Mind, Body and Society.* New York: Guilford Press.

Meyer, C.H. (1995) 'The ecosystems perspective: Implications for practice.' In C.H. Meyer and M.A. Mattaini (eds) *The Foundations of Social Work Practice.* Washington DC: NASW Press.

Meyer, C.H. (1976) *Social Work Practice: The Changing Landscape,* 2nd edn. New York: Free Press.

Morrison, T. (1993) *Staff Supervision in Social Care: An Action Learning Approach.* Harlow, Essex: Longman.

Parton, N. (2000) 'Some thoughts on the relationship between theory and practice in and for social work.' *British Journal of Social Work 30,* 449–63.

Perry, B.D. and Pate, J.E. (1994) 'Neurodevelopment and the psychobiological roots of post-traumatic stress disorder.' In L.F. Koziel and C.E. Stout (eds) *The Neuropsychology of Mental Disorders: A Practical Guide.* Springfield: Charles C. Thomas.

Professional Practice Board Working Party (2002) *Psychological Debriefing.* Leicester: British Psychological Society.

Rapp, C.A. and Hanson, J. (1988) 'Towards a model social work curriculum for practice with the chronically mentally ill.' *Community Mental Health Journal 24,* 4, Winter, 270,19682.

Rothschild, B. (2000) *The Body Remembers: The Psychophysiology of Trauma and Trauma Treatment.* New York: W.W. Norton.

Sachdev, P. (2001) 'The impact of colonialism on the mental health of the New Zealand Maori: A historical and contemporary perspective.' In D.L. Bhugra, R. (ed) *Colonialism and Psychiatry.* Oxford: Oxford University Press.

Shapiro, F. (1995) *Eye Movement Desensitization and Reprocessing: Basic Principles, Protocols, and Procedures.* New York: Guilford Press.

Thyer, B.A. (2002) 'Developing discipline-specific knowledge for social work: Is it possible?' *Journal of Social Work Education 38,* 1, Winter, 101–13.

Turia, T. (2000) *Speech to NZ Psychological Society Conference. NZ Psychological Society Annual Conference.* Palmerston North: Unpublished.

Valent, P. (1999) 'Traumatology at the turn of the millennium.' *Australasian Traumatic Stress Points,* December 1999, 2–4.

van der Kolk, B.A. (1996a) 'The body keeps the score: Approaches to the psychobiology of posttraumatic stress disorder.' In A.C. McFarlane, L.Weisaeth and B.A. van der Kolk (eds) *Traumatic Stress: The Effects of Overwhelming Experience on Mind, Body, and Society.* New York: Guilford Press.

van der Kolk, B.A. (1996b) 'The complexity of adaptation to trauma: Self-regulation, stimulus discrimination, and characterological development.' In B.A. van der Kolk, A.C. McFarlane and L.Weisaeth (eds) *Traumatic Stress: The Effects of Overwhelming Experience on Mind, Body and Society.* New York: Guilford Press.

van Dijk, J. and Igreja, V. (1999) 'Transcultural aspects of research on post-traumatic stress symptoms in rural areas in Mozambique.' *Psychotraumatology, Clinical Practice and Human Rights.* Istanbul: Interium.

World Health Organization (1992) ICD-10: *International Statistical Classification of Diseases and Related Health Problems,* 10th revision. Geneva: World Health Organization.

Yassen, J. (1995) 'Preventing secondary traumatic stress disorder.' In C. Figley (ed) *Compassion Fatigue: Coping with Secondary Traumatic Stress Disorder in Those who Treat the Traumatized.* New York: Brunner/Mazel.

Chapter 4

Integrated Practice in Mental Health Social Work

Mathew Keen and Kieran O'Donoghue

This chapter concludes the ecological systems section and is presented in the form of a conversation on the topic of integrated practice in mental health social work. The areas covered in this conversation are the authors' interpretation of integrated practice and its place in the ecological systems tradition, its application in the inpatient mental health setting and with the indigenous and settler populations living in Aotearoa/New Zealand. The chapter concludes with an evaluation of integrated practice. Before presenting the conversation we will briefly describe the setting and environment where the conversation takes place.

Mathew and Kieran meet in the main corridor outside the doors of Ward 21, in Palmerston North Hospital. Ward 21 is a 24-bed purpose-designed acute inpatient mental health ward, with six of these beds capable of being separated into two three-bed areas for consumers requiring the high needs assessment and treatment. The ward opened in November 2001. Mathew swipes his card to let us in and we walk through the open layout of the ward past the windowed office and a series of interview rooms to Mathew's office in the staff section.

Our initial conversation concerns how the new ward environment has affected the consumers, staff and practice. Mathew reports that a number of consumers who had experience of the old ward prefer this new ward, because of its cleaner and more pleasant appearance. Mathew also said that for the staff, the new working environment had helped in a key 'mindshift' into the recovery focus that has been a significant part of a wider culture change in mental health.

After discussing the unit we talked about Mathew's role as sole inpatient social worker. He described it as diverse, providing social work services at the concrete end of the spectrum: assisting consumers with basic living needs such as accommodation and income, addressing legal matters, network development and family work. His role also includes advanced clinical social work services: cognitive-behavioural approaches, professional supervision for social work students, social workers and colleagues from other disciplines; and critical stress incident debriefing for both consumers and staff. After locating ourselves in relation to the setting and Mathew's role, the conversation turns to integrated practice.

Kieran: Mathew, in the theory chapter, the integrated practice framework is referred to as based upon an ecological approach.

Mathew: I would certainly agree that the integrated practice framework is based upon an ecological approach and that person-in-context factors lie at the heart of both. For me, integrated practice provides a critical conceptual framework that assists the practitioner in enacting an ecological practice. In this sense, integrated practice could be constructed as an applied ecological practice in which the practitioner, as well as assessing the consumer and their environment, has begun by critically reflecting on who they are as a practitioner: their own values, beliefs, history, sense of 'self'. It is these factors that draws the practitioner to theoretical orientations, at both the socio-political and the clinical levels, that reflect awareness of self or the practitioner as a person.

Kieran: So integrated practice starts with the practitioner being able to examine their assumptions and locate themselves in terms of worldview, theoretical orientation and their own social context, before they engage with someone else and their social context?

Mathew: Yes, the practitioner is both self and socially aware with that awareness being continually contested and reconstructed as they develop. One thing I like about integrated practice, and this is something that I am learning more and more about, is that the people who use our service come with their own values, their own spiritual space, their own sense of self, or loss of sense of self. They also come with their sense of how the world operates together with the reasons why they think they have the so-called problems that have been ascribed to them or to which they have subscribed.

Kieran: I am reminded of Gitterman's (1996) point that both the person using social work services and the social worker bring their ecology, functioning, adaptiveness, stressors, status and niche with them to the practice encounter. I want to come back to the point you made about the practitioner in integrated practice and the processing and bringing together of their personal and professional philosophy, qualities and attributes with their knowledge, methods and skills, because it appears to me to be where integrated practice differs from other ecological approaches such as the life model.

Mathew: This takes me back to my first encounters with integrated practice and Dr Prasad in the late 1980s. Prasad (1993, p.7) described the integrated framework as a 'heuristic device to facilitate learning'. He based it on the ecological perspective and focused it on the practitioner, with the explicit purpose of them learning to explain, examine, critique and justify the rationale for their assessment and intervention. I have tentatively constructed an integrated psychiatric/mental health social work practice as:

> the culturally appropriate application of knowledge(s) and skill(s) reflecting an integration of the practitioner's personal and professional experiences, philosophy and values with critical socio-political and clinical theories informing a process of critical analysis and change-oriented intervention(s) to address problems as experienced by persons directly or indirectly affected by psychiatric illness. The primary focus for such intervention lies at the interface between the consumer (be it an individual, family, whanau, couple, group, or community) and the structural context or social environment. Intervention is applied via appropriate modes of social work practice (for example, casework, group work, family work, community work) with a goal of maximising human potential and social justice. (Keen 2001, pp.40–1)

Kieran: There are two more features, which for me further differentiate integrated practice from ecological systems theories. The first is the ongoing reflective process in which the practitioner is engaged, and the second is the anti-oppressive stance taken in the framework. Wakefield's (1996) critique of ecosystems theories indicates that the ecological metaphor of adaptation helps people adapt to their oppression rather than work toward changing that oppression.

Mathew: I see that reflection process occurring through the integration of self, reflected in a critical social science, and a psychological stance informed through that critical social science, together with the application of these at the clinical coalface via an ongoing reflective process. It is this reflective integration that constructs social work as a distinct profession. What this means for the practitioner is that integrated practice offers a frame for organizing and conceptualizing issues that present in practice, as well as inviting the practitioner to engage in an ongoing process of action-reflection through which they evaluate their practice.

> Just a point on theory, which is that theory matters! It informs our practice and transforms it from technicist function to praxis. If we do not know or understand why we do what we do or the way we do it, then it could be said that we do not truly know or understand what we are doing, and that has to be a concern for consumers. I think theory needs to be accessible and my own view is that it must have street-level applicability (Keen, 2001).

With regard to the integrated practice framework's response to oppression, Prasad (1993, p.8) required 'the "integrated practitioner"…to address conditions that disenfranchise people as well as personal troubles and public issues'. So, for me as a psychiatric/mental heath social worker it means addressingissues such as stigma and discrimination experienced by mental health consumers through humanizing mental health and contesting the stigma. One example of this is found in the 'Like minds, like mine' project, which has been promoted nationally by the Mental Health Commission (for further information see http://www.likeminds.govt.nz/).

Kieran: So far we have discussed integrated practice in terms of its location within the ecological systems tradition and its areas of convergence and divergence. I would like to change tack now and discuss integrated practice as a practice framework or perspective. In starting this part of our conversation I want to recognise that for Prasad (1986, 1988, 1993) it:

- accepts that there is nothing inherently radical or conservative about the social worker

- focuses on the practitioner and provides a way of thinking about social work that is comprehensive

- accepts that there is no standard approach to social work practice and avoids imposing one by accepting that different practitioners begin from varying philosophical positions

- accepts that practitioners will choose to highlight particular theories of change and models of practice

- recognizes that all practitioners are required to articulate what informs their analysis and action, and therefore, demonstrate the specific knowledge that informs practice and ensures that interventions meet professional and ethical standards.

It is claimed that the integrated practice framework is very different from the unitary approach to practice, and Specht and Vickery's (1977) integrated model (Prasad 1993). Prasad (1993, p.9) argued that the differences are that the unitary approaches did not adequately address the political dimensions of people's lives, were not explicit about the theories that informed their models of practice, and did not address the person of the practitioner in intervention.

Mathew: My starting point is with the key features of the integrated practice framework which, for me, are that it comprises an integration of a social worker's personal and professional philosophy, with critical socio-political and psychological approaches, that are applied in the various modes of practice to address presenting concerns within the field of practice. Added to this is a continual critical reflection, through multi-level analysis, and features such as culture, gender, class, sexuality and (dis)ability. What this means for me as a psychiatric/mental health social worker is that as a person I am looking at who I am, what matters to me, where my values come from and how my values are influencing me as a person and a practitioner. I also consider my history, how I am presenting and issues and perceptions concerned with culture, age, gender, ability etc.

The next layer involves the lenses that I use to make sense of the world, which for me, are the critical social science theories. This is where I consider my worldview and how I am constructing this view. In other words, what discourses or stories am I subscribing to about consumers, mental ill-health, family, social work? For example, do I perceive consumers as people with problems to be fixed or people who have not been able to access their strengths or community resources? Likewise, am I constructing mental ill-heath according to the *Diagnostic and Statistical Manual of Mental Disorders IVTR* (DSM-IVTR) and the bio-medical tradition or from an ecological and contextual frame? In each of these examples, as an integrated practitioner, I am questioning, what is the understanding I have of the world? What informs that understanding? What assumptions am I operating from? And what are the implications of this for the consumer?

The layer that follows is the clinical theories of social work and field of practice specific theories. These theories are concerned with the knowledge that I use as a practitioner to conceptualize personal/clinical issues and the structural and environmental context. Two examples of these theories come to mind: one is when working with a consumer experiencing depression. I may use cognitive-behavioural theory to help them to identify and address negative thoughts. Whilst doing this, I then might also recognize from the consumer's story that they have subscribed to a narrative in which they have been oppressed and constrained by the depression and as a result work with them, drawing on their own strengths, using a metaphorical frame from narrative therapy to deconstruct their story and access times when they managed their depression. In this process the consumer and I would work on recreating a story and an audience that is supportive of the consumer's personal and contextual recovery from depression using a range of available personal, medical and community resources (including medication) as part of the consumer's care.

In this sense, as a clinical theorist I would be informed and guided by knowledge(s) specific to social work, knowledge(s) shared with other disciplines, and by knowledge(s) and policies specific to psychiatry as a field of practice. It is the integration of all of these layers (namely, the person, the critical social science theorist and the clinical theorist) that leads to the next layer, that of the practitioner as a critically informed actor, which concerns my awareness of the techniques and strategies that I use that are reflective of my critical social science and clinical orientation. This means I have an informed understanding concerning why I choose to use processes from narrative therapy with the consumer experiencing depression, and why I may not use such techniques or intervention strategies with the consumer experiencing acute paranoid schizophrenia. ·

Furthermore, in each situation I recognize the worldview behind each level and how it relates to me as a social work practitioner in each situation. The result of this cycle of reflection is that the practitioner becomes critically informed and integrated, contesting, reviewing and evaluating themselves as a person and as a practitioner engaged with knowing, decision-making and action. Figure 4.1 below illustrates the layers I have just described and it also attempts to show the reflection that occurs throughout integrated practice.

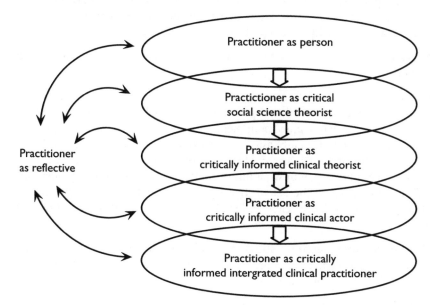

Figure 4.1 The levels of integrated practice

Kieran: Your detailed description of the levels of integrated practice has for me emphasized the depth of reflection required and the breadth of knowledge needed as a social worker.

Mathew: And that is why supervision is a necessity for integrated practice: because it is a forum where the practitioner can engage in a reflective discourse that explores and examines the knowledge(s) that informs practice as well as the effectiveness of the techniques and strategies used. Supervision will also reflect upon the acting person of the practitioner and their influence in social work practice.

Kieran: Let's pick up the point you have just made about supervision later on in our conversation. In the meantime, perhaps, we could discuss the relevance of the integrated framework in the mental health field and with particular groups. I wonder what your views are of the description of the integrated framework as an informed form of eclecticism that is practitioner-, rather than theory-driven?

Mathew: I am extremely disquieted by the word *eclectic,* because of how it is sometimes used as a catch-all when people, a) cannot articulate what informs their practice, and b) as rationale for an uninformed mixing and matching of theories. That said, the differentiation you have made concerning an informed form of eclecticism, that is practitioner-driven, means that the practitioner has intentionally planned and thought about their choices of theories and models and that they are also aware of how these theories and models relate to both them as a person and the practice situation. In other words, they have an understanding of how they have integrated ideas and concepts from a range of sources, as well as why they have brought them together in this fashion.

Kieran: So they can account for and justify their use of a range of sources and authorities?

Mathew: Yes, and I think that this ability to articulate, rationalize and account for one's practice is the real strength of integrated practice and why it is really relevant in social work practice in mental health. The contemporary practice environment, with its emphasis on clinical accountability, evidence-based practice, rights, and consumer and family involvement, demands that as a social worker, I am upfront about what informs my professional knowing, decision-making and action to the extent that, when I write either an assessment or a clinical note, I need to be clear and explicit about my analysis and action and what informs it.

Kieran: You raise questions about the challenges that practitioners face who use the integrated practice approach in the 'just do it' environment of direct practice. What are your views on this?

Mathew: I think there are challenges, because what seems to count at the coalface is the completion of tasks and the achievement of goals. The process and rationale that underpins task achievement and goal attainment is not measurable in the sense that tasks and goals are. That said, the reasons for a practitioner's professional judgement do come to the fore in multi-disciplinary team meetings, and it is important for me as a social worker to argue my points and provide clear and understandable reasons for them. Another time when the practitioner's clinical reasoning becomes important in mental health is when things go wrong.

Kieran: Perhaps the point you made concerning when things go wrong is poignantly illustrated by the New Zealand Health and Disability Commissioner's report into Southland District Health Board's mental health services. This report recognized that the social worker concerned was working in a 'dysfunctional system' in which roles and responsibilities were ill-defined and that Southland DHB had employed the social worker in a position that 'he was not equipped to fulfil' (HDC 2001, p.68). At the same time, the report was critical of the social work practice performed by the social worker; for example, it stated that: 'Social Worker A demonstrated limited understanding of mental illness and its impact and noted that he was not "psychiatrically trained", so his practice was oriented towards tasks and he relied on his colleagues for psychiatric input' (HDC 2001, p.68).

The picture that emerges from the report is arguably one of a social worker who is not engaged in the critical reflection upon themselves as a person, their worldview, the knowledge, theories and methods that inform their practice and their actions as a social work clinician.

Mathew: I think that the report you have referred to also points to the challenge that demands, such as time and case-loads, make upon the critical reflection required for integrated practice as well as the need to have social work colleagues with whom you can discuss your practice. It also highlights the importance of continually reviewing, evaluating and developing one's integrated approach to practice. With regard to integrated practice, I think it also points to the risk that a practitioner could turn the integrated practice framework into a shopping list, containing their espoused theory of social work practice with a full stop placed at the end of it. Such a position would be characterized by statements like 'This is my practice! These are my critical social science theories!' It neglects questions such as:

- Why is it like that?
- Will it be like that tomorrow?
- How do you know?
- Is nothing going to happen between now and next year or three years time that will change you, your value base, your practice theories, your community, your field of practice?

So the risk is that integrated practice and the integrated practitioner become stagnant, particularly if you reduce the concept of integrated practice to a shopping list of theories and interventions.

Kieran: I want to change direction again in our conversation and discuss the question of how does integrated practice address our professional obligations under Te Tiriti O Waitangi? In raising this question I want to first acknowledge that while we are treaty partners, both you and I are non-Maori and that Dr Prasad, to whom the development of the framework is attributed, is also non-Maori.

Mathew: One of the things about integrated practice is that it is not limited to the theoretical and self components and that it takes the context of practice seriously. Since our context is that of Aotearoa/New Zealand and the treaty is a major cornerstone in the development of this country and its social services, it applies to both the work we do as citizens of this country and the work we do with tangata whenua. It is of prime relevance within the context of practice and for social workers.

Kieran: So you are saying that if we use the integrated practice framework in Aotearoa/New Zealand, we firstly need to recognize that we are in a treaty context, and that Te Tiriti o Waitangi is a given in the integrated practice that occurs.

Mathew: Yes. Absolutely. You have to recognize where you are and know where you are, know the history – and when I say the history, I don't just mean what happened years ago, I am also meaning how that history is lived in the present. For me it is in this sense that the Treaty of Waitangi is a living document.

Kieran: What are the challenges you face as a non-Maori social worker using an integrated practice perspective in this setting working with tangata whaiora?

Mathew: The challenges would be the same for any non-Maori practitioner. They include recognizing my limitations. I am not tangata whenua. That said, there is a phrase I love that says 'You don't have to live somewhere to know what it is like to live there, but you have to listen to someone who has been there to know'. Even then you don't ever know the full story. For me, it's about listening and being open and, ultimately, a partnership based in absolute positive respect and regard, which recognizes each person as the expert in their own experience, is an aid in facing such a challenge.

Kieran: You mentioned recognizing your own limitations and working in partnership. I wonder about the question of the knowledge that we don't have and our obligations to seek that out for consumers from elsewhere?

Mathew: The use of cultural consultation and supervision is important here as well as using existing networks within the organization, profession and wider community. My preference is for Maori to be working with Maori and to facilitate and support this happening. It is about recognizing who has the knowledge and skills and connecting tangata whaiora with those people.

Kieran: What I hear you saying in terms of the articles of Te Tiriti o Waitangi is that you enact Articles 2 and 3 by facilitating and supporting tangata whenua, exercising self-determination in relation to their wellbeing and by working to provide tangata whaiora with the best service you can that will meet their needs.

Mathew: Another way for me of meeting my obligations under the Treaty of Waitangi is the awareness of tangata whenua theories and models when working cross-culturally. One such model is te whare tapa wha, which is a holistic framework and model of Maori health that consists of the four walls of: taha wairua (spiritual dimension), taha whanau (extended family), taha hinengaro (mental dimension) and taha tinana (physical dimension) (Durie 1994). I see some similarities between this framework and integrated practice. That said, I want to be clear that I am not saying they are the same nor do I want to equate one with the other, nor colonize te whare tapa wha with the integrated framework. I was particularly impressed with a participant in my Master's research who reflected the model so beautifully and with such passion, that it became clear to me that te whare tapa wha reflects a way of being, as well as a way of thinking and conceptualizing and acting. Integrated practice has the risk that practitioners will engage in a more compartmentalized approach, and that integration will be not nearly as perpetually intertwined.

Kieran: So you are saying they are not the same, but there are similarities. What then are the areas of convergence?

Mathew: I think that you could go through integrated practice and apply each dimension of te whare tapa wha to each layer of integrated practice. It addresses similar issues to those of integrated practice. As I start to conceptualize te whare tapa wha in this way, I realize that my non-Maori mind is compartmentalizing things and separating them out, and that I am doing this from an individualized worldview rather than from a collectivist kin-based one. And, therefore, te whare tapa wha challenges me to look again and see that it is holistic, interwoven, collective. And that the divisions in my language and mind concerning the heart and head, the spiritual and the physical, being, thinking, feeling and doing, with the whole being the sum of its parts, are just that in my mind and in my language, constructed by my cultural context.

Kieran: I am just reflecting on one of the challenges that Jane and I faced in writing the chapter on the ecological metaphor in Australasia, concerning whether we include te whare tapa wha as an ecological systems theory. As you are aware, having read that chapter, we didn't include it. One of the reasons for not including it was because it is based in te ao Maori (the Maori world) and because it belongs to that world. The minute we, as non-Maori, start to explain it within a framework of our construction, we are extracting it from its world and it becomes colonized much in the same way that whakapakari whanau (whanau decision-making) has been when it is described as a form of family group conferencing (Tauri 1998). In other words, by locating or integrating the indigenous theory within our worldview, we reconstruct it within that worldview, rather than relate to it within its own world. Therefore, if we located te whare tapa wha within the ecological systems tradition as indigenous form of ecological systems theory, we are creating the situation whereby it becomes viewed and labelled within that frame and may be construed and reduced to being a Maori ecological systems theory rather than being seen as te whare tapa wha with all of the nuances that come from it being located in the tangata whenua world.

Mathew: Yes, I think you have just given a good example of the challenges we face when we are critical of how we engage cross-culturally and as non-Maori practitioners who refer to and use te whare tapa wha. It seems to me the question we have to ask is: Whose house are we visiting, restoring and supporting? Do we see the whare as a whare rather than as a Maori version of a house? I believe tauiwi practitioners need an ongoing awareness and regard for te whare tapa wha, but it would be risky to claim an explicit application of the same. As

Oscar Wilde would put it: becoming actors playing parts that were not written for us.

Kieran: How well do you think the integrated framework addresses the needs of other population groups?

Mathew: My thesis was based on the application of integrated practice with same-sex oriented men and I think that it works really well, because it is based in an ecological approach. This is important because it provides the background for seeing multiple gay communities, and that gay people tie into a range of communities, as well as the need for practitioners to critically examine their worldview and positioning. For me, integrated practice also promotes approaching the other person with absolute regard and I think that this positive regard and respect for people helps opposite-sex oriented practitioners to work with consumers across the sexual orientation range. That first key component of integrated practice concerned with self-awareness and knowing how I come across, I think, is key in working with difference and diverse populations.

Kieran: Thanks for those comments. In terms of 'where to next' in this conversation I suggest that we talk some more about supervision, then evaluate integrated practice and finish by reflecting upon the conversation itself. What do you consider important in the supervision of a practitioner who uses an integrated practice approach?

Mathew: Apart from the obvious matter of finding a supervisor and having a choice of supervisor, it would be important to have a supervisor who:

- can contest without condemning
- can challenge without patronizing, and
- can support, engage and apply integrated practice in the supervision process.

Kieran: You also provide supervision, and I am wondering how your integrated approach helps other practitioners reflect upon themselves and their practice.

Mathew: I think that it helps in two areas. The first is in engaging the supervisee and the second is the discourse, and here integrated practice supports an open exchange and open invitation to think out loud. It also supports the reflective process that occurs in supervision. I see supervision as our point of reflective accountability. Through the supervision process, the social work practitioner, as a critically informed integrated practitioner, is a reflective practitioner who is provided with the opportunity of reflecting on their practice and what informs it. They can also consider the implications of practice in context, and address training and personal and professional development.

Kieran: In reflecting on what informs our practice, how do you evaluate integrated practice?

Mathew: I think its strength is that it enables practitioners to articulate what informs their knowing, decision-making and actions and serves to help integrate this at a personal, critical social science and clinical level into an informed practice approach through which they can explain and justify both their assessments and interventions in practice.

Turning to the challenges that integrated practice faces, one of them concerns the ability to maintain the depth of reflection and the breadth of knowledge when you are facing a high and demanding workload, for example, when you have 15 consumers to see today. I think that this is when thinking about one's theoretical orientation, values and everything is easily pushed aside as you go from one thing to another, and perhaps, your only reflection space is supervision. I think the danger that emerges here is that the practitioner risks embracing a technicist practice style based on action and devoid of critical reflexivity.

There is always room for thought about the different aspects of integrated practice, particularly, how do we integrate our values, ideas and our sense of self, right through to the coalface? It also raise the questions for me such as, where is the opportunity for developing theory, ideas and techniques? There is not a lot of room for such questions in contemporary mental health services, because of the demand on our time and on services. My hope is that the discourse continues. I think it is important to keep the conversation concerning what informs our practice alive and continuing, because its transformative potential is great! I believe we are enriched and grow from such conversations, and if they are left to the likes of you and me in my office they are not going to grow a lot. This discourse needs other voices.

References

Durie, M. (1994) *Whaiora*. Auckland: Oxford University Press.

Gitterman, A. (1996) 'Life model theory and social work treatment.' In F. Turner (ed) *Social Work Treatment*, 4th edn. New York, Free Press.

Health and Disability Commissioner (2001) *Southland District Health Board Mental Health Services: A Report by the Health and Disability Commisioner, February-March 2001*. Auckland: Health and Disability Commissioner.

Keen, B. (2001), *'Queer Practice' A Consideration of Some Psychiatric/Mental Health Social Work Practitioners' Constructions of Gay Male Sexualities*. Palmerston North: MSW Thesis, Massey University.

Prasad, R. (1986) *Transitions in Foster Care – The Development of Training Programs for Foster Care Workers*. Palmerston North: PhD thesis, Massey University.

Prasad, R. (1988) *Towards A Theoretical Framework in Foster Care: A Framework for the Management of and Research into Transitions in Foster Care*. King George Virgina: American Foster Care Resources.

Prasad, R. (ed) (1993) *Book of Readings: 79651 Integrated Practice in Welfare and Development.* Palmerston North: Massey University.

Specht, H. and Vickery, A. (eds) (1977) *Integrating Social Work Methods.* London: Allen and Unwin.

Tauri, J. (1998) 'Family group conferencing: The myth of indigenous empowerment in New Zealand.' *Justice as Healing Newsletter 4,* 1, http://www.usask.ca/nativelaw/publications/jah/tauri.html, accessed 21 March 2004.

Wakefield, J. (1996) 'Does social work need the eco-systems perspective? Part 1. Is the perspective clinically useful?' *Social Service Review 70,* 1, 1–32.

Part II
Developing Communities

Introduction

This section moves to focus on practice in community settings, another level in the integrated practice framework. The challenge for social and community workers is to maintain a focus on social justice and to develop an understanding about what wider structures are impacting negatively on the lives of their clients. Central to this is knowing how to challenge current situations while working alongside groups to develop alternative structures that can be sustained over time and that ensure that all citizens can fully participate in their communities.

The chapters in this section clearly demonstrate a strong link between practice and achieve this by exploring some key principles of community development in action, from a range of perspectives. These include:

- *vision* – knowing that change includes challenging current structures that marginalize communities but identifying a vision for the future

- *indigenous frameworks* – having a clear understanding of the rights of indigenous populations and their central place in our communities

- *global and local contexts* – understanding the relationship between global issues and local challenges and choosing how to work to effect change on a number of levels

- *locating oneself* – this includes knowing how groups have arrived at their current positions and understanding how this will contribute to achieving positive change for their communities

- *understanding power relations* – knowing how to work within power relationships is a key strategy in community development practice

- *self-determination* – achieving self-determination and understanding the meaning of this will be done within cultural frameworks and the other frameworks that determine how communities wish to organize their daily lives

- *working collectively* – people work together and share resources and experiences to achieve positive change

- *social change* – the search for change that will result in participation for marginalized groups guides community development practice
- *action and reflection* – the process of change involves action and reflection on strategies in order to sustain the effectiveness of the change process.

The chapters demonstrate the diversity of community development practice. The first chapter provides a context for the other chapters and outlines the theory and practice of community development. Chapter 6 by Rachael Selby provides an example of community development within an *iwi* (tribal) context and shows how positive change can be achieved and sustained over time. Tracie Mafile'o describes community development practice from a Tongan perspective and provides an alternative interpretation of key principles. In the final chapter Mary Nash offers yet another view on community development by showing the contribution community development practice can make to working with migrant populations.

Chapter 5

Community Development: Principles into Practice

Robyn Munford and Wheturangi Walsh-Tapiata

Introduction

This chapter explores community development from a number of perspectives. While the discussion is situated in the Aotearoa/New Zealand context, the principles and issues outlined have relevance for a range of settings and contexts. The following guides the discussion: how are the core values and principles of community development mediated through local contexts? We argue that there are key principles underlying the practice of community development. These have relevance in international contexts and include social justice, redistribution of resources, self-determination and sustainability. What is required is an understanding of how these are interpreted within specific cultural, economic, social, political and religious frameworks.

Community development in Aotearoa/New Zealand operates within a bicultural context. Ruwhiu (2001) articulates the meaning of biculturalism and portrays it as the relationship between cultures co-existing alongside one another. In Aotearoa/New Zealand biculturalism has a particular meaning, as it will in other countries. Te Tiriti o Waitangi (the Treaty of Waitangi) as a constitutional founding document protects the rights of Maori as tangata whenua (the indigenous population and guardians of the land) and validates the existence of tauiwi (others who came to New Zealand after Maori) to live in this land (Munford *et al.* 2001). Within this context it is about understanding Maori as the tangata whenua and as the indigenous population and understanding how relationships are constructed with others who have come later to this country (tauiwi). Tauiwi embraces a wide range of cultural groups and they in turn will interpret their identities within the context of Aotearoa/New Zealand. In this way multiculturalism and the world-views of all populations living in Aotearoa/New Zealand are built on an understanding of the relationship of the indigenous population with all others living in this land. While these ideas are increasingly informing our practice in Aotearoa/New Zealand, it must be stated that we have many challenges ahead in order to achieve a total commitment to bicultural practice in all aspects of social and community work.

There are many definitions of community development. We have synthesized the definitions of other writers, such as Craig (1987), Derrick (1993) and Ife (1995), and suggest that the following depict the key elements of community development:

- It involves working alongside groups to identify discourses, structures, policies and practices that require transformation.

- It often involves working with groups who have been marginalized and excluded from participation. Community workers assist these groups to gain control over their situations and to achieve positive changes that will enhance their daily lived experiences in all domains (social, political, cultural, economic etc.).

- Community development involves a vision of how things might be changed so that sustainability and social justice can be achieved at global and national levels (Ife 1995).

- Community development workers adopt collective methods, harness existing resources and identify what is required to ensure that all populations can be fully involved as citizens in their communities. Identifying long-term strategies for development is a key activity of community development (Derrick 1993).

- A key focus is on working from people's own definitions of situations, ensuring that community development workers are partners for change. Community workers work with groups and throughout the change process they model actions that embrace social justice, including an understanding that in top-down approaches the local and indigenous knowledge of communities is likely to have been subjugated (Munford and Walsh-Tapiata 2000).

We view community development as a process and a way of perceiving the world. Community development should not be viewed as just a 'job' but as a 'mindset' that characterizes a particular perspective on the world. While many workers will be employed as community development workers, others (for example, social workers) will be able to use community development principles in their daily work and to use these principles and community development practices to analyze and identify how the individual situations of social service clients can be transformed (Munford and Walsh-Tapiata 2000).

This chapter will explore principles that we have found to be useful in defining community development in action. It is based on an understanding of the links between theory and practice – praxis. Praxis is the dialogical relationship between theory and practice and provides a foundation for community development. As Kenny (1994, p.54) states:

> When we bring the two terms *theory* and *practice* together, we are talking about the links between theories, explanations and assumptions, on the one hand, and everyday activities, processes, task, skills and strategies, on the other. Thus community development integrates theory and practice. This integration is sometimes referred to as praxis. Praxis regards people not just as objects of study, but also as agents of history... For community development the integration of theory and practice brings together our theoretical understandings of the way in which society works and our vision of how we would like it to work, with specific strategies and tasks.

We have used this assertion to guide our practice and we have also identified a number of key principles derived from our own practice and from those of other writers. These are:

- having a vision for our future
- indigenous frameworks
- interpreting local contexts
- locating oneself in community development practice
- understanding power
- achieving self-determination
- working collectively
- bringing about positive social change
- action and reflection.

These will be discussed in turn and the final part of the chapter will look at the challenge of applying community development principles in practice. This includes how we can respond to these so that we develop robust strategies for maintaining community development practice and achieving change for marginalized groups whose participation and opportunities are compromised and who may have suffered long-term disadvantage as a result of this.

Key principles

Having a vision for our future

It is important for community workers to work with the community to build a vision. This can be broad, such as social justice for all, or it can be very focused, a goal that the community wishes to achieve for themselves. Having a vision forms the basis of finding a direction for achieving positive change and sustaining this change. The building of a vision involves 'listening to what individuals and communities know about themselves' (Beilharz 2002, p.v). Beilharz (2002, p.23) suggests 'developing a shared vision is a perquisite for change and is also a democratic process.'

In Aotearoa/New Zealand, the tangata whenua have a particular interpretation of articulating a vision. This is called moemoea. Here the people of the indigenous nation articulate their dreams, within these are stories from the past and for the future. This process connects people to their tipuna (ancestors) and these connections are interpreted within current contexts. Moemoea sustains people in the change process and is returned to time and time again.

Indigenous frameworks

In the Aotearoa/New Zealand context, it is essential to have an understanding of the Treaty of Waitangi and its importance in enabling us to understand the relationship between Maori and the Crown and with tauiwi. Community workers constantly think about why there have been transgressions against the articles of the Treaty and are challenged to articulate possibilities for the creation of more equitable relationships between Maori and tauiwi. The challenge for community workers is to translate the articles of the Treaty into their daily practices. For example, if we take partnership as a key element to be addressed, how can we form real and meaningful partnerships between Maori and tauiwi in organizations and communities?

We have argued elsewhere (Munford and Walsh-Tapiata 2000, p.12) that successful community development workers will always look for new ways of making the Treaty of Waitangi relevant to the contexts in which they are working. Indigenous frameworks, due to colonization, could have been lost. However, alternative structures based on indigenous frameworks are emerging; for example, the creation of Te Kohanga Reo (early childhood language centres) that introduce the Maori language to children. These movements often begin from the grassroots and indeed their success is attributed to this strategy. Funding and formal policies often follow their implementation, but those involved work hard to maintain the vision and essence of these initiatives. In addition to developing indigenous frameworks for practice, we are also constantly reminded as community workers that the needs of tauiwi become more diverse as increasing numbers of migrant groups come to live in Aotearoa/New Zealand. Other countries around the world will face similar issues. Community workers will need to work to foreground the needs of indigenous populations and local ethnic groups, while working to include new migrant populations as citizens in their communities.

Interpreting local contexts

This principle is linked to the discussion on indigenous frameworks above and includes an understanding of communities within their local contexts. We argue that community workers need to understand how global issues and national events and policies are played out in local communities. They must ask themselves whether local communities are supported or hindered by wider forces. Do these forces function to enhance community life or to marginalize populations? For example, do the economic policies of national governments and international organizations, such as world financial and trade agencies, support rural economies? Or do these policies result in the closing down of local factories with a negative impact on the livelihoods and sustainability of rural populations?

Linked to the above is the understanding by community workers that local structures must exist to support local communities. Do communities have access to adequate local resources that provide appropriate infrastructure to the community (Beilharz 2002) and contribute to building strong networks? In contrast, do families and individuals seek support from outside the community, which may be difficult for those with minimal material resources and which also means that local structures are not contributing to local networks of support? For example, local health agencies do not only provide for the health needs of individuals, but may also make a positive contribution by providing a focus for groups to come together to address local health needs.

A third meaning of local contexts includes the foregrounding of local knowledge 'as the common sense wisdom that comes from everyday life activities rather than formal learning' (Van Vlaenderen 2004, p.138). It refers to 'what is' and 'how things are done' and 'to the whole system of knowledge, including concepts, beliefs, values, goals and perceptions and the processes whereby these are acquired, stored and transmitted' (Van Vlaenderen 2004, p.138). The challenge for community workers is to understand that local knowledge is a central aspect of the change process and that without an understanding of this knowledge, community workers can often make the wrong decisions about and interpretations of local issues. This knowledge may have been previously ignored and the strengths and successes that the community has already achieved may not be immediately evident. The overwhelming effects of current struggles may diminish the community's sense of efficacy and control. Effective community workers work alongside communities in ways that enable local knowledge to emerge as a foundation for addressing current challenges in order to achieve change. This process in itself can be part of a larger process that enables communities to take control and see that they have a central role in determining their own futures. A key role of the community worker may involve presenting the possibilities for change in local contexts that can then impact on regional, national and international contexts.

Locating oneself in community development practice

Being able to locate oneself within one's own community development practice is an important principle and is strongly connected to understanding and interpreting local contexts. To effectively locate ourselves in our practice, we need to have a clear understanding of our background and position in society and the way this determines how we see the world. Locating oneself requires us to look critically at our previous experience and how this may influence our perspective and interpretations of key events.

Linking personal experience to public issues and events is a key component of locating oneself. It includes thinking of our worlds from a number of perspectives, for example, our family experience, education, significant events, influential people in our history and cultural and religious experiences, to name but a few. A key strategy is to think about how these personal experiences have been influenced by wider issues and identifying how these wider issues may have expanded or restricted life opportunities. By telling our stories and situating ourselves in a particular historical, social, economical and cultural position (Munford and Walsh-Tapiata 2000), we can begin to make sense of our world and how negative circumstances could be transformed.

Different cultures will have different ways of locating themselves. For Maori the critical question is concerned with knowing about where you are from as a foundation for knowing who you are. Knowing your iwi (tribe) and your tribal connections is central and tells others about your connections and relationships, now and in the past. One locates oneself not as an individual, but as part of a collective with a history that defines current contexts and relationships.

The process of asking oneself who we are in the world and what/who has influenced this, is an excellent tool for beginning a relationship with community groups. It enables groups to make connections with one another and with the community worker. Community workers use this process to establish a strong foundation for the change process.

Understanding power

One of the key foundations of community development is acknowledging that power relations do exist and that a key role of community workers is to identify the nature of these relations. An important element of understanding the nature of power relations is exploring who benefits from the existence of these, who is disadvantaged by these, how they are maintained and how they can be transformed. Community workers do not just accept current reality that may place certain groups in marginalized positions, as if this is a commonsense and expected state of affairs. Community workers work alongside communities to find out why certain situations exist. This will include an analysis of historical and current power relations at all levels – policy, community, organizational and individual levels.

We have used the analysis of writers such as Foucault (Munford and Walsh-Tapiata 2000) to understand the complexities of the relations of power. This includes an analysis of the discourses (the social practices, behaviours, rituals, structures that determine everyday life) that function to maintain power relations. Foucault argues that power is present in all social relationships and that to understand this one needs to carry out an 'analytics of power' (Gutting 1994). We must explore what power looks and feels like for those who are experiencing the negative consequences of power relations. Power is multi-faceted and operates differently at different sites and we cannot utilize a unitary and unchanging view of power. Moreover, power can be productive and will not always be repressive. For example, groups experiencing marginalization as social service clients may at times experience positive aspects of this situation. They may therefore feel ambivalent about challenging those aspects that have a negative impact on their lives.

If community workers are to understand how power operates in all aspects of social life and how these may be transformed, they need to explore how power operates in the daily practices of their communities. This exploration demonstrates how power is maintained but also the situations where it has been overcome and transformed. A framework that utilizes an understanding of how power operates in different situations is extremely useful in community development practice. It reveals the complexity of power and why some groups may not be able to challenge power relations. They may at times be productive for the group, or the discourses may have been taken for granted and seen as 'natural': an accepted way of operating and unable to be challenged. Power relations can be so invasive that individuals and groups are unable to see how life could be any different. The community development worker can assist groups to understand the operation of power, in order to move from positions of immobilization and passivity to a situation where they can begin to understand the nature of power and how it can be challenged.

Achieving self-determination

There are two key elements of self-determination: having one's voice heard and having opportunities for developing knowledge so that participation can be extended and strengthened. Participation is active, meaning that one can have a say about what is going on in one's community and in the wider society. In democratic societies it is more than exercising one's right to vote every number of years. It is about being able to exercise choice in a range of settings on a daily level. In our understandings of self-determination we incorporate the acknowledgment of the diversity of individuals and the right to be treated with dignity, no matter what your subject position. We see self-determination as being strongly connected to the understanding of power relations. Here we understand how some groups are subject to power relations in such a way that their identities are devalued, resources are inadequate and they are unable to exercise self-determination.

Self-determination is a complex concept. It involves walking alongside individuals in order to understand their world and to understand why they cannot become self-determining, why their dignity and diversity is minimized and why they are not able to make choices in their lives. It includes understanding why access to resources may be closed off and how these situations can be challenged so that participation and citizenship can be achieved.

Self-determination is central to social justice (Beilharz 2002). In Aotearoa/New Zealand one way this is played out in practice, is through tino rangatiratanga, a concept used by Maori to provide full meaning to the notion of self-determination. Durie (1995) identifies three principles associated with tino rangatiratanga:

- *nga matatini Maori* – the principle of Maori diversity, which recognizes that Maori now live in many diverse realities

- *whakakotahi* – the principle of Maori unity, which acknowledges the potential for solidarity in the Maori community, based on a sense of belonging and a common destiny

- *mana motuhake Maori* – the principle of autonomy and control which acknowledges that Maori are no longer prepared to let others decide policies for them, or to make key decisions on their behalf but want to determine their own futures, control their own resources and develop their own political structures.

Tino rangatiratanga guides the relationships between iwi, hapu (sub-tribe), whanau (family) and au (individual) and how these are connected in the pursuit of collective self-determination. Other societies will demonstrate particular interpretations of self-determination. Whatever the interpretation, the central theme remains: the ability to have voice, to participate and to exercise control over one's destiny.

Working collectively

One of the key elements of community development is to work alongside communities and groups in order to identify issues and to examine why these groups may be marginalized from decision-making processes and from resources. It challenges 'top-down' approaches that define the issues for the community. Community development requires a certain mindset on behalf of the worker. A key commitment of the worker is to carry out collective analyses with the community to find ways to share their knowledge with these groups and to ensure that the community worker does not take on the role of the 'expert'. Community workers resist the role of the expert and instead work with the community to identify an understanding of issues and how knowledge can be shared in order to address these issues. At times, community workers will take a lead role in terms of analysis and use of knowledge, given that communities will be at different stages of development and will need time to address issues and bring about change. However, the goal of a community worker is to work alongside communities and enable communities to be self-determining and gain knowledge and skills that help them achieve self-determination. At times this is a frustrating and challenging process for community workers, but they must resist returning to a situation where they hold power to make decisions and where they do not uphold the sharing of knowledge. They must always be prepared to work towards taking on a less significant role in the change process.

Working collectively forms the essence of community development practice and takes many forms. Maori call working collectively mahi tahi, working together towards a common goal. Having a commitment to working together for change requires commitment and practice, compromise at times and continual reflection in order to ensure that this is being achieved. There is an ongoing commitment to change for everyone rather than for just a few privileged individuals, an integral part of a community worker's worldview and vision for a just society.

A key aspect of working collectively is to learn how to direct decision-making towards approaches that strive for consensus. This is essential, given that many of the groups we work with are used to handing over decisions to others, and may have difficulty in believing that they can be agents in their own change processes. Achieving this belief begins with having opportunities to be active in group processes and decision-making and to see how others are partners in the change process.

Bringing about positive social change

Community development includes understanding how structures, policies and discourses can be challenged and transformed. A key element of community work practice is to ensure that any positive change is maintained and can be extended to have benefits for other groups. For example, disabled women working for access rights may achieve the development of policies that will ensure that all disabled people can have ease of access to all environments. An essential element of community development is sharing knowledge, so that new initiatives can benefit from the successes that have gone before and have been achieved by other groups.

Social change requires that people believe that they have agency and can achieve change. A challenge for community workers is to assist the community to believe that change is possible. This will involve identifying a vision, with clear goals on the pathway to change. We have used structural analysis processes with groups to bring about change (Munford and Walsh-Tapiata 2000). This includes taking groups through a process of locating themselves within the issues, naming clearly the issues to be addressed, identifying the vision for change, analyzing all the forces involved in the issues and working through and evaluating strategies for change. It ends with reflection on the process and identifying how change can be sustained. This includes evaluating how the change process may have spin-off benefits for other issues. For example, success in one area can provide impetus for challenging other areas that require transformation. It also includes an analysis of the potential negative outcomes of social change. For example, placing individuals in public roles that may open them up to challenge and criticism.

A key challenge is also to cope with the setbacks that may come in the change process and to find ways to maintain the energy to keep working towards our goals. In Aotearoa/New Zealand, Maori have shown the importance of grassroots change. There have been many success stories both historically and within current contexts. For example, the development of the Kohanga Reo movement has demonstrated outstanding change that has had 'buy-in' from a range of groups and long-term benefits that have been maintained and contributed to the development of other educational initiatives. While various government departments can be acknowledged for participation in the development of this early childhood initiative, it was the local communities, kaumatua (older Maori people) and women who made the commitment to develop this initiative in their respective communities. This was the essence of the success of the movement; a government directive or policy would not have made this initiative work. In this example, the decision-making power of the collective led to the overall positive development of a group of people who were not previously seen to be successful in the education system, in their communities and in wider society.

Being involved in bringing about positive change can be demanding but is also profoundly rewarding. All of the key phases leading to change require critical reflection and a commitment to modifying strategies along the way. It also includes celebrating the successes and the commitment to social change.

Action and reflection

Action and reflection are key community development principles. Action and reflection include a continual commitment to reflecting on one's actions in order to analyze the success and failures and to identify more effective strategies to bring about change. The key phases of change are to engage in planning, and analysis, action and reflection. We have developed a number of tools for carrying out action and reflection (Munford and Walsh-Tapiata 2000). These include:

- role-playing possible strategies for change

- stopping the planning processes to identify possible positive and negative outcomes of change

- vision exercises to ensure that the long-term goals are still clearly focused

- keeping a journal of events that includes processes for reflecting on the change process.

Action and reflection are critical, as groups may become so entwined in their issue that they do not create the opportunity to step back to see the processes in action and the influence of a wide range of factors on the issue and on group processes. Action and reflection are excellent foundations for developing formal procedures for evaluating the change process and outcomes. This includes understanding how the community has been able to define its own goals and priorities and how it has invested in the change process (Beilharz 2002). It is important to establish at the beginning of the process strategies for understanding how plans are to be defined and agreed upon and how success will be monitored and evaluated throughout the key stages of a project. These strategies also keep community workers accountable, with a commitment to reflect critically on their practice.

Making the principles come alive – challenges for practice

The challenge for community workers is to ensure that the principles discussed above guide all aspects of their practice. The following discussion identifies some of the challenges, but also some of the strategies, for ensuring that these remain central to community development practice. These are not in order of priority, as all of these points are key aspects of successful change projects.

Maintaining the relationship between theory and practice

Community workers will often work alongside those groups who are at the margins and whose lives have been negatively influenced by factors such as economic globalization, market liberalization and the accompanying political discourse of neo-liberalism (Williams, Labonte and O'Brien 2003, p.33). As Williams *et al.* (2003) suggest, we need to understand that these communities are likely to have had little influence on the shape of policy discourse and on decision-making and minimal opportunities to engage in politics as active citizens. Williams *et al.* (2003) suggest that community development workers have a key role in supporting such groups to find opportunities to assert their own cultural expression and to exercise agency. We see that a key component of this work is to foreground the strong links between theory and practice. It is the role of the community worker to encourage a dialogue between theory and practice, whereby the different kinds of knowledge that are brought to community development practice are given equal weight. We argue that all community development work must have a commitment to praxis and to understanding the dynamic interplay between different kinds of knowledge. As we discussed earlier, giving value to one's knowledge and traditions, and seeing these as important as the formal, intellectual knowledge that may be used in practice, is a significant part of the change process.

Praxis ensures that our actions are well grounded and that we are not merely reacting to events but are systematically working to understand our world and to bring about change. In our work with groups, we begin with exploring the meaning of praxis and how we can equip ourselves with the knowledge that will help us challenge dominant structures and to transform these. Freire's (1972) legacy of challenging the 'culture of silence' and working to support groups to find out about their worlds is an important keystone in our community development practice.

Keeping the vision alive

The discussion in the previous section is strongly connected to thinking about how we can keep our vision alive so that it can sustain the change process and keep us going through difficult times. As with our commitment to praxis, a vision exercise needs to happen right at the beginning of a project and forms part of the relationship building between group members and the community worker. Time needs to be taken to identify dreams and aspirations and to turn these into concrete goals that can be achieved by the group. One of the biggest challenges to groups is to maintain the motivation of a change process when times become difficult and energy is dissipated. We believe that a structural analysis approach will provide a framework for guiding the change process and for keeping the vision alive (Munford and Walsh-Tapiata 2000). This framework includes: establishing the group, identifying issues and framing goals, analyzing the issue, developing strategies for change, and evaluating the project through its key phases. Here we use a number of tools in each of the phases to ensure that all group members are involved and are active participants in the group. Facilitation of group meetings is shared and members are encouraged to develop their own tools of analysis that highlight their own knowledge and understanding of the issues. Many creative ideas have emerged from this process, with people's hidden talents (such as in visual arts) coming to the fore as they work to understand the many perspectives on an issue and on the change process.

The framework can be modified according to the needs of the group. What it does is provide a systematic way of dealing with issues, so that groups do not become overwhelmed. It assists us to maintain our passion and keep our vision alive and in the process of carrying out a range of creative activities, it enables group members to share their knowledge and to learn new skills that will be transferable to the other activities with which they may become involved in the future. This process supports real power sharing, where the process of change is congruent with the end goal and where active participation and exercise of agency are cornerstones of the change process.

Maintaining collective strategies and upholding self-determination

In our work we spend much time practising how we can maintain our commitment to working collectively to find shared strategies for change. We continually critique our practice, and central to this is consideration of whether we are upholding the commitment to achieving self-determination and what this actually means in practice. Self-determination, as we saw in the previous discussion, is culturally and context specific; this needs to be factored into our evaluation of how self-determination is being enacted and agency is being exercised. We have brought maintaining collective strategies and upholding self-determination together in this discussion, as we believe that they are strongly connected. Self-determination is not achieved for individuals in isolation from the collective. It is likely that it is more effectively achieved when interdependence and collective support is sought, rather than independence and freedom to act as an individual, without reference to one's position as a member of a community, culture or organization. As Furlong (2003, p.186) suggests, a key question to be asked is whether the self is understood as free-standing, rational and unitary or whether it is 'relational' and connected to kin affiliations and related positions. Our concern in community development is to be aware of what this means in practice and to position the achievement of self-determination within an understanding of collective and social good. It includes understanding how interdependence and strong affiliations with one's reference groups and society (in an environment free from abuse and harm) is likely to result in increasing opportunities for individuals to actively participate in their communities in the long term.

Furlong's (2003) discussion is helpful, for it reminds us to critically evaluate the meaning of self-determination and to understand its position within the promotion of social justice and within the domains of belonging and connection. We can ask the question: does self-determination enliven the prospects for inclusiveness and accountability (p.191)? And does it uphold collective responsibility and entail 'an expectation of mutualistic citizenship' (p.193)?

Working collectively also involves community workers in critical reflection on their attitudes towards the groups with whom they are working. At times, community workers have been accused of being paternalistic when they have slipped into care roles that are imbued with control and authority over clients (Tonkens and Duyvendak 2003). Again, we agree with Tonkens and Duyvendak (2003) and argue that given the nature of our society, paternalism is likely to be inevitable. But for us the important questions are about ensuring that a striving for social justice and active citizenship is driving our efforts and relationships with communities.

Believing that change is possible and working to sustain this change

An understanding of how self-determination is played out is strongly connected to how communities come to recognize their ability to effect change. Beilharz (2002) discusses how communities who have traditionally been seen as victims and the causes of their own problems, will often accept their plight and may feel powerless to change their situation. This is particularly so in impoverished communities (Munford *et al.* 2001) where people may have limited means to change their circumstances, and where they may have internalized their oppression to the extent that they accept their current situation as 'natural' and expected (Pease 2003). Many groups have been let down by traditional helping agencies, which means that the community worker needs to work hard to gain the trust and confidence of the community.

We need also to understand the role social capital (networks, associations, social groups etc.) has in encouraging individuals to participate in their communities. We have argued elsewhere (Munford, Sanders and Andrew 2003) that impoverished communities cannot be expected to have stocks of social and economic capital and that this will need to be addressed as part of the change process. As DeFilippis (2001) argues, social capital is linked to economic capital and it should not be expected that communities that are lacking economic capital will be able to harness large stocks of social capital, as these are also likely to be diminished. However, what a framework such as this does is give us a starting point for community development action. The change process will include an analysis of social networks and the support of these networks in order to expand and realize social and economic capital (DeFilippis 2001). He suggests that it is important to build on existing networks, but it is also important to get inside these networks to ensure that they are beneficial to the groups concerned. For example, in one of our research projects we have shown that young people may join gangs that meet their needs for connection and belonging, but in the long term are likely to have negative consequences for their health and wellbeing (Munford and Sanders 2003).

The change process is complex and strategies need to be put in place that will ensure that successes and achievements can be harnessed to sustain change over the long-term. To make a commitment to a change process, communities need to receive something from the process and to believe that the end goals will have a positive influence on their current situations. As Beilharz (2002) suggests, community workers are involved in creating optimism that change is possible and life circumstances can be transformed. Beginning with small goals is a key strategy, as success in these will support groups to take on further challenges. A key challenge for the community worker is to be clear about their commitment to change and to maintain a community development approach while ensuring that the daily needs of individuals are addressed. Being realistic about goals and strategies, knowing how to negotiate differing views on what is required, working collectively, knowing who will support the group through the difficult times and keeping that vision about social justice in front of you, are just some of the factors that will encourage communities to become involved in their own change processes and sustain this change over the long term.

Conclusion

This chapter has given the reader one view of community development. We see community development approaches as central to achieving social change. Community development requires a commitment to engaging with communities, to support them to be agents in their own change processes. The challenges are many, but so are the rewards; one of the most important being enhanced participation and involvement of communities in developing their own futures and destinies.

Questions for reflection

1. Reflect on the principles and the challenges in community development practice in terms of your own work.

2. What theoretical ideas inform your community development practice?

3. Identify the relationship between community development and the struggles of indigenous groups. What is the relationship between community development and indigenous frameworks? How can community development enhance and make visible the experience of indigenous groups? And other populations?

4. Reflect on a piece of social change in which you have been involved. Are there other strategies that could have been used?

References

Beilharz, L. (2002) *Building Community: The Shared Action Experience.* Bendigo, Australia: St Luke's Innovative Resources.

Craig, W. (1987) *A Community Work Perspective.* Palmerston North: Massey University.

DeFilippis, J. (2001) 'The myth of social capital in community development.' *Housing Policy Debate 12*, 4, 781–806.

Derrick, E. (1993) *Community Development and Social Change.* Auckland: Auckland District Council of Social Services.

Durie, M. (1995) 'Tino Rangatiratanga: Maori self determination.' *He Pukenga Korero, A Journal of Maori Studies 1*, 1, 44–53.

Freire, P. (1972) *The Pedagogy of the Oppressed.* London: Penguin.

Furlong, M.A. (2003) 'Self-determination and a critical perspective in casework: Promoting a balance between interdependence and autonomy.' *Qualitative Social Work: Research and Practice 2*, 2, 177–196.

Gutting, G. (1994) *The Cambridge Companion to Foucault.* Cambridge and New York: Cambridge University Press.

Ife, J. (1995) *Community Development: Creating Community Alternatives – Vision, Analysis and Practice.* Melbourne: Longman.

Kenny, S. (1994) *Developing Communities for the Future: Community Development in Australia.* Australia: Thomas Nelson.

Munford, R., Sanders, J. and Andrew, A. (2003) 'Community development-action research in community settings.' *Social Work Education 22*, 1, 93–104.

Munford, R. and Sanders, J. with Andrew, A., Butler, P. and Ruwhiu, L. (2003) 'Action research with families/whanau and communities.' In R. Munford and J. Sanders (eds) *Making a Difference in Families: Research that Creates Change.* Australia: Allen and Unwin.

Munford, R. and Sanders, J. with Andrew, A., Butler, P., Kaipuke, R. and Ruwhiu, L. (2001) 'Aotearoa/New Zealand – Working differently with communities and families.' In C. Warren-Adamson (ed) *Family Centres and their International Role in Social Action.* Aldershot: Ashgate.

Munford, R. and Walsh-Tapiata, W. (2000) *Strategies for Change: Community Development in Aotearoa/New Zealand.* Palmerston North: Massey University.

Pease, P. (2003) 'Rethinking the relationship between the self and society.' In J. Allan, B. Pease and L. Briskman (eds) *Critical Social Work: An Introduction to Theories and Practice.* Australia: Allen and Unwin.

Ruwhiu, L. (2001) 'Bicultural issues in Aotearoa/New Zealand social work.' In M. Connolly (ed.) *New Zealand Social Work: Contexts and Practice.* Auckland: Oxford University Press.

Tonkens, E. and Duyvendak, J.W. (2003) 'Paternalism – caught between rejection and acceptance: Taking care and taking control in community work.' *Community Development Journal 38*, 1, 6–15.

Van Vlaenderen, H. (2004) 'Community development research: Merging communities of practice.' *Community Development Journal 39*, 2, 135–143.

Walsh-Tapiata, W. (1999) 'The more we go into the future the more we depend on the past: Strategic planning Maori style.' *Te Komako III: Social Work Review XI*, 4, 21–24.

Williams, L., Labonte, R. and O'Brien, M. (2003) 'Empowering social action through narratives of identity and culture.' *Health Promotion International 18*, 1, 33–40.

Chapter 6

Dreams are Free:
Nga Moemoea a te Hapu

Rachael Selby

This chapter illustrates community development in action. Ngatokowaru Marae is nestled beside the Hokio Stream, west of Lake Horowhenua, five kilometres from the Tasman sea and with a view of the Tararua ranges to the east. The family and marae have been located there, on the lower west coast of the North Island, since the early nineteenth century. The families, who built the first houses in the late nineteenth century, worked the land, milked cows and used the stream as a source of food and water for the community. The matriarch, Ema, gave birth to 14 children in the latter part of the century. They belonged to the land and stream, each regarded as gifts of their ancestors. The children who were born and raised there, were later taken to the local school by horse and trap or they walked the dusty road to the town until a school bus service began.

The community marae was self-sufficient, providing for its members and bringing in cash by selling surplus crops to the market and by selling milk to the local dairy factory. In the distance across the lake, they watched the forest being felled, the arrival of Europeans and the building of a railway connecting the city in Wellington, 100 kilometres south, with the city in Auckland to the north. Eventually, the steam from the trains could be seen in the distance. A new town emerged from the forest with a wide main street and wooden shops built from the timber on the hills. The railway linked the town with the growing communities along its route.

The Hokio stream flows from east to west along the northern boundary of the marae. It was important to the community living on its banks because it provided food: shellfish, flounder, an abundance of eel and freshwater crabs. The watercress, abundant on the edge of the stream, was a lush green vegetable. The stream was also used as a place in which to store food. In the late summer and early autumn when the eels migrated from the lake to the sea, the family trapped the eels and stored them in large wooden boxes which rested against the bank in the steam. The boxes were a metre long by half a metre high and wide, with holes at each end for the water to continue to flow through. A lid was attached and lifted each day to check the condition of the eels and to retrieve some for dinner. The eels were prepared in many different ways and over the winter were a primary source of protein. They were, for centuries, a staple food consumed several times a week. Vegetables were grown in the garden at the back of the homestead.

Children used the stream for swimming and exploring the environment. Favourite swimming holes were given names. Trees provided platforms from which to dive. Teenagers met friends to go eeling in the evenings. The stream neighbourhood was the playground, providing a wealth of experiences to children growing up in the area. They walked the banks of the stream to move from lake to sea, from house to house. They watched the fish life under the water and cooled off in the summer swimming and playing in the clear cool stream.

The healers in the community used the stream as a source of water to perform the cleansing and spiritual healing rituals. When members of the community were unwell, or travelling to distant places, water was used to bless the travellers and to provide protection. As the community also practised Christian rituals, water was used in baptism.

In 1952, the town council across the lake made the decision to discharge its sewage into Lake Horowhenua. The lake, located less than a kilometre east of the community fed the Hokio Stream. Within a short time, the raw sewage floated in the lake and down the stream beside the marae. It hung together in clumps, a filthy reminder of the growing modern European community on the other side of the lake.

Families living along the stream moved to the town anticipating that life on the stream could no longer continue as in the past. For the next three decades the effluent polluted the lake and stream. The population of the town grew, industry grew and the effluent increased. Development of the town was of greater importance than the survival of the community on the stream. The health of the lake and stream, were sacrificed in the name of progress. Durie (1998, p.54) describes urbanization as the 'unmarshalled force' pushing and pulling as Maori moved from rural to urban areas after the Second World War. The sewage disposal gave an extra push to families who saw the deterioration in the quality of the stream and the disappearance of fish species in it.

From the 1950s to the 1970s the marae was used less and less. When families attended functions at the marae, the children were forbidden to go near the stream. It was fenced off and older children designated to ensure that no children went down the slope to the banks of the stream, banks now overgrown with vegetation encouraged by the effluent. For 20 years the marae was seldom used. Many of our elders saw themselves as the last generation to use the marae as a gathering place where family celebrations occurred. Twenty-first birthdays and weddings were held in church halls in town rather than at the marae. A generation of children lost the connection with the stream, forbidden to venture near the unhealthy, polluted water. They also lost the skills needed to interact with the stream as a giver of food.

Until the Second World War, the marae was a bastion of tikanga Maori, where te reo Maori was spoken by the elders, where there was no question about the customs and traditions which were practised. It was an environment where Maori customs and traditions were the norm. It was a place where European influence had not penetrated in a way that would undermine Maori culture. After the Second World War and during the 1950s, this changed. Ngatokowaru was no longer used as a place of permanent residence, but primarily as a place to farewell the last generation to have been born there at the turn of the century.

When children and young people attended functions at the marae, it was accepted that after the war, they were brought up in a Pakeha world, speaking English, and their grandparents admired the success they had in school, in sports teams and in integrating into the Pakeha world. If they transgressed at the marae, they were forgiven as it was more important for them to know how to live in the Pakeha world than in the Maori world. That it was a formula leading to the demise of the community was of less concern than the success they could enjoy by being Pakeha, especially if they had a Pakeha parent and were fair-skinned.

Since the late nineteenth century, it had been predicted that the Maori race would die out (Durie 1998, p.53). A government official, Dr Isaac Featherstone 'echoed liberal European sentiment in the late nineteenth century when he spoke of the responsibility to "smooth the pillow of the dying race"' (King 1997, p.38). King describes the attitudes of Pakeha during the twentieth century towards Maori who came to be seen as unhealthy and living in substandard conditions. 'There were, in effect, two New Zealands: Pakeha New Zealand, served and serviced by comprehensive systems of national and local administration; and Maori New Zealand, largely ignored by both, except when those systems wanted to appropriate resources such as land, income or manpower.' (King 1997, p.43). In many ways the hapu community was invisible on the banks of the stream and the impact of refuse and effluent in their backyard was ignored by the local council, as were its origins.

For much of the mid-twentieth century, being Maori had been a negative experience for many of our people. Colonization, immigration and the growth of the non-Maori population had swamped Maori life, customs, beliefs and values. Many felt that intermarriage would result in people leaving the Maori world behind and in Maori becoming more Pakeha. In essence, many Maori lived as Pakeha, and survived in the Pakeha world. At school, young Maori who entered the academic streams learned European languages, mainly Latin,

French and German, which were considered to be 'useful' as opposed to te reo Maori, which some of our elders claimed 'would never put bread and butter on the table'.

Those who wanted to maintain their links with the Maori world learned to live in both the Maori and non-Maori worlds. They learned to live a double life – being Pakeha during the week and daylight hours and inserting a part-time Maori life into the evenings and weekends. Being Maori, in many instances, inhibited Maori children from belonging to social organizations and sports teams, in the interests of maintaining cultural ties. Relationships with partners and friends of other cultures could at times be severely strained when Maori were pulled in different directions trying to meet hapu and whanau cultural obligations.

During the 1960s the remaining families who maintained the customs and traditions at the marae travelled to Hokio to meet those obligations, as there were no longer permanent residents living there. Most of those who had been born there had died and been buried at the cemetery on the hill, closer to the lake.

Throughout New Zealand, urban Maori protest groups were emerging, and groups of young Maori leaders at Auckland and Victoria universities thrust Maori into the media, beginning a decade of protest and revival. They demanded 'teaching of Maori language in schools, Maori control of Maori land and Maori finance...' (King 1997, p.96) and joined with other groups who organised a land march to Parliament and occupations of land illegally taken, such as Bastion Point and Raglan Golf Course. The process of assimilation of Maori was challenged and halted.

The Maori population was no longer in decline. A revival began around the country. Maori, young and old, wanted to learn te reo Maori and to claim their identity as Maori. A decision was made by Ngati Pareraukawa to build a new, larger meeting house and to redevelop the complex for future generations. While many were energized and excited with this plan, there was also opposition. Some felt that the marae was a relic of the past and that future generations would be integrated into the dominant Pakeha society and have no need of it. Others felt that because the marae had been clearly under-utilized since the early 1950s, and many families had moved away from the area to other towns and cities, they would be unlikely to want to maintain links with the area. Many could not remember exactly why the families had moved to town. A new complex could well be a white elephant and might be interpreted as Maori wanting to go backwards rather than forwards into the modern world. Events occurring nationally spurred many to return to the area and to reconnect with the land and marae.

At the same time, the Raukawa Trustees, a body with responsibility for the maintenance and use of the parent marae, Raukawa Marae in Otaki, made a decision that was to have long-term impact on the people of the tribal group.

Their plan was decisive and provided a clear, long-term vision for the future. They launched Whakatupuranga Rua Mano – Generation 2000. It was labelled as an experiment in tribal development. It promoted a 25-year programme of educational and cultural development of the local people. It included the human and spiritual development of the people, the physical development of the marae, its buildings and surroundings and the strengthening of the people (Winiata 1979).

The hapu at Ngatokowaru supported the development initiative and the marae became one of the centres of learning, regularly hosting seminars, conferences and educational hui. Weekend gatherings were scheduled regularly, to promote the educational attainment of the people, and to provide opportunities for families that had become distanced from the marae to return and learn about their history, values and cultural background. The children of Ngati Raukawa were encouraged to stay at school longer and to seek higher qualifications. The children and the parents of Ngatokowaru Marae committed to hapu development. The marae was revived, new buildings planned, fundraising undertaken and new facilities completed. Most important, the families learned about our own history, the ancestors who had left us the marae, and focused on the positive aspects of being Maori. The community took responsibility for the development of the buildings, the development of the people and the development of the wider environment. It was for many a programme of decolonization.

The decision to build a new meeting house in the early 1970s and to support the Generation 2000 initiative in 1975 had a long-term impact on the people of Ngati Pareraukawa. The new meeting house, opened in 1978, brought many families back to the marae to attend meetings, to contribute to the building programme over the following three decades and to focus on the positive aspects of being Maori. However, being Maori and being a hapu member was usually a weekend activity. Many families lived at a distance, an hour or more from the marae. For many families with competing interests, it was a cause of frustration, a tension between wanting to maintain the ancestral links to the marae, and satisfying the needs of teenagers who wanted to spend weekends at home and nearer to friends, or playing sport in teams that travelled to other centres at the weekends. Inevitably, many families could not maintain the links.

At the end of the twentieth century, the community spent time reflecting on what had been gained as a result of 25 years of the Generation 2000 programme. We noted we were in a stronger position culturally than 25 years earlier. The question was whether as a hapu, as a tribal group, we would be in a stronger position in another 50 years, or in another 100 years time. We noted other gains, such as the buildings having become smoke-free, a commitment to providing a healthier environment. The menus had changed over the previous

20 years as we had become more conscious of presenting healthy meals. Health professionals from the hapu presented seminars on relevant health issues.

On New Year's Eve 1999, a group of families quietly spent the evening at the marae. They were aware that none of them would be here in another 100 years. They asked questions about what vision they had for the marae in 2100, what life would be like for our descendants in 2100 and what might be the gifts that we would leave for them. It was a time for more reflection than usual.

Over the next two years, the hapu as a community debated whether we would survive as a hapu for another 100 years and if we did, what we might do now to ensure that the hapu was in better health in 2100. We often talk about the gifts of our ancestors. We wanted to name them and identify those we wanted to leave for our descendants. We pondered whether the marae and its environment were a treasure that should be maintained and developed for future generations and asked ourselves whether we were indeed holding on to a relic which had no relevance in the future.

The new millennium prompted our hapu as a community to look to the future. We were aware that we had put much energy and financial commitment into redeveloping the buildings at the marae. There had always been a view, that in order to survive, it would be necessary to focus on the development of the people. Hence in 2003, a series of meetings was devoted to developing a hapu plan for the future.

Strategic plans had become popular in the 1980s. It was proposed that the hapu develop such a plan, which would focus on the future. Early in 2003, the community came together on a Sunday afternoon with planning in mind.

A six metre long, one metre wide sheet of paper was spread along one end of the dining room covering three long trestle tables. The date, 1900, was marked at one end and the year, 2000, at the other. Everyone was invited to record historical events on the paper. The questions posed were: what would you like to record as a part of the history of our hapu? What do you want your grandchildren to know about the twentieth century?

Some of the elders wrote their own birth dates on the paper: 1920, 1922, 1930. Others recorded the birthdays of their children. Some recorded the dates that family members had died. Others wrote about events such as the year there was a significant eel run. The first meeting of the marae committee was held in 1946.

The totara logs that were used for the new meeting house were removed from the Rangitikei river by the army in 1974 (Selby 1999). This was recorded by one of those who was present. The 'old' meeting house had been dismantled and burned to ashes in 1976. The new meeting house was opened in March 1978. The new dining room was opened in 1981. Some families recorded whanau reunions that had taken place. Weddings, birthdays and social events were recorded. The year the local council stopped pouring sewage into the lake went down: 1978. The year the neighbour's stinking piggery was closed down was also recorded: December 1999.

The dining room was abuzz with noise as cousins, aunties, uncles and children all chatted and recalled events of significance to them. Initially, personal recollections were not placed on the paper. As enthusiasm grew, everyone was encouraged to write their memories down, to see them as important, then more memories spilled on to the paper.

The next session was designed to move the hapu as a community, into the future. We focused on what we wanted to leave to the next generation. Given that in 1975, we had made a decision to commit to a rebuilding programme, a revitalization programme and an education programme, we focused on what we wanted to do in the next five years and ten years to ensure our survival. This was community development in action.

Individuals and groups went to work at each of the stations around the room where a 'prompt' sheet sat beside piles of paper and pens. The prompt sheets were headed with topics that had been identified as important to the hapu. Everyone was asked to move around the room and write their hopes and dreams for the future on paper at each station. The topics were: buildings, language, waiata: special songs, karakia: prayers, landscaping, environment, Hokio Stream, history, wairua-spirituality, education, health, research, iwi participation, local and regional government.

The response was astonishing. People of all ages, from children to the elderly, quietly worked as if in examination mode. They wrote carefully. They contemplated seriously. They pondered deeply. They gazed out the windows looking to those who had walked on the marae before them as if for guidance. When they spoke to someone near them, they spoke in whispers, not to muffle what they saying, but because it seemed the right volume in which to speak. People thought out loud, but softly. They remembered and the memories pushed the pens and were recorded. Those who had not intended to write anything, sat and wrote whole pages recording their visions for the future. Some who had doubted that such an exercise would excite any imagination were clearly excited about the idea of recording their views, about not having to compete with others to present their views, not having to speak out in a forum, but being given as much time and paper as they needed to write whatever came to mind.

While convening a forum and asking people to speak out could have been the medium for collecting information, most seemed to enjoy the writing exercise. It was uninterrupted. It was personal. There were no time constraints. As the afternoon wore on and the sun dipped and sent its rays through the western doors, families moved around the workstations and added thoughts and suggestions to the pages on the tables. When they departed, the pages were all collected into a large basket ready to be collated, examined and transferred into batches of information that could be used to plan the future.

The week following the hui a small group met to look at the responses. The themes were clear: a strong desire to strengthen the marae-based hapu, acknowledging that many of our people also live around the world, a commitment to ensure that the marae and people are stronger in 2100 and that we take responsibility for ensuring the survival of our hapu as a non-resident community spread around Aotearoa and overseas.

Not surprisingly, when the papers were reviewed, it was found they settled easily under four headings. These four concepts were adopted as the guiding principles for the Generation 2000 – Whakatupuranga Rua Mano experiment in tribal development begun in 1975. They were embraced 'as guiding principles' (Winiata 2000, p.33) for the school of higher learning, Te Wananga-o-Raukawa in 1981.

The same four principles emerged again.

1. Our people are our wealth: develop and retain.

2. The marae is our principal home: maintain and respect it.

3. Te reo is a taonga: halt the decline and revive.

4. Self-determination.

These principles have become guiding principles for many of the community and iwi development initiatives which have occurred in Ngati Raukawa in the past 30 years. They surfaced logically again in 2003 for the hapu of Ngati Parerauka. The hopes and dreams of the hapu were compiled under the four headings and goals set to reflect the aspirations of the people.

Principle 1: Our people are our wealth: develop and retain. The following goals were then set to reflect the shared visions written down by the people.

1. Compile a hapu register that includes the whereabouts of our whanau and hapu and their skills.

2. Compile a complete hapu whakapapa.

3. Plan for five hui each year to promote whanaungatanga.

4. Learn about our hapu and people.

5. Enhance our skills.

6. Increase our knowledge.

7. Promote a healthy marae and healthy lifestyles.

8. Support research about our people and our history.

9. Promote educational attainment.

Principle 2: Our marae is our principal home: maintain and respect it. The goals which would reflect this principle were then set.

1. Maintain and develop the buildings, landscape, flagpole and stream.

2. Conserve and restore our taonga.

3. Promote the use of the marae.

Principle 3: Te reo is a taonga: halt the decline and revive. The following goals were identified.

1. Promote the use of te reo Maori.

2. Increase the number of whanau who know our waiata.

3. Support kaikaranga and kaikorero.

4. Increase the numbers of Ngati Pareraukawa attending Te Wananga-o-Raukawa.

5. Offer Marae-based studies at Ngatokowaru marae.

Principle 4: Self-determination. The final goals were then set.

1. Increase the numbers actively participating at Ngatokowaru.

2. Develop active groups to promote whanaungatanga activities.

3. Identify whanau with business skills and knowledge.

4. Record our history.

5. Identify our resources and multiply them.

Fifteen goals were then identified for us to achieve in 2003. They enabled the marae committee to focus the activities for the year and to measure our achievements. At meetings, when individuals brought good ideas, rather than try to act on them immediately, we were able to defer them until the next year, noting that we had committed our energy to the following goals. Each goal is linked to one or more of the four principles and expands on the concept, if required for further clarity.

Goal 1:   *To build a new ablution block*
Link: Our marae is our principal home
            Promote the use of the marae

Goal 2:   *To learn about three waiata and learn to perform waiata as a hapu*
Link: Te reo is a taonga
            Our people are our wealth
            Self determination – tino rangatiratanga

Goal 3: To encourage whanau to learn karakia to open and close meetings
Link: Our people are our wealth
Te reo is a taonga
Self determination – tino rangatiratanga

Goal 4: Support research about our people and our history
Link: Our people are our wealth
Self determination – tino rangatiratanga

Goal 5: Increase the numbers actively participating at Ngatokowaru
Link: Self determination

Goal 6: Copy the Marae Committee minute books as an historical record
Link: Self determination – record our history

Goal 7: Compile a register of members of Ngati Pareraukawa
Link: Self-determination – identify our resources, record our history
Our people are our wealth

Goal 8: Promote educational attainment
Link: Self-determination – identify our resources and multiply them

Goal 9: Clean up Hokio Stream
Link: Our marae is our principal home – maintain and develop the stream

Goal 10: Maintain flagpole
Link: Our marae is our principal home – maintain the flagpole
Conserve and restore our taonga

Goal 11: Support Koputara Trustees
Link: Self-Determination – identify our resources and multiply them

Goal 12: Promote participation in hapu sports
Link: Our people are our wealth – promote a healthy marae and healthy lifestyles
Self-determination – increase the numbers participating at Ngatokowaru and develop active groups

Goal 13: Update the Marae Trustees
Link: Our marae is our principal home

Goal 14 Participate in regional and local government
Link: Our marae is our principal home

Goal 15   Make the marae wheelchair-friendly
Link: Our marae is our principal home
           Our people are our wealth

These goals were accepted by the committee and used as the basis for our activities over the next 12 months. The building of a new ablution block was a top priority, as it is the last building to be renewed within the complex. The family were also clear that they did not want to put all their energy into further physical development. Hence Goal 2 identifying traditional waiata, which had been composed by women from whom we descended and expressed our desire to preserve those waiata within the family. Over the next year we copied the words and sent tape recordings to many whanau who committed themselves to learn them.

The goals reflected the range of important issues for the community and enabled more members to be active in helping to achieve them. Some were about recording history: for our children to read in 2100, recording stories on audio-tape and copying the five original minutes books carefully preserved for over 60 years. Others were about improving the environment: clean up the Hokio Stream, participate in local and regional government and make the marae wheelchair-friendly. Another group of goals highlighted improving the skills and knowledge of the people: waiata, karakia and educational attainment. Another set of goals focused on increasing the numbers participating in marae life.

The people reinforced that the community was a priority, that it should be promoted and preserved as a fortress of those things that had been left to us by the original owners of the marae who had built the community 150 years earlier. The buildings should be maintained, the environment respected and cleaned up – even in the face of opposition from larger communities looking for easy options in terms of 'waste management'. Most important, the people wanted to learn more about their own history, people, traditions and values.

The regional council agreed to clean up the stream and to assist with the planting of native trees along the banks. They assisted in removing alien species. More young people attended hui and family from far away began to ask for tape recordings of waiata to be sent to them. Others asked that a website be set up so that they could visit the 'principal home' on the web – from London and New York, Paris and Sydney.

The Sunday afternoon of dreams gave the community the opportunity to focus on goals as individuals and as a family. The goals have become a reality. In the first year, all 15 goals have been worked on and most completed. More people are actively participating in the life of the community and taking responsibility for its long-term survival. The momentum that began slowly in 1975 provided a strong base on which to build at the end of the century.

There have been small steps made to reclaim our environment in the past decade. The town across the lake has grown and the sewage is no longer poured into the lake – it is piped to the south of the marae and poured into the contours of the land. The eels migrate in the autumn along the stream, no longer in the multitudes of the past, but research and restoration projects are in place to assist their recovery. Native trees will be planted on the banks in the winter of 2004. The elders who remember how to construct an eel trap and net in the stream have offered to take the young men to the stream next summer to learn skills only held in the hands of a few now. Children do not yet swim in the stream, as the nutrients from the land and the market gardens in the area seep into the lake and cause unhealthy excess growth. Our great-grandmother left us a clear clean lake. The councils responsible for the environment in the second half of the twentieth century have done more damage to the environment than all the previous tenants over the past thousand years. The community will have to fight many battles if we are to leave the environment in a better state than it was at the end of 1999. It will need a community development action plan to succeed.

Questions for reflection

1. What are the key principles that inform this case study of community development?

2. What makes them so successful?

3. What can you learn from them for your own practice?

References

Durie, M. (1994) *Whaiora: Maori Health Development.* Auckland: Oxford University Press.

Durie, M. (1998) *Te mana, te kawanatanga. The politics of self-determination.* Auckland: Oxford University Press.

King M. (1997) *1000 years of Maori history: Nga iwi o te motu.* Auckland: Reed Publishing.

Ngatokowaru Marae Committee Minute Books (unpublished)

Selby, J. (1999) 'The day of the logs.' *Te Ukaipo 1*, December, 4–8.

Winiata, W. (1979) 'Generation 2000: An experiment in tribal development.' In *He Matapuna: Some Maori Perspectives.* Wellington: New Zealand Planning Council.

Chapter 7

Community Development: A Tongan Perspective

Tracie Mafile'o

Takanga 'enau fohe
(Mates at their oars, perhaps, their oars are mates)

Introduction

This Tongan proverb points to the importance and nature of community for Pacific peoples and has been explained as follows:

> In treacherous seas the persons at the oars must be equal in strength and ability, and they must row together in unity... Thus, we use this proverb...to express our vision...that Tongans...('diasporic communities') work collaboratively and communally, forge new alliances, map and re-map new social relations and socio-political networks, all for the betterment of our Tongan people as a whole. (Ka'ili 2004)

Tongan community development is about working together for our collective good.

This chapter discusses community development as expressed and practised by Tongan social and community workers who took part in a study of Tongan social work practice in Aotearoa/New Zealand. Community is central to working with Pacific populations, involving an integral link between macro and micro approaches. Although the study focused particularly on Tongan social and community work practice, this discussion has particular applicability to work with other Pacific peoples' groups, given many shared cultural characteristics and realities. In addition, much community development occurs with a pan-Pacific focus, harnessing political alliances between Pacific groups. Further, many of the themes emerging in this study have relevance for work amongst other non-Western, ethnic minority and indigenous groups.

The discussion begins with an exploration of the terms *community, Tongan community* and *Tongan community development.* I then briefly refer to community development theoretical approaches as they relate to work with non-Western communities. An outline of the research project that substantially informs this chapter follows. Drawing on practice scenarios and reflections in regards to Tongan social and community work, I move on to illustrate how community work theory is utilized and adapted with non-Western communities existing in a largely Western nation context. Key practice principles around the position of the practitioner, the source of the solution, the calibre of collectivity, defining distinctiveness and macro analysis are examined. Finally, I will offer critical reflection on the challenges of community development approaches for Tongan community development.

Exploring terms: community, Tongan community and Tongan community development

The concepts of *community,* the *Tongan community* and *Tongan community development* are key terms used in this chapter. My understanding of community is taken from Ife's definition (1995, p.90–1), where community is explained as being a form of social organization possessing five interrelated characteristics. First, a community is on a human scale where people can readily know each other rather than being a large impersonalized and centralized structure. Second, members of a community gain a sense of identity and belonging to it. Third, members of a community have obligations to contribute to the life of the community. Fourth, there are structures and relationships whereby people interact with each other as 'whole people' rather than as limited and defined roles or categories. Finally, a community allows the production and expression of local culture.

Tongan communities are formed on the basis of shared ethnic identity. Furthermore, the Pacific diaspora has culminated in Tongan communities existing transnationally (Morton Lee 2003). The traditional Tongan community is considered to be the most highly stratified society in the Pacific (Latukefu 1997). This hierarchy largely continues to the present day where the ha'a tu'i (royalty) is at the top of the hierarchy, followed by hou'eiki and matapule (chiefs and their attendants) and the majority of the people, who are kau tu'a (commoners), are at the lower level. Within this stratification, kinship-based lines provide the basis of the structure for Tongan communities. As a collective culture, interrelationships and mutual responsibilities are a cohesive force for Tongan communities.

Contemporary Tongan community development work is part of an historical, cultural, social and political context. Well before Europeans first visited the Pacific, traditional Tongan values and social systems provided a form of social care. It has been suggested that in pre-contact Tonga, the nature of the kin-based structure 'prevented any permanent political hierarchy' (Gailey 1987, p.47). Colonization in the Pacific ushered in Christianity, class relations, state formation and subsequent 'dramatic social upheaval' for Tonga (Gailey 1987, p.145). Although Tonga was never formally colonized, it was extremely influenced by the West, for example, British concepts of justice and law were adopted (Latukefu 1997). As a part of this process, religion became a key point of identity and community organization in Tongan society.

Pacific peoples, and Tongans in particular, have a high religious affiliation compared to the general population of New Zealand (Statistics New Zealand, 2002). The church is a significant aspect of Pacific communities, and community development often occurs in the context of the church. As such, much of the following discussion about community and community work involves both the institution of the Christian church and attention to aspects of hierarchy.

In the post World War Two period New Zealand's immigration policies were relaxed to encourage labour migration from the Pacific islands. There are over 40,000 Tongans living in New Zealand, of whom 53 per cent are New Zealand-born (Statistic New Zealand 2002), compared to the 1996 Tongan census which reported that there were 97,000 Tongans living in Tonga (Morton Lee 2003, p.293). In the New Zealand context, Tongans have experienced accelerated cultural and social change, particularly in the last 30 years as part of the processes of migration (Macpherson 2001). Many Tongan cultural values have persisted, albeit expressed differently in the contemporary context. It is in this context that Tongan social and community work has also developed. The practice of Tongan community development stems significantly from Tongan cultural knowledge and is not solely informed by Western social science theory or experience within the Western context.

Theoretical approaches and non-Western community development practice

It has been noted that there is no unified community work theory; rather there are a number of macro theories from which community development derives (Munford and Walsh-Tapiata 2001; Popple 1995). These theories include pluralist, radical and socialist, feminist, black and anti-racist critique (Popple 1995) and critical and post-structural approaches (Munford and Walsh-Tapiata 2001).

Broadly speaking, anti-racist theory is directly relevant in Tongan and other non-Western community work. Anti-racist theory critiques the modern welfare state as being 'a characteristic form of the developed capitalist state securing the interests of capital and of white people...at the expense of ethnic minorities' (Pierson 1991, p.82). The experience of Tongans as migrant labour in the post-war period, and the subsequent racialization of Pacific peoples, epitomized by the 'overstayer' campaigns when economic downturn set in, raises issues about 'how' Pacific peoples identify and belong in the New Zealand context (Southwick 2001). A similar phenomenon has also been experienced by other migrant peoples internationally. Tongan peoples largely occupy positions of disadvantage within the welfare state, where they experience lower levels of income, inadequate housing and poor health in comparison to the national population (Statistics New Zealand 2002). Tongan community development is therefore about having a critical analysis of this positioning of families and communities and is about mobilizing the community to develop counter structures that create new realities for Tongans.

Core community work theories were developed within non-Pacific societies. These theories of community development have arisen in the context of largely Western-industrialized countries in response to failures of the welfare state to advance wellbeing for some of their families and communities. I am not suggesting here that the explanation and analysis given by such theories has no relevance for Pacific communities. Rather, there are helpful intersections between Tongan or other indigenous knowledges and Western social theory that, in synergy, powerfully make sense of what is occurring for Tongan families and communities and guide social and community work practice with these populations (Howe 1997).

There is growing interest in the 'indigenization' of social work; there is mutual exchange between cultures and 'locally appropriate forms of social work may draw on and adapt Western models' (Payne 1997, p.12). Nimmagadda and Cowger (1999) demonstrate, for instance, how Indian workers use core concepts of dharma and karma in their practice. Graham (1999) goes further to argue the need for African-centred perspectives in social work that challenge existing dominant paradigms for theory and practice. Ife (1995, p.97) asserts that 'it is beginning to be acknowledged that in many cases indigenous people's spiritual and social values form a more solid basis for tackling social problems than do the conventional mechanisms of the welfare state'. The application of indigenous knowledge in social and community work in Western national contexts will be explored in the rest of this chapter.

The research

The project on which the content of this chapter is based was PhD research which explored Tongan social work models of practice. It was an exploratory qualitative study that investigated Tongan ways of conceptualizing and practising social work.

The participants were Tongan social workers in New Zealand, including both island-born and New Zealand-born, from a range of fields of practice. Participants included some who identified with professions or roles other than social work (for example, counselling or pastoring), but who were perceived by the Tongan community as being 'social workers'. There were 20 participants located in Auckland, New Zealand's largest and fastest growing city and where 78 per cent of Tongans in New Zealand reside (Statistics New Zealand 2002). There were seven participants in Wellington, the capital city, where 5 per cent of the New Zealand Tongan population reside (Statistics New Zealand 2002).

Three stages of data collection took place. The first stage consisted of an in-depth individual tape-recorded interview. The focus was on a description of participants' practice experience and what they perceived were Tongan charac-teristics of their practice. The second stage consisted of five focus groups in which key themes and concepts arising out of the individual interviews were discussed. These were bilingual and also tape-recorded. The third stage con-sisted of follow-up individual interviews. The practitioner quotes and examples below are drawn from the data collected in this research.

Key theory and practice themes

I now move to highlight intersections between community development theory and Tongan community development. I draw on practice reflections and scenarios presented by Tongan social and community workers to show how social and community work practice within non-Western, migrant and indige-nous communities is developing. The themes discussed are:

- the practitioner as internal to the community
- solutions sourced at the community level
- collectivity as a strength
- culturally distinctive structures and processes
- the importance of having a macro critical analysis.

There is an implicit understanding that whether practitioners are employed in a community development role or other roles such as 'casework', it is possible to work from a community development perspective. The scenarios below there-fore represent a range of social work and community work contexts.

Position of the practitioner: internal, integrated, inclusive

The first characteristic of community development noted here is the position of the practitioner or community worker as internal and integrated into the com-munity, and inclusive in their approach. Tongan social and community workers report making conscious efforts to be a part of the Tongan community as an integrated part of their lives. That is, their contact with the Tongan community is not something that is done simply 'as a job'. Rather, they integrally identify as Tongan and participate in Tongan events such as attending a Tongan church, weddings, funerals, faikava (kava drinking ceremonies) and by helping and being of service to their family and other Tongans in the community. A statutory social worker stated: '…even when you're not working, it's good to be involved in your Tongan community… prior to working here I didn't think that was important…and I find myself going to church more'.

A community agency social worker/counsellor revealed the following: 'I deliberately attend the Tongan church so I can build up their trust in me'.

The internal practitioner then has a voice that will more likely be heard and understood by those they work alongside in the community, as commented on by one community youth worker who was raised in the community where she is now working:

> Sometimes in forums where I'm not supposed to speak, I speak. I think because I've been working within their community for three years or more, because I ran a youth group in our church prior to that and I know the community people here and my parents know them, that I get away with a lot that a lot of young PI [Pacific Islander] graduates would not get away with.

Discussion in the literature on community development often includes direction for making initial contacts with communities (Craig 1987; Twelvetrees 2002). In a Tongan sense, however, community workers may already be insiders to the communities with which they work and such contact occurs as a part of growing up and living in a community. This notion of internal community workers is supported by Ife (1995 p.266–7), who warns that the 'external approach runs counter to the ideals of empowerment, local initiative, self-reliance and autonomy, and effectively reinforces the community's dependence on external resources'.

Integration into the community also means that community service is an important aspect of community development work with Pacific communities. Writers on community development tend to differentiate between community development and community service. It is argued that the latter does not lead to changing the source of social issues but rather contributes to creating dependence and merely maintaining the status quo (Elliot 1978). Within Pacific cultures, however, being of service is given high value. Autagavaia (2001, p.80) explains that the value of tautau, which in a Samoan context is 'to be a servant in character and behaviour at all costs', is an important ethical component of Samoan social work. She highlights the Samoan proverb 'O le ala i le pule o le tautau' (the path to authority is to serve) as the basis of this.

Pacific community development must therefore include service activities if development outcomes are to be realised. Community workers serve by being willing and able to play multiple diverse roles appropriate to their age, gender and status. This may include practical assistance such as preparing food or assisting with immigration applications. It is this attitude and action of service that is key to being internal to a community and therefore positions a community worker to facilitate community development. What differentiates community service in a Pacific context from the dependency creating and potentially paternalistic activities of service in other cultural contexts is the position of the practitioner as part of an interdependent collective.

Finally, practitioners in Tongan social and community work use an inclusive approach with the use of inclusive language as a means to join with families. This was explained in the following way: 'When you approach them you have to include yourself in the family. For example, ("I have come here regarding our children"). You have to include yourself so they can feel that you want to be a part of them.' In this way, even in practice situations where there is a clear power relationship present because of the statutory social work role, the approach of Tongan social workers was to seek inclusiveness and to be internal in some way.

Source of solution: community grounded

The second practice theme of community development explored here is that of the role of community itself as the source of solution and holistic intervention. The community is a source of learning, education and training required for community work that is not necessarily accessible in established, formal educational institutions. A young practitioner related that:

> Growing up in our schools (in New Zealand) hasn't really taught us how to relate to our elders. You know, and that's something that I've really learnt only being around our parents and in the church.

A senior practitioner aptly described how one can learn in the community:

> First of all, look to where the community is…and take away your knowing… There is another classroom; it's to go down to the community. There is a faikava [kava drinking ceremony] – go and listen to the way they talk. There is a funeral – go there and listen to what they do and why they do this… The king arrives in Auckland; people go there – go there and learn why they do these things…the things we do in a Tongan way to get the word of faka'apa'apa [respect]…there are two classrooms, one in the community and one in the institution.

The community is a place for learning the values, protocols, processes and skills important, not only for life, but for Tongan social and community work.

The community is also central to intervention whether in community work per se or in individual or family-focused work. A mental health support worker commented, for example, that she takes clients to their family church and to major Tongan community events as a means to foster connection. In this case, rather than facilitating special meetings or counselling sessions to integrate people back into their families, the community provides a centre for intervention. In a similar vein, many Pacific groups, including churches, operate youth groups, fono (workshops/meetings), women's groups and so on that provide an important resource for Pacific families. In one example given, a church ran a youth forum where youth identified their issues around education, social and cultural issues. There was then general feedback given to the parents in the church. This provided a safe mechanism to bridge generation and cultural gaps, building awareness and understanding between diverse groups within the community. It was particularly effective in that many of these issues may not otherwise have been aired or addressed as young people may not have felt they could 'talk back' by raising issues on an individual basis. Using the community as the point of intervention serves to build strength into structures that will provide long-term sustained change.

Community centred and grounded intervention is also holistic. Ife (1995, p.85) comments that: 'Holism requires the breaking down of...the physical/social dualism which has characterised the "partitioning" of knowledge and understanding. It requires a broadening rather than a narrowing of the knowledge base...'

One youth worker raised concern about a compartmentalizing approach and suggested how this may be prevented with the use of community:

> many of our kids do, they go into five programmes, they just get cut into pieces. They need to be serviced holistically...and then you service them in a way that takes them back to their family. I think in a way that's where our programmes that implement family visits and family esteem and dealing with Pacific principles that are based around family and community work, kind of empowers them to go back.

The specialization characteristic of many human services may serve to disempower families and communities by not working holistically.

Calibre of collectivity: enhancing collective strength

An emphasis on enhancing the collective is common to community work. Kenny (1994 p.20), for instance, states: 'Community development work assists people in a community to identify their needs and obtain resources, and collectively empowers people to have more control over their lives.' Tongan kin-based interdependent social structures go hand in hand with cultural values that are highly context specific and 'other' focused. This has been categorized elsewhere as an interdependent view of self, as opposed to the independent view of self that is more common to Western cultures (Markus and Kitayama 1991). Helu (1999 p.25) has identified Tonga as a shame culture where 'people value more their interpersonal and group relationships and spend time shining their public image' as opposed to a guilt culture where people 'worry over things like justice, truth and rights'. It is this interdependence that characterizes collectivity in Tongan communities.

Tongan community development in New Zealand has drawn on the collective strengths found within Tongan culture. Working together was a necessary part of life and survival in traditional Tonga. The toutu'u, for instance, consists of a system of community gardening in Tonga where community members help work on each other's plantation. Toulalanga or koka'anga are occasions when women work on weaving or tapa cloth-making respectively. These koloa (riches) are not an individual, but a group effort. Such fetokoni'aki (helping each other) is a basic structure of Tongan communities and is integral as a value. These processes and values have been utilized in Tongan community development in the New Zealand context with community gardens. A community health worker reported negotiating to use a waste piece of council land as a community garden. Clients of the service were allocated a patch of garden and grew fresh produce for their families and for sale at markets. It was noted that an outcome of this initiative was that rather than the service giving food parcels to families, families were giving produce to the agency.

Another implication of the collective emphasis in Tongan culture is that the power, strength and resource gained from possessing a Tongan identity for Tongan community members cannot be underestimated. Despite factors such as poverty or poor health statistics, there is reprieve in the strength gained in particular Tongan values such as 'ofa (love or compassion), fakatokilalo (humility), faka'apa'apa (respect) or fetokoni'aki (helping each other). A social worker in this study described her position:

> I'm different because... I've got the culture; I've got the language and the value[s] of a Pacific islander... It really makes me proud...of being Tongan... Everyone can study and become a psychiatrist, everyone can study and become a psych nurse, but being a Tongan is very special. It's being a Tongan and having the values of a Tongan inside you.

It is perhaps this ability to transcend seemingly limited physical and economic means by the holding onto a greater ideological, philosophical, cultural or spiritual reality that resonates with Rees' (1991 p.34) discussion of the unravelling of biography. He states:

> Physical containment does not necessarily imprison either spirit or intellect, whereas imprisonment of a capacity for criticism and vision may occur even when a human being is not constrained by four walls. The closed mind of the influential senior executive staff, the resistance to change of the conservative bureaucrat, the acceptance of the status quo by the fearful student, the debilitating grind of poverty or of stigma, also have stifling effects. By unravelling the biography which reveals these other forms of imprisonment, expressions of powerlessness become the means of achieving change.

Importantly for Tongan community work, biography reveals more than forms of imprisonment, it unleashes the freedom to be, to belong and to become.

Defining distinctiveness: culturally distinctive structures and processes

Community development with ethnic minority groups is not only about creating changes within those ethnic communities, it is necessarily also about carving out distinctive spaces and creating changes within the wider socio-political systems so that those groups can determine their own destiny and thrive at all levels. Creating structural change is therefore an aspect of Tongan community work.

The focus of the structural change, however, is less on the political economy and more on cultural aspects. At odds with the assumption of conflict imbedded in radical perspectives (Shaw 1994) is the Tongan tendency to work towards harmony and to sacrifice self in order to maintain relationships for the good of the group. This has meant that radical strategies that openly challenge those in power have not been commonplace in Tongan community development efforts. In fact, there is considerable focus on assisting Tongans to adapt to the New Zealand or palangi environment, albeit in a way that maintains essential Tongan cultural values. In this way, resistance has been less political and more cultural in focus. There is, however, increasing willingness to employ overt protest, as the pro-democracy movement in Tonga, for example, gains momentum.

Tongan social and community workers are inherently in positions where they need to negotiate diverse paradigms. They are provided with values, processes and skills from a Tongan knowledge-base and yet operate in Western contexts of the agency, society, funding requirements etc. An example was given by a community worker who was given the task of conducting a pedestrian audit in a community with a high Pacific population. The community worker discovered that the Pacific church in that area was more interested in their need for a piano. The worker therefore worked with them to purchase a piano before moving on to the audit. The same community worker commented: 'What (the agency) wants is different from what our Pacific communities are really wanting. To work with the church I've got to be creative…'

As illustrated in this example, community work with non-Western communities involves the employment and advancement of culturally distinctive processes and structures.

Analysis and critical awareness: having a macro understanding

The final practice theme to be discussed here is that practitioners have a macro analysis of micro situations. Internal social and community workers are more likely to have shared experiences associated with life in the islands and issues of migration to New Zealand. This shared knowledge and understanding of the context allows sharing to occur in a way that is mutually understood. Further, the practitioner with a critical awareness and analysis of the circumstances surrounding those collective experiences is positioned to take more appropriate action. For example, an understanding of the economic benefit to New Zealand gained from Pacific labour in the post war period reveals other aspects of an individual's story that are collectively realized aspects at the society level.

In the case of Pacific peoples in New Zealand, there is also an historical and cultural link between Pacific peoples' groups and tangata whenua (Maori) that stands in addition to relationships set up under the Treaty of Waitangi. Earle (1995) postulates that from a south Pacific regional perspective, Pacific peoples are indigenous to the Pacific as are iwi Maori (Maori peoples). Pacific peoples therefore have integral historical, geographical and cultural links to iwi Maori and to New Zealand (Ministry of Justice and Ministry of Pacific Island Affairs 2001). Such analysis of Pacific peoples' presence in New Zealand opens up possibilities for pathways to wellbeing that transcend individual wellbeing to include collective political and economic alliances and action.

Critical awareness is also important for Tongan community development so that community workers and community leaders are not trapped by the ambiguities of seeking adaptation and 'success' within the adopted country of New Zealand while at the same time seeking liberation from hierarchies of domination within their Tongan community. Freire (1972) posed a dialogical theory of action where the oppressed are active subjects in transforming structures in order to liberate themselves. He argues that if the oppressed are not critically aware and are 'drawn into the process as ambiguous beings, partly themselves and partly the oppressors housed within them,' (p.97) that they will not truly rise to power. Critical awareness then assists with an analysis for working with individuals and families and gives important perspective for development at the community level.

Critical reflection on the challenges of such an approach

Those involved in social and community work practice are constantly faced with the dilemmas involved in cultural change. The issues are intensified when, as a migrant and minority community, there are tensions between efforts to adapt and succeed in the new context of New Zealand while seeking to maintain Tongan culture. This tension was highlighted by Tiatia (1998), who carried out research revealing that Pacific young people in New Zealand are caught between cultures in terms of family, education and church. There was some concern expressed by Tongan social and community workers as a result of their observation of changes in Tongan culture within the New Zealand context:

From the island we have been brought up [in] fetokoni'aki (helping each other)... If I've got enough for my family, I tokoni (help). And then maybe not [that] you will tokoni back, but your children will grow up and tokoni. These days, they expect you to tokoni and you tokoni me straight, you know? See the value[s] of the Tongans is start[ing] to fade...the spirit of fetokoni'aki is not there anymore.

The collective good is something that we don't think enough about, and we just think about the individual good. One of the dangers about that is that as we think about our individual wellbeing, if we don't think about it in the context of the greater wellbeing of our families and communities, we become more and more separated. We become more and more disconnected from one another.

These challenges highlight the need for maintaining minority cultural values amidst a majority culture in a way that enhances and does not undermine the essence of those values. The specific challenge for community development is the need to at once allow cultural change to occur without reinforcing processes of cultural domination. There are fine lines to walk between promoting values of equality, freedom and justice for cultural minority groups in a Western context and ensuring indigenous cultural values are upheld.

Conclusion

The community is central to non-Western social and community work. In relation to the social challenges facing Pacific communities, Matsuoka (2001 p.451) concludes that it is becoming increasingly clear that 'the unit of analysis and the target for system intervention is the community'. Ife (1995, p.90) goes so far as to suggest that perhaps 'the community is the institution which will succeed the family, the Church, the market and the state as the primary focus for the meeting of human need'. While essentially within a Tongan perspective family identity is central and church is highly significant as an institution, perhaps for those who have undergone social and cultural change to the extent that they are now divorced from those Tongan structures, the community will eventually become the linchpin to meeting their needs. Void of a community work element, social work with Pacific peoples will only perpetuate a growth in the need for social services. An approach that is not couched within community undermines the collectivity and interdependence of Pacific peoples.

The first theme of non-Western community work explored here was that the practitioner is positioned as being internal and integrated into the community with which they work. In this way there is promotion of the notion of working within your own ethnic group. In Pacific communities, the community worker has a rounded role that includes a degree of community service activities in addition to purely development roles. The importance of internal positioning is also highlighted in work with individuals where inclusive language is used to join the worker and the client and their systems. Second, the source of solution is community grounded in terms of both training and resourcing the practitioner and providing holistic intervention. The third theme centres on the interdependent nature of the collective. This has provided a sound base from which to implement such initiatives as community gardens and provides a spiritual strength in terms of a resourceful ethnic identity. A fourth practice theme in non-Western community development is the assertion of culturally distinctive processes and structures. Finally, a critical awareness at a macro level sheds essential light and understanding for work with both individuals and communities. Community development with Tongan, Pacific and other non-Western minority groups in a Western context will always be about walking a fine line in the context of cultural change. Cultural change is inevitable in both Western and non-Western contexts. It is incumbent upon community development practitioners to navigate through cultural change in a way that ultimately enhances the wellbeing of those communities that are excluded and disadvantaged, to the benefit of society as a whole.

Questions for reflection

1. What are ways in which collectivity can be enhanced amongst Pacific or migrant communities in a Western nation?

2. How might community development with Euro-Western populations differ from community development amongst Tongan, Pacific or indigenous groups?

3. How do your values compare to the key practice themes outlined in this chapter?

4. Which experiences have given you relevant knowledge or skills to work effectively as a community development worker with those who are culturally different from yourself?

Acknowledgements

I thank the Tongan social workers who participated in this project. Malo 'aupito kiate kimoutolu hono kotoa.

References

Autagavaia, M. (2001) 'Social work with Pacific island communities.' In M. Connolly (ed) *New Zealand Social Work: Contexts and Practice*. Melbourne: Oxford University Press.

Craig, W. (1987) *A Community Work Perspective*. Palmerston North: Massey University.

Earle, D. (1995) 'Pacific islands people in Aotearoa/New Zealand: Existing and emerging paradigms.' *Social Policy Journal of New Zealand 4*, 14–23.

Elliot, M. (1978) 'Towards an understanding of the nature of community work.' *Ripple Community Volunteers Newsletter 14*.

Freire, P. (1972) *Pedagogy of the Oppressed*. Harmondsworth: Penguin.

Gailey, C.W. (1987) *Kinship to Kingship: Gender Hierarchy and State Formation in the Tongan Islands*. Austin: University of Texas Press.

Graham, M.J. (1999) 'The African-centred worldview: Developing a paradigm for social work.' *British Journal of Social Work 29*, 2, 251–252.

Helu, I.F. (1999) *Critical Essays: Cultural Perspectives from the South Seas*. Canberra: The Journal of Pacific History.

Howe, D. (1997) 'Relating theory to practice.' In M. Davies (ed) *The Blackwell Companion to Social Work*. Oxford: Blackwell Publishers.

Ife, J.W. (1995) *Community Development: Creating Community Alternatives – Vision, Analysis and Practice*. Melbourne: Longman.

Ka'ili, T.O. (2004) 'Coverage of the Tongan History Association Conference.' Retrieved on 19 February 2004 from www.plantet-tonga.com/events/tha_conference/takanga.shtml

Kenny, S. (1994) *Developing Communities for the Future: Community Development in Australia*. Melbourne: Thomas Nelson.

Latukefu, S. (1997) 'The impact of the British on the Tongan traditional concept of justice and law.' In H. Hiery and J. MacKenzie (eds) *European Impact and Pacific Influence: British and German Colonial Policy in the Pacific Islands and the Indigenous Response*. London: German Historical Institute.

Macpherson, C. (2001) 'One trunk sends out many branches: Pacific cultures and cultural identities.' In C. Macpherson, P. Spoonley and M. Anae (eds) *Tangata o te Moana Nui: The Evolving Identities of Pacific Peoples in Aotearoa/New Zealand*. Palmerston North: Dunmore Press.

Markus, H.R. and Kitayama, S. (1991) 'Culture and the self: Implications for cognition, emotion, and motivation.' *Psychological Review 98*, 2, 224–253.

Matsuoka, J.K. (2001) 'Evaluation and assessment in Hawaiian and Pacific communities.' In R. Fong and S. Furuto (eds) *Culturally Competent Practice: Skills, Intervention, and Evaluations*. Boston: Allyn and Bacon.

Ministry of Justice and Ministry of Pacific Island Affairs (2001) *Pacific Peoples Constitution Report*. Wellington: Author.

Morton Lee, H. (2003) *Tongans Overseas*. Honolulu: University of Hawaii Press.

Munford, R. and Walsh-Tapiata, W. (2001) *Strategies for Change: Community Development in Aotearoa/New Zealand*, 3rd edn. Palmerston North: Massey University.

Nimmagadda, J. and Cowger, C.D. (1999) 'Cross-cultural practice: Social worker ingenuity in the indigenization of practice knowledge.' *International Social Work 42*, 3, 261–276.

Payne, M. (1997) *Modern Social Work Theory*, 2nd edn. Houndmills: Macmillan.

Pierson, C. (1991) *Beyond the Welfare State? The New Political Economy of Welfare*. Cambridge: Polity Press.

Popple, K. (1995) *Analysing Community Work: Its Theory and Practice.* Buckingham: Open University Press.

Rees, S. (1991) *Achieving Power: Practice and Policy in Social Welfare.* Sydney: Allen and Unwin.

Shaw, R. (1994) 'Radical social work.' In R. Munford and M. Nash (eds) *Social Work in Action.* Palmerston North, New Zealand: Dunmore Press.

Southwick, M. (2001) 'Culture and identity from a Pacific perspective.' *Social Work Review / Tu Mau 13*, 3, 19–22.

Statistics New Zealand (2002) *Tongan – Population.* Wellington: Author.

Tiatia, J. (1998) *Caught Between Cultures: A New Zealand-born Pacific Island Perspective.* Auckland: Christian Research Association.

Twelvetrees, A. (2002) *Community Work*, 3rd edn. Houndmills: Palgrave.

Chapter 8

Responding to Settlement Needs: Migrants and Refugees and Community Development

Mary Nash

This chapter focuses on community work in the context of what is arguably a new field of practice, namely settlement work (George 2002) with migrants and refugees. Elements of civic social work, defined by Powell (2001, p.163–65) as 'a concern for the rights and needs of citizens' are also involved in this field of practice. Community work may be defined as different in kind from social work, or as related, but at the far end of the caring spectrum from social work. As agents for change wherever there are structural and social injustices resulting in the oppression of minority groups, community workers and social workers can meet philosophically and professionally in settlement work. Refugees and many other groups of migrants are growing and recognized minorities with whom both community and social workers are involved. The skills of community work are as essential as those of social work in this new field of practice. Effective settlement workers will have a critical analysis of the social structures and political pressures, international as well as local, which lead to both voluntary and forced migration and eventual settlement. This, together with knowledge of human rights and social justice issues, provides a foundation on which to build the necessary community work skills for appropriate intervention in this complex field.

What this means for practitioners in New Zealand as well as internationally will be illustrated using findings from two nationwide postal surveys, one of social workers (Nash and Trlin 2004) and one of non-government organizations (NGOs) (Nash and Trlin forthcoming) carried out in 2001.[1] These surveys gathered information about programmes and services available to migrants and refugees and information about current service provision in relation to government resources. Twelve follow-up interviews with a targeted sample of NGO workers who completed the second survey provide community development insights.

Information from this research will be referred to generically as 'the research' and in this chapter it will provide examples of community work practice at macro, meso and micro levels (Bronfenbrenner 1979) as well as illustrating aspects of theory-based practice (George 2002). A selection of key practice principles derived from the research findings and recent literature in this field brings this chapter to its conclusion.

Immigrants and refugees

The movement of people (voluntary or forced) across borders is an international phenomenon, an expression of globalization[2] with implications for nations and their economic and political stability as well as their cultural identity. New Zealand, by virtue of its distance from other landmasses, and absence of close border conflicts, is not threatened in the same way as so many other states by the prospect of unmanageable numbers of asylum-seekers and refugees seeking to establish themselves here. It is helpful to define commonly used terms for different types of migrant referred to in this chapter.

An immigrant is someone who moves in a planned way, from one country to another in order to settle permanently in the new country. Immigrants know that they may, if they choose, return to their country of origin. This is not the case for refugees. It is estimated that there are about 19.5 million refugees in the world (www.unchr.ch, basic facts page 6 March 2003). According to the United Nations 1951 Convention on the Status of Refugees, a refugee is a person who:

> Owing to well-founded fear of being persecuted for reasons of race, religion, nationality, membership of a particular social group or political opinion, is outside the country of his nationality and is unable or, owing to such fear, is unwilling to avail himself of the protection of that country. (www.unchr.ch)

Asylum-seekers, in contrast to immigrants and refugees, are people who enter a country without legal documents, or whose documents expire once they have arrived and who claim refugee status. New Zealand, as a signatory to the 1951 UN Convention Relating to the Status of Refugees, has a responsibility to determine the citizenship status of all asylum-seekers.

Community work with immigrants and refugees

Research and publications concerning issues and processes of settlement for immigrants and refugees indicate a developing conceptualization of this work into a field of practice for resettlement or citizenship and new research findings indicate that frameworks for practice in this area are taking shape (George 2002; Healy 2001; Nash and Trlin forthcoming; Potocky-Tripodi 2002; Powell 2001; Valtonen 2001; Whelan *et al.* 2003). Recent New Zealand literature suggests a growing interest in this field of practice, documenting the need for social workers to recognize the multi-cultural needs of refugees and migrants (Briggs 2001) and developing models for social workers in this area (Chapman 2002). Policy recommendations by community-based agencies call for an integrated approach to service provision (Cotton 1999) and strategic discernment in the matter of the New Zealand Refugee quota selection criteria (Cotton 2002). Chinese social workers and researchers have produced a number of insightful publications concerning social work with Chinese and Asian migrants (Ho *et al.* 2000; Wang 2000; Ngai 2000; Wong 2000 and Chu 2001). Interest in this area of social work is supported by a growing body of helpful overseas material. In a comprehensive handbook on practice for social work with refugees and immigrants, Potocky-Tripodi (2002, p.3) argues that this work 'requires specialized knowledge of the unique issues of these populations'. She systematically explores the complexity of factors that practitioners need to recognize as important in the lives of this diverse client group, using an ecological framework of macro, meso and micro levels of analysis. This framework, used by many theorists in this field, is also used in this chapter. Examples of settlement work at each level in the framework are introduced below, using information from the Friendly Support Network, which stretches across New Zealand, and is a self-help organization (mainly, but not exclusively) for people of Dutch descent, many of whom arrived in the 1950s and have brought up their children in New Zealand.

At the macro level, settlement work highlights human rights and social justice, taking into account the economic and international contexts influencing the various types of migrant, as well as national policies and provisions for them. Practitioners need to know about legislation affecting immigration generally. Knowledge of human rights legislation and the work of the United Nations High Commission on Refugees (UNHCR), including relevant aspects of international and local law surrounding immigrants and refugees, is essential. Structural analysis and social justice are key aspects of this level of community work, which aims to develop good social policies and service provision. At a macro level, the Friendly Support Network is involved in policy development, seeking support from government for its efforts to provide services to elderly migrants from Holland. It addresses such problems as family reunification (where retired family members seek to live in New Zealand and cannot settle because they feel isolated, their grandchildren cannot speak Dutch, and so they want to return), language regression (a high percentage of the very old will lose their second language ability) and pension issues.

Working at the meso level, practitioners will have a good working knowledge and critical analysis of agency networks and resources in the wider community. They will be familiar with service delivery systems available to their client groups and they need to be knowledgeable regarding key problem areas such as health, mental health, family dynamics, cultural diversity, language, education and economic circumstances. The NGO workers interviewed in the research expressed a range of insights and knowledge at this level, reflecting their organizations' commitment to being change agents. At this level, the Friendly Support Network has developed its own home care services, 'ThuisZorg', which attend to the personal needs of people trying to remain independent in their own homes. Members of the Network liaise with relevant organizations and groups in the community to ensure that they are a recognized referral point, and also that they know where to refer their own clients.

At the micro level, practitioners need to be culturally competent and have the requisite knowledge and skills to work appropriately with their immigrant or refugee clients. The Friendly Support Network is a good example here as it fulfils the need for the Dutch speaking community to request and receive assistance from a culturally and linguistically appropriate source. For instance, the services provided by ThuisZorg include assessment and personal care provided by 'care workers who are trained, bilingual and reliable people who have a sensitivity towards the Dutch culture' (ThuisZorg, Waitakere Community Resource Centre 2001).

These three examples of settlement work at the macro, meso and micro levels are included to emphasize the ongoing nature of settlement, and the importance of an awareness of how settlement continues to affect people at different stages of the human life-cycle.

George (2002, pp.468–71), in a review of the literature on settlement service delivery, discerns two broad approaches: theory-based and practice-based. Two categories in the theory-based approach offer frameworks for conceptualizing settlement services and ways in which they are provided. The first category features cultural competence and client empowerment. Ecological models as well as empowerment approaches are their key features. Intervention occurs at the international, political, community and family levels. The second category of settlement service delivery is typically a continuum model that considers the processes and stages by which migrants and refugees shift from pre-movement to acclimatization, followed by adaptation towards integration.

Practice-based approaches are characterized by their ethnic-centred and grassroots ethos and origins or, if they are mainstream agencies, by their focus on providing culturally appropriate and well-informed services. Examples of these models in action can be found by examining services for migrants and refugees in New Zealand.

New Zealand services for immigrants and refugees

In New Zealand, the state and community provide certain services to assist new immigrants (voluntary, or economic, as well as refugee) in the settlement process. The extent of help available varies geographically and depends on the migration category to which people belong. The interplay between state and community organizations is influenced and shaped by policies that affect the provision of services; these are often fragmented and complex. An overview with examples of some of the services (statutory and national as well as local NGOs) available to support settlement into New Zealand society helps to contextualize service provision. Some of these agencies serve the general population and some of them are specifically for refugees and sometimes for voluntary migrants (see Table 8.1).

Table 8.1 Services supporting settlement into New Zealand

Statutory services	New Zealand Immigration Service
	Mangere Refugee Resettlement Service
	Work and Income New Zealand
	Ministry of Internal Affairs
	Office of Ethnic Affairs
	Housing New Zealand
	Ministry of Social Development
	Hospital and other statutory health services
	Schools
National non-government organizations	Citizens Advice Bureaux
	Refugee and Migrant Services
	Refugees as Survivors
	New Zealand Federation of Ethnic Councils
	Human Rights Foundation
	Dutch Friendly Support Network
Locally based non-government organizations	Auckland Refugee Council
	Shakti
	Chinese New Settlers Service
	Refugee Resettlement Support Service

The New Zealand Immigration Service is responsible for the Mangere Refugee Resettlement Agency, which provides an intensive six weeks' induction and health programme for newly arrived refugees. No such induction programme is run by a state service for newly arrived economic immigrants. Work and

Income New Zealand and the Ministry of Internal Affairs are as available to new immigrants as to other residents and citizens, provided they meet the necessary criteria. The Office of Ethnic Affairs is run out of the Ministry of Internal Affairs and serves ethnic populations apart from tangata whenua, the indigenous people of New Zealand (Ministry of Maori Affairs) and Pacific Island communities (Ministry of Pacific Island Affairs).

Using George's continuum model of settlement referred to above, the Mangere Reception Centre for refugees caters for the acclimatization end of the continuum, while social and community workers who are involved with refugees in the community are assisting them through adaptation and towards integration into local communities. The Refugee and Migrant Service, as well as Refugees as Survivors and other dedicated organizations, are particularly involved in the adaptation phase, while self-help groups and mainstream agencies become involved predominantly, but not exclusively, in the integration phase of settlement. NGOs vary considerably in size and target many different causes.

Both Valtonen (2001, 2002) and George (2002) argue that community development and self-help policies are effective in the pursuit of successful resettlement. They emphasize the importance of self-help and ethnic groups for supporting new settlers as they adapt and integrate into their new communities. They call for the introduction of policies that will enable immigrants, refugees and asylum-seekers, who have become integrated into their new communities, to work with newcomers whose experiences they share. Whelan *et al.* (2002, p.19) endorse this approach when they describe the valuable input of refugee women helping their own people and reflect on how this promotes an empowerment based approach to the oppressed (Ife 1995).

Community work and settlement services

It is argued here that an ecological model can promote best practice from a community work perspective in this new field. Research referred to above indicates that the community workers involved with refugees and immigrants frequently refer to macro, meso and micro levels of analysis and interaction when explaining and discussing their work. Examples of their work at each of these three levels, together with some of the reflective observations made by respondents, are provided in this section.

Macro level community work with migrants and refugees

> You have got to be able to have a structural analysis, you have got to be able to have a global analysis... Because in this sector...if you only have case work skills, you only have...a micro-base approach to your work, it is not going to work, it will be very soul-destroying. (Respondent, Nash and Trlin fothcoming)

This succinct statement encapsulates the macro level approach taken by community workers with migrants and refugees. Respondents who questioned whether resource people in community organizations should be social workers, or educators for the people who are actually working with individuals and families at the grassroots, agreed that working only at the micro level was soul-destroying. One could too easily get so involved in case by case situations that it would be impossible to do the enabling or training component of the job. They argued that specialized workers were needed to enable others to do the work (by providing training and good supervision) rather than to do it themselves, getting overwhelmed and ending up achieving very little or nothing.

The Refugee and Migrant Services exemplify this way of working, for they have a significant advisory role in relation to government policy for quota refugees and asylum-seekers. They produce well-informed discussion papers with a macro-level analysis of key topics such as family reunification and policy and selection of quota refugees, and they work on a macro level. Together with Refugees as Survivors, they were very clear that while casework services for individuals are essential, to be most effective they will probably be supported from within a community-based agency. This point is consistently made by those with experience in this field, and was made by Whelan *et al.* (2002) who, while working in Australia with 400 displaced Kosovans, developed a community, rather than a counselling approach to their clients.

For some respondents, social justice and advocacy formed an integral part of the services they offered and they found a macro level analysis was very useful. Others stressed the need for a much stronger resettlement approach with a structured model of support providing better access to free English teaching for a realistic period of time, together with good financial help with resettlement. Several respondents were frustrated at what they described as the lack of 'really good help for people, many of whom are highly skilled in their own country, to actually translate their skills into something that would help them quickly assimilate, if you like, into New Zealand'. This concern for the provision of a national settlement programme leads naturally into the meso level of analysis, which focuses on community service provision.

Meso level community work with migrants and refugees

Using an ecological framework, the meso level denotes organizations and agencies providing services in the wider community that could be regarded as relevant to the functioning of a particular client group. Practitioners involved with refugee work were sometimes unaware of the existence of a network of agencies with specialist skills and knowledge (Nash and Trlin 2004). This was more likely in generic agencies that did not offer refugee specific services, particularly if they were situated outside the main centres for refugee and migrant settlement. Most people in the resettlement field would be quite well aware of agencies dealing with refugees.

Respondents working directly in this area gave useful illustrations of their work and how they felt it could be enhanced. For example, one respondent was very sure that her agency could greatly improve meso level services if it 'were better resourced, by direct or indirect government funding...because it would enable us to increase our profile, and put a bit more time into the training aspects that can't be done – training for other agencies'. As it was, her agency, which focused on settlement work, encouraged good working partnerships with other less specialized agencies.

A respondent from an agency offering generic services agreed that many agencies needed to be better informed and more aware of what services were available to immigrants and refugees. However, in her own case, she felt that her multi-disciplinary team of social workers, nurses and therapists who worked with refugees and asylum-seekers knew most of the main services, had good relationships with the people within them and knew who the key people were. They had worked hard to build strong relationships with the main refugee and asylum seeker organizations which, she felt, sometimes depended on her agency for resources, onward referrals and information. Many respondents felt that social and community workers needed to be well trained about networking. Community work in this new field is very demanding of the practitioner, who needs to have knowledge of both international and local matters affecting migration and settlement. Most of the respondents to the two surveys, as well as those interviewed, voiced their concerns about the difficulties they face when they lack information about the cultural needs and networks of the immigrants and refugees they work with and for. This was a particular issue for practitioners working at a micro level with clients from different cultural backgrounds overseas.

Micro level community work

Community work at a micro level entails working one-on-one with individuals and families, using the skills of intervention more often associated with counsellors and social workers (but which are also essential for community workers) while at the same time being mindful of the macro perspective. The research findings illustrate this: respondents indicated a clearly perceived need for improved cultural services, staff training and interpreter services. They showed awareness of the need to further develop practice knowledge and skills in what Russell and White (2002), in their Canadian-based research, refer to as multi-faceted perception of self and other. Respondents also saw a need for training in brokering for services and advocacy, skills that Russell and White (2002, p.639) refer to as proactive service provision. They were very aware of the need to offer a comprehensive range of services to this client group that spanned the social change, community development and social work spectrum.

The respondents who were surveyed by Nash and Trlin (2004) had similar views and their observations illustrate micro-level community work with individuals. They pointed out that interviewing refugees or asylum-seekers in crisis is labour intensive. It can involve interpreters, cultural advisors and time building trust and rapport: 'To be able to assess you need to know the client's politics, ethnicity, social status.'

With regard to cultural training, one community worker discussed two projects, each relevant in an international context. One involved people from a particular culture, such as Somali, doing a half-day seminar on their culture and its meaning, providing a Somali luncheon and providing contact with the Somali community. The other involved setting up new settlers teams, where there would be specific people within each office who could work with all the refugees and asylum-seekers, and who may be of a different nationality as well. Examples of cultural training recommended by those working in this area were detailed and useful and some are included below in an adapted form, as examples of the micro skills required.

Recommendations for cultural training

Practitioners require a basic training in terms of what is different about cross-cultural work, what is significant about how you deliver services to groups who have had traumatic mental health experiences.

Workers need exposure to people of different cultures who live their lives in a completely different way. They need the confidence to ask the right questions of their clients, but that is not what they have been trained in. They have been trained to have enough background to know, and when they don't have the requisite information, they feel disempowered, vulnerable.

We have to impart knowledge about respectful ways to inquire. We may need to simply check out with someone whether shaking hands is appropriate in their culture. One of the things our agency tries to do is to re-empower, to request: 'Teach me about your culture, teach me what I could do that would be helpful, what I could do that would be non-helpful.' It is such a respectful, empowering thing to do.

The micro level skills described above emphasize the belief that cultural competence and client empowerment are particularly important aspects of the practitioner's repertoire when working within an ecological framework.

This section has provided concrete examples of settlement work at the macro, meso and micro levels. The information, derived from social and community workers surveyed and interviewed in 2001 about their work and how they felt it could be improved, is both grounded and practical, and relevant to an international setting.

Theory-based and practice-based frameworks

Findings from the two nationwide surveys referred to at the beginning of this chapter provide examples of theory-based and practice-based frameworks for settlement service delivery. For example, the cultural competence, empowerment and ecological analysis characteristic of the first broad category of theory-based approaches, express the vision of community development (Ife 1995, pp.96–7, Munford and Walsh-Tapiata 1999). This is founded on ecological/social justice values, and gives space to the wisdom of the oppressed, which informs and gives hope to communities that recognize their obligations to humanity. In relation to these models, social and community workers surveyed in New Zealand showed awareness and concern about the need to develop their cultural skills in order to communicate and assist migrants and refugees. Many wanted to strengthen their knowledge of human rights and international issues affecting their clients and to use an ecological model to inform their practice.

In relation to the second broad category of theory-based approaches, the continuum models, respondents invariably commented that services should be more co-ordinated, integrated and better resourced. They also drew attention to several other countries in which this is the case. Practitioners recommended three areas for policy development relating to resettlement.

1. The provision of an integrated model of care from arrival to readiness for employment.

2. The empowerment of people going through the re-settlement process to live independently in New Zealand society.

3. The provision of free pre-school education and English language education to immigrants, who should be treated sensitively and respected for their ethnic derivation.

One community worker made similar points with reference to voluntary migrants thus:

> I would like to see the new government provide some help to the new migrants. There is a settlement programme for refugees but we don't have immigrant settlement policy. There are three things needed. We have a three stage process: pre-immigration, and departure, and settlement. At pre-migrant stage we should give accurate and appropriate information to the people who are waiting to come to New Zealand. Then when they arrive in New Zealand we should provide the settlement programme, like orientation, to teach them

New Zealand meals... legislations, and they all come from new cultures. Even though little things, it is very important for them, for example, everyday life. And another part I think is important is employment providing some skilled training of New Zealand employment culture. Teach about the New Zealand labour market, different from dole.

The sound principles that underlie these policy recommendations reflect an ecological approach to practice, as well as an awareness of the continuum model of resettlement (George and Fuller-Thompson 1998) and recognition of some of the basic humanitarian needs of immigrants, refugees and asylum-seekers, all consistent with the tenets of community work. Community work involves both human and material resources, and the social and community workers who responded to the two surveys mentioned above were unanimous that there is insufficient funding for NGO settlement service provision in New Zealand.

Typical situations where practice-based models for settlement service delivery can be seen are those in which settled migrants have organized themselves to provide information and other services to immigrants and/or refugees from their own culture in order to assist them in the process of settlement. Examples in New Zealand would be the ethnic community councils in many of the urban centres, and more specific examples would be the Dutch Friendly Support Network already mentioned or the Auckland Latin American Community Inc. The mission statement of the Auckland Latin American Community Inc. provides an excellent illustration of the underlying empowerment philosophy and values informing this category of settlement service delivery:

> We intend to provide a holistic, bicultural, bilingual safe and accessible social and community service for the Latin American People, giving priority to the development of programmes aimed at children, young persons and their families and the wider community in Auckland. (ALAC Inc. 2001)

Key practice principles

International literature has many examples of practice principles relevant to community and development work, as well as settlement service delivery. Healy (2001, pp.288–9) in her work on international social work, includes the UN Summit for Social Development – Ten Commitments, while Powell (2001) argues the importance of civic social work by challenging social workers to broaden their horizons and acknowledge the centrality of citizenship and inclusion in their work.

Powell proposes ten core practice principles, including the promotion of social inclusion, trust and respect for clients and for their views on what works for them in order to develop user participation and empowerment. Multiculturalism and sensitive recognition of poverty are crucial attributes for civic social work and Powell argues that, to be effective, social work must function with the support of the state as well as of the service users. In similar vein, George (2002) identifies 'full and equal participation of newcomers in Canadian society' (George 2002, p. 468) as the aim of the Canadian Council for Refugees. She views resettlement in two ways: first as a two-way process in which both new-comers and the host society have to adapt to one another and second, the provision of resettlement services can be seen as a duty based on human rights (2002, p.468).

George notes that the Canadian Council for Refugees identifies values such as inclusivity, empowerment, respect for newcomers, cultural sensitivity, collaboration and reliability of services as important in resettlement work. In addition, short-term measures of success include gaining employment, as well as social and civic integration, while long-term measures involve career advancement, social participation and access to institutions. In New Zealand, social and community workers give priority to working in a bicultural manner, mindful of the Treaty of Waitangi that, signed in 1840 by the Crown and many of the indigenous peoples of New Zealand, gave Maori customary rights and protections.

Policy recommendations for the migration and settlement of refugees (Bloch 2002) place importance on citizenship and its associated rights while settlement practice principles, put forward by Potocky-Tripodi (2002), are also grounded in community development and human rights values. The principled concerns and values held by many of the social and community workers surveyed and interviewed in the research referred to in this chapter echoed similar practice and development principles to those described above. Respondents highlighted the following practice principles and requirements as essential for effective community work in this area:

- the development of high agency standards
- the employment of qualified, experienced, committed and respected staff
- commitment to ethical practices and respect for people from minority groups
- a sound macro view approach and a good analysis of the bigger picture
- to value advocacy, social justice and inclusion
- the creation of a comfortable place for the new migrants
- the integration of new settlers in the local community: enabling them to participate in the life of the school or the community

- ongoing networking with clients
- reflection and future directions.

Community and social work in the settlement field require strong community development skills and knowledge including theoretical knowledge, structural analysis, networking, advocacy, co-operation and collaboration, understanding of social policy (how to influence and change it) and, in this field especially, knowledge of human rights and citizenship law. The receiving communities of migrants need to be well prepared if they are to accept immigrants and refugees. Host populations need to be educated through publicity campaigns and integration projects to assist the settlement process for immigrants and refugees. Host children need to know more about the lives and customs of children from different ethnic backgrounds.[3]

While globalization sets up countervailing pressures on people to acknowledge and celebrate their own local identity, it is time to consider what is happening and explore the tensions between globalization and national identity (Midgley 2000). How are social and community workers responding to these countervailing pressures? Will they gather the best from international sources while maintaining high practice standards appropriate to local conditions? Informed answers are important in order to ensure that practitioners and students receive appropriate and cutting edge education and training for practice and so that clients can have confidence in those who work with them as knowledgeable and well trained practitioners.

Questions for reflection

1. What are the key characteristics of work with immigrants, refugees and asylum-seekers that suggest this is a new field of practice for social and community workers?

2. What do you consider essential knowledge for practitioners in this new field of practice?

3. What policies would you like to see introduced or supported to enable immigrants, refugees and asylum-seekers to become integrated into their new communities?

Notes

1 These surveys were conducted through the New Settlers Programme, which explores the experiences of new settlers in New Zealand. The Programme Leader is Associate Professor Andrew Trlin and the Programme is funded by the Foundation for Research, Science and Technology. Mary Nash was Principal Researcher for the surveys and follow-up interviews.

2   For more on globalization and social work see Ramanathan and Link (1999).

3   A good contemporary example of such campaigns from the NGO sector is the Caritas Aotearoa/New Zealand social justice series, *Welcoming the Stranger: Refugees and Migrants in the Modern World* (Caritas New Zealand 2002).

References

Ahmad, Y., Woolaston, S. and Patel, S. (2000) 'Child safety in Indian families.' *Social Work Now 15*, 13–19.

Bloch, A. (2002) *The Migration and Settlement of Refugees and Migrants in Britain*. Houndmills, Basingstoke and New York: Palgrave Macmillan.

Briggs, L. (2001) 'Refugees and migrants: Issues of multi-culturalism in Aotearoa/New Zealand.' In M. Connolly (ed) *Social Work in New Zealand*. Oxford, New York: Oxford University Press.

Bronfenbrenner, U. (1979) *The Ecology of Human Development: Experiments by Nature and Design*. Cambridge, MA: Harvard University Press.

Caritas New Zealand, (2002) *Welcoming the Stranger: Refugees and Migrants in the Modern World. Social Justice Series 7*. Wellington: Caritas New Zealand.

Chapman, A. (2002) 'Social work with refugees and migrants.' In R. Truell and L. Nowland (eds) *Reflections on Current Practice in Social Work*. Palmerston North: Dunmore Press.

Chu, K., Cheung, V. and Tan, R. (2001) 'Working with the Chinese in New Zealand.' *Social Work Now 18*, 12–18.

Cotton, P. (1999) *The New Zealand Refugee Quota: Quota Selection Recommendations*. Wellington: Refugee and Migrant Service.

Cotton, P. (2002) *Refugee Resettlement Policy in New Zealand: An Integrated Approach*. Wellington: Refugee and Migrant Service.

George, U. (2002) 'A needs-based model for settlement service delivery for newcomers to Canada.' *International Social Work 45*, 4, 465–480.

George, U. and Fuller-Thompson, E. (1998) 'To stay or not to stay: Chartacteristics associated with newcomers planning to remain in Canada.' *Journal of Regional Science 20*, 1–2, 181–194.

Healy, L. (2001) *International Social Work. Professional Action in an Interdependent World*. New York, Oxford: Oxford University Press.

Ho, E., Cheung, E., Bedford, C. and Leung, P. (2000) *Settlement Assistance Needs of Recent Migrants*. Wellington: New Zealand Immigration Service.

Home Care Services. (2001) *ThuisZorg*. Auckland: Waitakere Community Resource Centre, Auckland.

Ife, J. (1995) *Community Development*. Melbourne: Longman Australia.

Midgley, J. (2000) 'Social work and globalisation.' *Social Work, July, 13–28*.

Munford, R. and Walsh-Tapiata, W. (1999) *Strategies for Change*. Palmerston North: Massey University.

Nash, M. (2002) 'Social work provision in relation to immigrants, refugees and asylum seekers in New Zealand: Some preliminary findings.' *Social Work Review 14*, 4, 26–31.

Nash, M. and Trlin, A. (2004) *Social Work with Immigrants, Refugees and Asylum Seekers in New Zealand*. Palmerston North: New Settlers Programme, Massey University.

Nash, M. and Trlin, A. (forthcoming) *Report into Non-Goverment Not For Profit Agencies and Organizations Providing Social Services to Immgrants and Refugees in New Zealand*. Palmerston North: New Settlers Programme, Massey University.

Ngai, M. (2000) *Overview of Chinese Social Services and Networks*. Auckland: Chinese Social Workers Interest Group.

Potocky-Tripodi, M. (2002) *Best Practices for Social Work with Refugees and Migrants*. New York: Columbia University Press.

Powell, F. (2001) *The Politics of Social Work*. London: Sage.

Ramanathan, C.S. and Link, R.J. (1999) *All Our Futures: Principles and Resources for Social Work Practice in a Global Era*. Belmont, USW: Wadsworth.

Russell, M.N. and White, B. (2002) 'Social worker and immigrant client experiences in multicultural service provision: Educational implications.' *Social Work Education 21*, 6, 635–650.

United Nations High Commission on Refugees (1951) *Convention Relating to the Status of Refugees*. www.unchr.ch, accessed 6 March 2003.

Valtonen, K. (2001) 'Social work with immigrants and refugees: Developing a participation-based framework for anti-oppressive practice.' *British Journal of Social Work 31*, 955–960.

Valtonen, K. (2002) 'Social work with immigrants and refugees: Developing a participation-based framework for anti-oppressive practice, Part 2.' *British Journal of Social Work 32*, 113–120.

Wang, J. L.J. (2000) *Highlighting Two Gaps in Existing New Zealand Social Services: Settlement Programmes and Asian Services*. ANZASW Biennial Conference, Auckland 2000.

Whelan, J., Swallow, M., Peschar, P. and Dunne, A. (2002) 'From counseling to social work: Developing a framework for social work practice with displaced persons.' *Australian Social Work 55*, 1, 13–23.

Wong, J. (2000) *Agencies Providing Social Services for the Chinese Community. Paper presented by M. Ngai at the ANZASW Biennial Conference, Auckland 2000*.

Part III
Working with Strengths

Part II
Working with Strangers

Introduction

This section explores how strengths approaches contribute to the integrated practice framework. Strengths-based approaches have become a strong influence in social work practice and have been developed in a diversity of practice settings. These range from mental health settings, statutory organizations and in non-government agencies that work with families, children and young people.

The chapters in this section explore the key elements of strengths approaches and develop these within a particular context and perspective. The key themes include a focus on the following:

- A belief that those with whom social workers work bring strengths and resources to the helping relationship and that these contribute to finding solutions to current challenges.

- A belief that a focus on strengths does not diminish the importance of identifying 'risks' and developing strategies for finding ways to protect clients from situations of harm and from causing harm. However, strengths approaches challenge us to think about what it is to that enables people to survive and grow and to identify the moments when solutions were found and positive change was achieved.

- A belief that within the wider environment of clients' lives there will be resources that can assist in the change process. The challenge for the social worker is to see the world with a different perspective, one that enables them to be creative in seeking out resources and opportunities for supporting the change process.

- A belief that fundamental to strengths approaches is the building of strong relationships and partnerships with clients. They, not the social worker, direct the change process.

The three chapters in this section focus on working with families (Robyn Munford and Jackie Sanders), working in statutory settings (Rodger Jack) and using strengths approaches to guide the supervision of practice (Chris Thomas and Sharlene Davis). In reading these chapters we encourage the reader to reflect on their own practice and to identify how strengths approaches can enhance the efficacy of their practice.

Chapter 9

Working with Families: Strengths-based Approaches

Robyn Munford and Jackie Sanders

Social and community workers are involved in the daily lives of families. Their work requires them to make judgements about how families can be supported to care for their children. In Aotearoa/New Zealand the general population is concerned about the high rate of child abuse and violence towards children. Horrific events sharply focus our mind on what is happening inside families and beg the question about communities of support for families, who face so many daily challenges that they require assistance to care for their children. Social and community workers often struggle to find more effective ways of working with families. Strengths-based approaches have become a strong influence in addressing the challenges with which families are confronted (Saleeby 2002). This chapter, based on research on families in Aotearoa/New Zealand (Munford and Sanders 1999; Munford *et al.* 2001, Munford and Sanders 2003), examines how strengths-based approaches can contribute to our understanding of working with families.

The chapter begins by exploring current ideas on social work practice and how they connect with a strengths-based approach. It then provides a context for understanding the lives of families and children and briefly considers the Aotearoa/New Zealand context. The chapter then focuses upon key themes in strengths approaches. Finally, we consider the ways in which the principles of the strengths approach have been applied in social work practice with families. Here we discuss in detail the way in which the broad strengths philosophy has informed practice. There are connections here to community development given that a key strategy of strengths-based approaches is to harness informal and 'naturally occurring networks' to support families within their neighbourhoods and communities of interest (Munford and Sanders 1999, p.94).

Theorizing social work practice

Strengths-based approaches encompass and reflect particular contexts and in this case, those in Aotearoa/New Zealand. The learning from this country has relevance for social work practice internationally. It is argued that strengths-based approaches go right to the heart of relationship building with clients and challenge social workers to examine their positions and roles in helping relationships. Social workers are encouraged to critically explore what empowerment and positive change actually mean in practice and in the daily lives of families (Munford and Sanders 1999). Critical social work and community work, postmodernism and constructive approaches (Allan, Pease and Briskman 2003; Cooper 2001; Fook 2003; Healy 2000; Ife 1997; Parton and O'Byrne 2000), provide a helpful foundation for understanding the potential of strengths approaches to transform practice. These approaches encourage social workers to interrogate notions of power, to appreciate how knowledge is constructed, to critically explore the nature of the social work task and the relationships between workers and clients, including the way that they address difference and diversity. Writers in this tradition urge us to understand how social work is mediated through meaning systems with a key focus on defining how formal knowledge acquired from intellectual endeavours interacts with practice knowledge and the perspectives clients bring to the social work intervention (Cooper 2001).

Central to these views is an understanding of how theory and practice interact with one another and contribute equally to knowledge development. The constructivist approach challenges social workers to foreground the authority of clients as 'engaged' subjects and to understand that clients 'will be undertaking their own active synthesis and interpretation of the social work intervention' (Cooper 2001, p.724). This view transforms the way we perceive the intervention process, where the definition of clients moves from seeing them as passive recipients of help (where the social worker as expert controls the change process) to a view that sees clients as active participants in the change process and experts on what will work in their lives (Ife 2001).

We are also challenged to evaluate the potential of social work to bring about change on the micro and macro levels and, as Cooper (2001, p.722) suggests, to understand that social work is 'on the boundary between private lives and public concerns' and that what happens within 'individual, specific applications' are strongly connected to wider issues. An inclusive and participative approach in work with clients (Cooper 2001) can facilitate the voices of marginalized groups to be heard and to challenge the dominant discourses that may function to exclude them from participation (Ife 1997). Allan (2003, p.71) argues that critical social work perspectives that bring together structural and postmodern approaches, require social workers to 'link the personal and the political and to ensure that people's immediate material needs are addressed and that also consider the need for longer-term social change'. A focus on narrative work (p.71) and on exploring 'alternative discourses' (p.68) provides opportunities for clients 'to deal with their internalised oppression and thus become actively engaged in actions aimed at social change' (p.71).

Social workers must also heed the challenge of writers such as Margolin (1997) who uses ideas from theorists such as Foucault to cross-examine social work practice and to provide a genealogy of the minutiae of social work stories in a range of practice settings. Margolin (1997) reminds us that social work is not removed from the operation of power and control and that on a daily level social workers juggle the challenge of mediating the demands of professional practice and agency requirements, and the desire to work in a way that can genuinely engage with, and challenge the structures and the discourses that prevent clients from participation and from taking control of their own lives. They need to be able to critique their own work and what influences the construction of their practice. One of the challenges is to understand how context contributes to defining the nature of the social work task and it is to this that we now turn.

Social work practice in context

A major challenge for nations around the world is to identify how their visions for the positive future of their children can be realized. In countries where many do not have enough daily sustenance, the questions to be faced are about survival. In some countries, the challenges are about addressing issues of child exploitation and abuse and providing safe living environments for children. In other countries issues including suicide prevention and minimization of harm and developing healthy lifestyles free of alcohol and drugs, occupy the minds of parents, social workers and policy makers. In the end, all of these challenges are about survival and encompass the common themes of material and social resources, health and wellbeing and questions about the nature and status of childhood and what it means to be a particular child in a particular place and time (Mayall 2002). Children are part of families as a key social institution. In formulating policy and developing practice frameworks, attention should be focused on what happens in this key social institution, including an understanding about how this environment may open up or restrict life opportunities. This is a central concern of social workers.

In Aotearoa/New Zealand, as in other countries, social workers are challenged to understand the particular contexts of their practice. Indigenous frameworks and understandings, as well as a desire to develop what it means to practice in bicultural ways, have exerted a powerful influence over the way in which social and community work practice has developed. It must be noted here that Aotearoa/New Zealand has a constitutional founding document, the Treaty of Waitangi (Te Tiriti o Waitangi) that protects the rights of Maori (tangata whenua) and provides validation for tauiwi (all those who have settled in New Zealand after the arrival of the Maori) to live in this land. Understand-ings of mulitculturalism are framed within the primary relationship between Maori and tauiwi. This relationship has been used to understand and construct relationships between other cultural groups. For example, Pacific Islands communities who have a strong presence in Aotearoa/New Zealand and have introduced a range of worldviews that have strengthened our social work practice frameworks (Munford 2003).

The context of social and community work practice in Aotearoa/New Zealand has resulted in particular interpretations of social work models and new ways of working have emerged. For example the Whare Tapa Wha model (Durie 1995) provides an indigenous interpretation of understanding health and wellbeing encompassing spiritual, psychological, physical and kinship dimensions. These frameworks of practice are to be seen across the fields of practice in a range of social service settings including state agencies, Maori-centred agencies, health settings and non-government agencies (Sanders and Munford 2001; Walsh-Tapiata 2002).

The commitment of social and community workers in Aotearoa/New Zealand to embrace new ways of working and be challenged by alternative frameworks is part of a search for models that support families and communi-ties. The emphasis has been upon finding local solutions by validating local stories and knowledge in order to build engaged communities that find strength in utilizing their own energy, resources and local talent (Mataira 2002, p.5). These models align with the knowledge underpinning strengths-based approaches that focus on hearing stories differently in order to find solutions and create positive change (Munford and Sanders 1999). Strengths-based approaches, as with many of the emerging models in Aotearoa/New Zealand, move away from a focus on deficits and on the dysfunctional aspects of family life. While not minimizing the enormous difficulties families may face, such as abuse, poverty, poor health and the loss of hope (Dawson and Berry 2002), the strengths-based approach aims to focus on the competencies families have used to overcome and survive difficult circumstances (Munford *et al.* 2001).

Strengths-based approaches – key themes emerging from research with families

Saleeby (2002, pp.12–18) elaborates five key principles of the strengths per-spective:

- every individual, group, family and community has strengths

- trauma, abuse, illness and struggle may be injurious but they may also be sources of challenge and opportunity

- assume that you do not know the upper limits of the capacity to grow and change and take individual, group and community aspirations seriously
- we best serve clients by collaborating with them
- every environment is full of resources.

The international social work definition also provides a useful foundation for strengths-based approaches in social work practice and has a strong resonance with these key principles. This definition promotes social change, problem-solving in human relationships and the empowerment and liberation of people to enhance wellbeing. Social work intervenes at points where people interact with their environment. Central to social work practice is an understanding of the principles of human rights and social justice. Indigenous and local knowledge define the context of social work and social workers seek to embrace humanitarian and democratic ideals addressing injustices and inequities in their daily practice (International Federation of Social Workers). A strengths approach will embrace many of these aspects, interpreting problem-solving in human relationships in a particular way by beginning at a different place with clients.

Moving to a focus on strengths

A focus on strengths moves us to think about what it is that enables families to survive and grow. Our research programme on families (Munford and Sanders 1999) revealed a number of key findings about how to construct effective practice with families. Central to this is a move from a focus on deficit to a focus on finding the strengths that families bring to the helping relationship. Frameworks of practice based on deficit models have been criticized for focusing upon dysfunctional aspects of families (Saleeby 2002). These approaches have failed to recognize that families have competencies and have managed to survive very difficult circumstances. What became clear in our research programme was that many families who had sought help over a period of time had been viewed as 'failed families'. The very process of becoming part of a social service system often reinforced their feelings of incompetence and failure. Those workers who viewed seeking help as positive used this initial contact to support families to examine areas of strength and competence in order to address the issues that had brought them to the agency. These workers clearly saw the family as the key agent of change and challenged others around them, both the formal and informal networks, to adopt this perspective and to adopt a consistent approach with families in the process of addressing issues and achieving positive change.

A focus on strengths does not diminish the importance of identifying 'risks' and developing strategies for protecting children and young people from situations of harm. However, a focus on strengths also moves us to think about what it is that enables families to survive and grow. Many writers on social policy argue that there is a preoccupation with the management of 'risk' (Ellis and Dean 2000) and a focus on individual responsibility and independence rather than a focus on interdependence and collective provision. Others (Mitchell 2000), using Foucault's writing on discourses and power, argue that while dominant discourses construct populations in particular ways, these populations can 'resist' and develop 'alternative practices and alternative accounts that challenge the orthodox and dominant' (Ellis and Dean 2000, p.xxii). The move to adopt strengths approaches is situated right in the middle of these debates. Social workers who use a strengths approach assist families to resist negative practices and walk alongside them to achieve positive outcomes, simultaneously building a repertoire of successes that can be harnessed to address future issues. As Gilligan (2000) suggests, when one works from a strengths perspective a whole new set of questions will need to be asked. The seeking of positive resources can unleash 'healing and developmental potential [that may] otherwise go unrecognized' (Gilligan 2000, p.16).

The move to a focus on strengths has challenges for social workers and these approaches provide them with opportunities to question the essence of their practice (Dominelli 1996). As Norman (2000, pp.1–2) argues, the historical preoccupation with dysfunction, deficit and disease has prevented social workers from harnessing the 'inherent push for growth' and that a deficit and problem-focused orientation can be ultimately counterproductive. We have argued elsewhere (Munford and Sanders 1999) that strengths approaches link individual troubles to public issues. They also challenge definitions of clients as mere consumers of services and critiques the wider discourses that see those who seek support as 'failed families'.

Entering the world of families

Workers must take time to understand the broader influences that may determine how families live their lives (Munford and Sanders 1999). Circumstances can be overwhelming for families (for example, poverty, inadequate housing causing overcrowding and ill-health) and in many situations positive change will not be achieved until key issues are addressed. Workers can work through these broad issues with their clients. Many families have difficulty identifying their competences and abilities when they are immersed in challenging times. The worker has a central role in assisting families to tell their story in a way that enables them to identify positive aspects of their experience and to build on this to create a vision for the future. This is exciting work, especially when it involves children and young people, as they too become part of the change process and learn to build on their successes in order to strengthen their solution-finding capacities so they can enjoy the present and achieve their aspirations for the future (Munford *et al.* 2001; Norman 2000).

Active listening and forming partnerships

It should be obvious that strengths work necessitates active listening in order for workers to build constructive relationships with clients (Egan 2002). Active listening expects workers to disrupt notions of the 'expert' and to critically examine how they view the knowledge and experience that clients bring to helping relationships (Munford *et al.* 2001; Sanders and Munford 2003). Forming constructive partnerships requires a genuine sharing of ideas and an understanding from the worker's perspective that clients have critical knowledge that can be harnessed in the change process. The forming of effective partnerships requires workers to understand that the achievement of positive change requires 'effective and high-quality unconditional support' (Munford and Sanders 1999, p.138) where support work is facilitative not directive and where families maintain control and identify priorities for what they want to achieve in family life. This will only be achieved if a 'real' partnership between the worker and the client has been formed. This partnership is based on an understanding that clients may hold narratives that portray themselves as incompetent and without agency over their circumstances (McQuaide 2000). A skilled worker is able to draw out the strengths in these narratives and assist the client to develop alternative meanings and interpretations of their situation.

Providing alternative meanings and interpretations

One of the challenges for families is to find the emotional resources to transcend their current situations and identify possibilities for the future. Our research included a number of sole parents. These parents often lacked adequate material resources and worked hard to find the social resources to support them in their parenting role. Many struggled to have access to 'naturally occurring networks' (Munford and Sanders 1999, p.94) and so workers have a key role in assisting them to develop these networks. Many of these families had been labelled negatively (for example, with the view that sole parents will not be able to parent well), and as a consequence expend much energy trying to overcome the feelings engendered by being labelled as incapable of providing adequately for their children (Schmitz 1995). Strengths work enables families to explore the impact of these factors and to find strategies for overcoming current challenges. Workers who adopt such practice may choose to work with organizations and networks that attempt to challenge and transform negative structural conditions. Some clients will join these workers in these activities; the helping partnership not only functions to address immediate problems but also may provide other opportunities and new roles for clients to take on.

An important finding from the research reinforces the significance of supporting families to achieve competence in at least one area early on in the intervention process. For example, for a parent having difficulty managing the sullen and angry behaviour of a teenager it may be about finding one place in the day where the interaction with this teenager can be positive, if even for only five minutes. Achieving success or competence, however small, enables families to transfer solution-finding skills to other areas of their lives. We must never overlook both the overwhelming effect of feeling not competent and the liberation that comes from being seen as successful. A re-framing and re-interpretation of challenges can help families see that seemingly hopeless situations can be managed and transformed.

The attitude of the worker and organizational practices will contribute to successful relationships with clients. Organizations adopting strengths approaches in their work need to be critically reflective of their practice and the degree to which organizational culture reflects the strengths philosophy (Zunz and Chernesky 2000). For the worker, participation in regular supervision that encourages them to reflect on practice and search for alternative meanings and interpretations in their work, is central to creating and maintaining effective practice.

Social work practice with families

In moving to adopt a strengths-based approach in social work practice, we suggest that a number of key elements emerge as central to this work. These contribute to a framework for practice and include:

- a commitment to reflective practice
- context-sensitive work
- finding strengths – building effective relationships and partnerships
- multi-levelled interventions
- understanding the daily lives of families.

One can argue that this list identifies the essential components of effective social work practice and we would agree. Strengths approaches remind us of what can be achieved in social work and as the following discussion demonstrates, many of the key elements of effective social work practice have been proven over time. The goal is to ensure that best practice can be maintained and that social work can adapt to the demands and challenges of the twenty-first century. By foregrounding the strengths dimension in practice, social work can provide an important corrective to pathology-based approaches to the provision of services (Norman 2000).

A commitment to reflective practice

An essential element of social work practice is supervision. Taking the time to critique one's work with clients so that all aspects of this work can be explored, and where strategies for improving practice can be identified, is critical to the ongoing development and maintenance of good practice. A key element of strengths approaches is reflective practice, being prepared to critique and change one's practice and where necessary, find ways to ensure that the practices that are working will be supported and maintained by the organization. When social service agencies have a commitment to reflective practice they are more likely to remain responsive to families, to test out what really works and to have a commitment to ensuring that organizational practices parallel the relationships that are being established with clients (Munford and Sanders 1999).

A commitment to reflective practice can provide a foundation for developing a more formal reflection on practice. Research and evaluation can emerge out of the practices of reflection. Having opportunities to meet in group supervision alongside individual supervision, can involve a focus on the monitoring and evaluation of practice. This can begin slowly and in a way that does not impact on the daily work of the organization (Sanders and Munford 2003). There are some creative ways of carrying out research within organizations. For example, O'Neil (2003) provides an excellent illustration of research in practice, showing how research can be built into the everyday practices of agencies and also demonstrating how clients can co-direct research processes and become researchers in their own right. Building on strengths-based principles, O'Neil (2003) describes how researching alongside clients can become a strategy for assisting clients to gain confidence to take control of the direction of their lives. It is a way of underlining and respecting the knowledge of clients and when built into the practice frameworks of agencies, the research can become an integral part of strengths practices that see clients as partners in the change process.

Reflective practice can be empowering for workers as it enables them to take charge of their work and to take time to critically engage with their daily practice. Research may provide an opportunity to analyze their practice so that good practice can be sustained over time. In partnership with clients, it may also be an opportunity to understand what it is that really does make a difference in the lives of clients (Munford and Sanders 1999, p.200). Self-reflective practice can give a 'voice to the voiceless', for clients and for workers, and will assist in defining effective service delivery strategies by re-analyzing situations to generate new knowledge and frameworks for practice (Allan 2003).

Context-sensitive work

Our research programme (Munford and Sanders 1999) reinforced the central importance of context in understanding family life. Families are part of many overlapping sets of relationships and systems including culture, the economy, political structures, religion, geographical location and household composition. The research programme has shown that responses to family issues may require intervention in a number of contexts in order to ensure that positive change can be achieved. One of the key contexts to consider is culture and in Aotearoa/New Zealand, this will involve an understanding of the meaning systems of both Maori and non-Maori. Social workers need to understand the cultural practices of each family and harness these in the process of change. For example, involving extended family members in the change process given that this is a usual way of operating for the family and a key aspect of how they run their lives.

One of the key elements of context-sensitive work is to understand how personal troubles are connected with public issues, and to know that what is happening in the daily lives of families is strongly influenced by wider forces and central and local government policies (Munford and Sanders 1999, p.200). Workers attempt to understand the current realities of family life by exploring the stories and practices of the family and by exploring the wider contexts that may function to marginalize families. The worker reflects on the nature of the family context and thinks about the key factors that are having an influence in the life of this family. This is wide-ranging and occurs at a number of levels. It may involve taking into account historical and cultural factors that are integral to the way that the family operates, an acknowledgement of the power dynamics within families and knowing how to work with these and understanding the place of factors external to the family, such as community networks and knowing how to harness 'naturally occurring networks' to support families.

Understanding the key contexts that influence family life enable workers to engage in well-informed practice. Strengths approaches are likely to be more effective when the social worker can critically understand the complexities of family life and harness a wide range of resources to assist in finding the strengths within families.

Finding strengths

One of the major challenges for social workers working with strengths approaches is to allow themselves to move from always listening to dysfunction in the lives of clients to listening to how people have managed many of 'life's ups and downs and [how they] grew emotionally and socially when they could tap into and use their own strengths and skills' (O'Neil 2003, p.114). In her research on families as clients and as partners in change processes, O'Neil (p.114) explored how 'sustainable change happened when the individual, family or community had the ability to choose a course of action that was built on their strengths. What was getting them into trouble was their lack of access to their own strengths and to the necessary outside resources.' O'Neil was motivated to look for social work practice that identified how families were utilizing their internal and external resources.

Norman (2000, p.2) also demonstrates how strengths approaches actually work in practice and argues for strategies that move away from 'teaching people evermore sophisticated formulations of their problems' to assisting them to 'learn to recognize and appreciate (and use) their own strengths, thereby enabling them to take control of their own lives and solve their own problems'. Strengths approaches are closely connected to an understanding of how resilient outcomes are achieved. And, as Norman (2000) suggests, those individuals who have developed strategies for dealing with stressful and adverse conditions and events can harness these protective factors to achieve positive change. These factors include personal attributes and environmental factors, such as being able to enhance resources external to the immediate situation (Munford and Sanders 1999). A sense of self-efficacy has been found to be a key factor in achieving resilience and involves having feelings of self-worth and believing that you are able to exert some control over your environment (Norman 2000).

The challenge for the social worker is to build a support relationship with the client so that strengths can be identified and can be harnessed to achieve positive change. This requires social workers to be creative and to assist the family to identify the spaces in their life where they have experienced success and to use these to achieve success in other areas. Strengths-based work takes time and, as Gilligan (2004) suggests, agencies will also need to change their stance in order to assist social workers to respond differently to clients. In talking about responding to a crisis in bureaucratized child protection systems, he argues for 'a new emphasis on relationships, strengths and the clients' social context in child and family work…that requires practitioners and students to reflect carefully on the nature of helping' (Giligan 2004, p.91). In our research, the factors identified above also emerged as significant components of working within strengths approaches. In addition, being able to work at different levels was also a key focus of strengths work and we now turn to a discussion of this.

Multi-levelled interventions

Our research (Munford and Sanders 1999; Sanders and Munford 2003) has clearly indicated that one of the most significant elements of strengths work is focused on building a strong relationship and partnership with clients. This relationship is central to the range of work families and workers do together. We found that workers who were able to work on a number of levels and could tap into a wide range of resources were often very successful in their work with families (Munford and Sanders 1999). We called these 'multi-levelled interventions' and these included working with individuals, families, groups, communities and informal networks, other agencies and formal helping systems.

Being able to work effectively at a number of levels and in different ways include:

- The ability to use a wide range of strategies in working with families.

- The ability to respond to a wide range of requests from the family and to address these in the style that is most appropriate for the family.

- Being able to understand the importance of practical assistance for families and to find ways to provide this as part of helping relationships.

- The recognition that families need to be supported to utilize their own networks where appropriate and where these are contributing to the issue, to be assisted to develop other networks that will provide ongoing support.

- The understanding that the helping relationship should not be central to families' lives and that what is important in strengths work is to firmly believe that clients are at the centre of their own change process (Gilligan 2004). This understanding is manifest in the work of social workers who are able to effectively harness the contexts within which families live their lives.

The factors above encourage us to find ways of understanding the daily lives of all families.

Understanding the daily lives of families

Our research has focused on key aspects of family life and central to this has been an exploration of the parenting roles within families. A central theme in this work has been to understand what it is that prevents families from being 'available to parent' (Munford and Sanders 1999, pp. 97–8). Many parents struggle to parent their children well, not because they do not desire to, but because many factors prevent them from doing so. They struggle with the daily tasks associated with being a parent. They may be poor, experience ill-health, parent alone and have negative experiences that prevent them from developing effective solution-finding strategies. We identify five key areas to be addressed by social workers when understanding the daily lives of families as part of the processes of finding strengths and supporting them in achieving positive change:

1. *Past history* – parents may have developed knowledge and skills needed to parent well but are unable to utilize these effectively because of past experiences. Their own negative experiences in childhood may prevent them from developing positive strategies with their own children. They will need support to achieve success as a parent and to achieve positive outcomes with their children. Many have not had the opportunity to explore what for them family life is about, including their vision and aspirations for themselves and their family.

2. *Discourses of family life* – many parents have internalized the discourses that have labelled them as 'bad' parent and unable to care adequately for their children (Munford and Sanders 1999, pp. 78–84). Those who find themselves in these situations (Allan 2003; Costello 2003; Pease 2003) will need assistance to address these feelings of inadequacy and powerlessness so that they can begin to take control over their own situation and effect change for the future.

3. *Material and social resources* – it is more difficult to parent effectively when resources are scarce. Families living in impoverished communities often find it difficult to access positive networks that can assist them in their daily lives (Gilligan 2004). This is where positive social and economic policies and well-resourced communities have a key role in supporting families to increase their material and social resources so that they can move from a focus on survival to a focus on development.

4. *Marginalization and isolation* – families who are struggling to find the basic resources for survival will often feel marginalized and isolated and unable to fully participate in their communities. Both the lack of material resources and the stigma attached to being poor may prevent them from joining in activities outside their immediate environment. Social workers can have a key role in developing innovative strategies for involving families within communities and making use of 'naturally occurring networks'.

5. *Understanding the daily lives of families* - here we listen to the stories about how families organize their daily lives. For many children, a lack of clear daily routines contributes to their confusion and uncertainty about their worlds and what they can expect from adults and others around them (Gilligan 2004). Families can be supported

to identify what daily routines work well for them and what gets in the way and disrupts these routines.

In strengths-based approaches, work in the areas identified above is carried out in ways that enable the family to identify what it is that they have achieved despite difficult circumstances. It is important that these factors do not become a checklist for what has gone wrong in the past, but rather that they provide a framework for thinking differently and creatively about what it is that have enabled families to survive despite these difficulties.

Conclusion

As Gilligan (2004) so aptly puts it, social workers need to identify their own strengths in order to work effectively with clients. They also need to understand that they are not the exclusive source of help and that they do not deliver help. Effective social work will occur when social workers understand the social contexts of clients' lives and know how to harness the strengths within these contexts (Gilligan 2004, pp.101–2). It will also happen when social workers are prepared to challenge those structures that may prevent clients from effectively harnessing their strengths on behalf of their families (Allan *et al.* 2003). We believe that strengths-based work demonstrates exciting potential, but as with all best practice it demands that social workers be critically reflective of their work and understand that, as has always been the case for good social work practice, they have the choice of being either an agent of control or an agent for change.

Questions for reflection

1. What are the key elements of a strengths approach?

2. What are some of the key questions that workers need to ask themselves when forming partnerships with families?

3. How would you identify the links between strengths approaches and indigenous frameworks for practice?

4. Why is reflective practice central to strengths approaches?

5. How could you incorporate a strengths approach into your current practice frameworks?

References

Allan, J. (2003) 'Practising critical social work.' In J. Allan, B. Pease and L. Briskman (eds) *Critical Social Work: An Introduction to Theories and Practice.* Australia: Allen and Unwin.

Allan, J., Pease, B. and Briskman, L. (2003) *Critical Social Work: An Introduction to Theories and Practice.* Australia: Allen and Unwin.

Cooper, B. (2001) 'Constructivism in social work: Towards a participative practice viability.' *British Journal of Social Work 31,* 721–737.

Costello, S. (2003) 'Families: Reconstructing social work practices.' In J. Allan, B. Pease and L. Briskman (eds) *Critical Social Work: An Introduction to Theories and Practice.* Australia: Allen and Unwin.

Dawson, K. and Berry, M. (2002) 'Engaging families in child welfare services: An evidence-based approach to best practice.' *Child Welfare League of America LXXXI,* 2, 293–317.

Dominelli, L. (1996) 'Deprofessionalising social work: anti-oppressive practice, competences and postmodernism.' *British Journal of Social Work 26,* 153–175.

Durie, M. (1995) *Whaiora, Maori Health Department.* Auckland: Oxford University Press.

Egan, G. (2002) *The Skilled Helper: A Problem-Management and Opportunity-Development Approach to Helping.* Pacific Grove, CA: Brooks/Cole.

Ellis, K. and Dean, H. (2000) *Social Policy and the Body: Transitions in Corporeal Discourse.* Great Britain: Macmillan.

Fook, J. (2003) 'Critical social work: The current issues.' *Qualitative Social Work 2,* 2, 123–130.

Gilligan, R. (2000) 'Family support: issues and prospects.' In J. Canavan, P. Dolan and J. Pinkerton (eds) *Family Support: Direction from Diversity.* London: Jessica Kingsley Publishers.

Gilligan, R. (2004) 'Promoting resilience in child and family social work: Issues for social work practice.' *Social Work Education 23,* 1, 93-104.

Healy, K. (2000) *Social Work Practices: Contemporary Perspectives on Change.* London: Sage.

Ife, J. (1997) *Rethinking Social Work: Towards Critical Practice.* Melbourne: Longman.

Ife, J. (2001) *Human Rights and Social Work: Towards Rights-Based Practice.* Cambridge: Cambridge University Press.

International Federation of Social Workers (IFSW) and International Association of Schools of Social Work (IASSW) *International Definition of Social Work.* www.ifsw.org

Margolin, L. (1997) *Under the Cover of Kindness.* Charolottesville: University Press of Virginia.

Mataira, P.J. (2002) 'Treaty partnering: Establishment of a charter for Maori community based programmes.' *Te Komako, Social Work Review XIV,* 2, 5–7.

Mayall, B. (2002) *Towards a Sociology for Childhood: Thinking from Children's Lives.* Buckingham: Open University Press.

McQuaide S. (2000) 'Women's resilience at midlife: What is it? Do you mobilize it?' In E. Norman (ed) *Resiliency Enhancement: Putting the Strengths Perspective into Social Work Practice.* New York: Columbia University Press.

Mitchell, M. (2000) 'Disciplinary interventions and resistances around "safer sex".' In K. Ellis and H. Dean (eds) *Social Policy and the Body: Transitions in Corporeal Discourse.* Great Britain: Macmillan.

Munford, R. (2003) 'And then there was social work.' *New Zealand Sociology 18,* 1, 46–54.

Munford, R. and Sanders, J. (1999) *Supporting Families.* Palmerston North: Dunmore Press.

Munford, R., Sanders, J. with Andrew, A., Butler, P., Kaipuke, R. and Ruwhiu, L. (2001) 'Aotearoa/New Zealand - working differently with communities and families.' In C. Warren-Adamson (ed) *Family Centres and their International Role in Social Action.* Aldershot: Ashgate.

Munford, R. and Sanders, J. (2003) *Making a Difference in Families: Research that Creates Change.* Australia: Allen and Unwin.

Norman, E. (2000) *Resiliency Enhancement: Putting the Strengths Perspective into Social Work Practice.* New York: Columbia University Press.

O'Neil, D. (2003) 'Clients as researchers: The benefits of strengths-based research.' In R. Munford and J. Sanders (eds) *Making a Difference in Families: Research that Creates Change.* Australia: Allen and Unwin.

Parton, N. and O'Byrne, P. (2000) *Constructive Social Work: Towards a New Practice.* Houndmills: Macmillan.

Pease, P. (2003) 'Rethinking the relationship between the self and society.' In J. Allan, B. Pease and L. Briskman (eds) *Critical Social Work: An Introduction to Theories and Practice.* Australia: Allen and Unwin.

Saleeby, D. (2002) *The Strengths Perspective in Social Work Practice.* White Plains, NY: Longman.

Sanders, J. and Munford, R. (2001) *Heart Work and Hard Mahi.* Palmerston North: Massey University.

Sanders, J. and Munford, R. (2003) 'Strengthening practice through research: Research in organisations.' In R. Munford and J. Sanders (eds) *Making a Difference in Families: Research that Creates Change.* Australia: Allen and Unwin.

Schmitz, C. (1995) 'Reframing the dialogue on female-headed single-parent families.' *Affilia 10,* 4, 426–441.

Walsh-Tapiata, W. (2002) 'Editorial.' *Te Komako, Social Work Review XIV,* 2, 1–2.

Zunz, S. J. and Chernesky, R. H. (2000) 'The workplace as a protective environment: Management strategies.' In E. Norman (ed) *Resiliency Enhancement: Putting the Strengths Perspective into Social Work Practice.* New York: Columbia University Press.

Chapter 10

Strengths-based Practice in Statutory Care and Protection Work

Rodger Jack

Care and Protection is far too important not to be strengths-based.
(Andrew Turnell, Keynote Address, *Gathering Momentum* conference,
New Zealand 2003)

Introduction

This chapter explores the application of a strengths-based approach in statutory child protection, drawing on examples from the experiences of front-line staff in Child Youth and Family Services, the statutory child protection agency in New Zealand. Strengths approaches to practice[1] have been adopted as the intentional practice approach in Child Youth and Family Services (Department of Child Youth and Family Services 2001, p.5), which established a practice development initiative in 2000 to explore the implications of and develop practice for this approach.

Strengths-based practice in the statutory setting is not an invitation to deny knowledge about risks and dangerous dynamics in child protection work or to minimize or collude with abuse, violence, neglect, offending or any other factors which are harming, or have the potential to harm, children, young people, and their families and whanau (whanau is the Maori term for extended family). Rather, it is a principled and transparent approach to statutory social work, based on legal and ethical principles. The social worker works intensively to engage the family/whanau in a partnership for change, while being very open with them about his/her role and obligations and about legal and safety requirements.

My objectives in this chapter are first to demonstrate that strengths-based practice is a robust challenging approach that is able to guide practice in statutory child protection (and improve the service delivery experience for the service recipient[2] and the worker), and to provide a guide that can support workers in exploring how they might use strengths-based practice in challenging settings.

To do this I briefly describe the child protection context in New Zealand, then how strengths-based practice is defined. I next describe how the principles and processes involved in strengths-based practice apply to the role of statutory workers in child protection.

The New Zealand child protection context[3]

The primary responsibility of the Department of Child, Youth and Family Services is towards children and young people who are at risk of abuse or neglect, or who are at risk of offending. The Department's mission statement encourages and promotes safe children, strong families and stronger communities. Families in need are supported to meet their care and control responsibilities. Child, Youth and Family's statutory role is defined by the following legislation: the Children, Young Persons, and Their Families Act 1989 (referred throughout as CYP and F Act), the Adoption Act 1955, the Adult Adoption Information Act 1986, the Adoption (Inter-country) Act 1997, and the Guardianship Act 1968.

The introduction of the CYP and F Act changed the child welfare perspective of the previous Children and Young Persons Act 1974 to an innovative family empowerment model placing the emphasis on the child and young person within the family/whanau, hapu (extended family), iwi (tribe), or family group. It emphasized the role and responsibilities of families/whanau in caring for their children and young people and protecting them from harm.

For the first time the law provided for jurisdictional separation between children and young people in need of care or protection and those who had offended against the law. It made provision for matters relating to care, protection and offending to be resolved wherever possible by the child or young person's own family/whanau.

The CYP and F Act ensures family group participation in decision-making and recognizes that the family (in its various forms) is the social unit most suited to meet the needs of children and young people, providing a suitable environment for their growth, upbringing and development. This contrasted with previous child welfare perspectives that took little account of Maori values and processes, often eroding the rights of family/whanau, and undermining their authority and whatever skills and resources they could provide for their children.

The CYP and F Act had an immediate influence on practice and a dramatic impact on the numbers of children in care – falling from 10,000 in the late 1980s to around 1,500 in the early 1990s. As with other government services where de-institutionalization occurred, the support, services and financial resources did not follow the clients. Since the passing of the Act, the provision of statutory child protection services in Aotearoa/New Zealand has been affected by the rolling back of the welfare state, the contractual environment and constant reorganization of service provision (Cheyne, O'Brien and Belgrave 1997).

The 1990s saw a tumultuous period for statutory child protection services. Review followed review with associated structural changes and instability. Efficiency gains and organizational change eroded the capability of the agency, at the same time there was an increased focus on the Crown's purchase agreement and the delivery of outputs. In 1999 the Department of Child, Youth and Family Services was created as a stand-alone department of state. One year later, the newly elected Labour government commissioned Judge Mick Brown to conduct a ministerial review into the Department of Child, Youth and Family Services, in response to concerns about under-investment and poor service quality in the face of increased demand.

Late in 2000, the Brown Report (2000) identified a number of issues relating to the Department's systems, capability and capacity. It found that the existing outcomes did not clearly demonstrate the achievement of positive results, specifically that long-term wellbeing is the outcome for all children and young people. The quality of both the Department's social work services and its client and stakeholder relationships required addressing.

The government injected extra funding to address demand and pressures. The response from the Department was a change plan, *New Directions in Action* (Department Child, Youth and Family Services 2001) the overall goal of which is to build an organization that advances the wellbeing of families and the wellbeing of children and young people as members of families, whanau, hapu and iwi. A major initiative of the *New Directions* strategy was the establishment of a project to introduce a strengths-based approach to practice in order to enhance the application of the CYP and F Act and improve outcomes for children and their families.

Defining and applying strengths-based practice in the statutory context

There are common threads in the definitions of strengths-based practice that locate strengths approaches first in the philosophical position of the worker and subsequently in their practice behaviours. It is thus more accurate to describe strengths perspectives as approaches to people rather than fixed models of practice. They are primarily about the positional stance the worker takes relative to the client in respect to their dignity, rights, uniqueness, commonalities, abilities, and capacity to learn, grow and change. Strengths approaches are about the assumptions social workers make about the service recipients and their experiences. They are based on core beliefs that change the nature of the client–worker relationship, and the language and behaviour of the worker.

Defining Strengths-based Practice

Strengths-based practice is principled and empowering work, guided by the worker's attitudes and beliefs, which is characterized by collaboration and ensures the client is understood to have strengths, resources, capacities and abilities that when mobilized by the client's aspirations and the worker's relationship, can generate change (Saleebey 1997).

Strengths perspectives do not seek to minimize or sanitize problems but rather seek to respond to problems in the context of the strengths, resources and wisdom of the people involved with that problem.

The care and protection role

There are three broad functions in child protection work - intake, investigation and assessment, and the provision of out-of-home care. The intake initiates the process and a decision is made whether to investigate the concerns. The investigation and assessment involves the assessment of the risk of danger and harm, or neglect to a child or young person and a determination whether the child or young person is in need of care or protection. The care responsibility is to provide safe and stable care arrangements for the child, preferably with their own immediate or extended family, and to ensure that parents are supported to have an ongoing close involvement with their child even in circumstances where they may no longer be able to have a direct caregiving role.

Arguably, the component of statutory child protection work that raises the most challenges for collaborative strengths-based practice is the investigation and assessment, so I will focus predominantly on this aspect. I will summarize the principles common to strengths-based practice and then develop their application in practice.

Principles common to strengths-based approaches

The principles discussed guide the strengths-based care and protection worker in their practice, behaviour, language, responses, and use of frameworks and models of practice. Turnell and Edwards (1999) note that these principles are aspirations for the worker to implement rather than assumptions. Workers should recognize that no one gets it right all the time. They should persistently aspire to implement the practice principles, but have the humility to recognize that even the most experienced worker will have to think and act carefully to implement them, especially when facing seemingly intractable problems or abuse in families.

ALL PEOPLE DESERVE RESPECT AS PEOPLE WORTH DOING BUSINESS WITH

The attitude of workers is crucial in developing a successful partnership. Unless the worker shows respect, and has hope that by working together the situation can change, it is unlikely that much will change. Nowhere is this more important than in the statutory setting where the experience of service recipients is all too frequently that of being blamed, isolated, unheard and unwanted in the planning and execution of service delivery. The strengths-based worker must be open, honest and transparent in all dealings with the service recipient. They need to be clear about what they are doing and when, how and why.

ALL PEOPLE, FAMILIES AND COMMUNITIES HAVE STRENGTHS, RESOURCES, CAPACITIES AND CAPABILITIES

All people, regardless of their history, have valuable capacities, resources, skills, motivations and visions that can help them resolve problems and gain more control over their daily lives and environment. The investigation and assessment process needs to actively seek out these potential resources and ensure they are mobilized in the intervention.

THE STRENGTHS, RESOURCES, CAPACITIES AND CAPABILITIES OF PEOPLE ARE NOT FOUND IN BROAD GENERAL OR DIAGNOSTIC DESCRIPTIONS OF PEOPLE

These are usually located in the specific detail that is often not immediately obvious. The worker must always search for detail, whether exploring negative or positive aspects of the situation. Potential solutions also arise out of details, not generalizations. People's solution-finding attempts can be hidden, not obvious to onlookers, and need to be searched for in conversation with them. Detailed information is needed about any solutions that have been tried and had some success; these will form a foundation for future successful outcomes.

WHERE POSSIBLE, USE NATURALLY OCCURRING RESOURCES FIRST

Given that families and communities can be a source of unexpected resources, these should be explored and brought into service prior to consideration of professional resources. This assists in breaking down the assumption that professionals have a more useful contribution to good outcomes than the service recipients, or that the parent who has harmed their child has no contribution to make in creating safety.

PEOPLE HAVE EXPERTISE IN THEIR OWN LIVES AND SITUATIONS

The worker has expertise from their training, professional and life experiences that contribute to outcomes, but the contribution of the service recipients and their wider community's own knowledge, wisdom, insight, experience and life experiences should not be underestimated. Investigation and assessment should actively seek to locate and highlight these strengths as resources for change.

THE PROBLEM IS ALWAYS THE PROBLEM: THE PERSON IS NEVER THE PROBLEM

The harm done or the risk of danger to a child is the problem, not the parent, their family or their community. The worker must be careful in their approach, language, behaviour and questions to demonstrate that the parent does not need to be fixed, but rather that safety and wellbeing must be created. The parent may be an ally in a solution to this problem. The parent is likely to need to make changes, but that is not the same as being the problem.

ALL PEOPLE ARE CAPABLE OF CHANGE AND GROWTH

Workers cannot know the limits of a service recipient's desire or capacity to learn, grow or change. Even where there is a repetitive pattern of abuse or neglect, there still remains the possibility of growth and change that must be considered. The worker's responses, questions, behaviour and language need to demonstrate this possibility.

ALL PEOPLE HAVE HOPES, DREAMS AND ASPIRATIONS

People are usually more motivated to work toward their own goals than those that are imposed. Workers elicit people's own goals and search for compatibility between service recipient and worker's goals, which are brought together to create a plan for safety and wellbeing.

CHANGE IS MORE LIKELY WHEN CONDITIONS ARE CREATED THAT ENABLE PEOPLE TO IDENTIFY, VALUE AND MOBILIZE THEIR STRENGTHS AND CAPACITIES

Conditions for change include:

- people feeling valued and validated
- uniqueness and cultural diversity being recognized and respected
- what works being highlighted – in every situation something works.

THE LANGUAGE WORKERS USE AND THE WAY QUESTIONS ARE ASKED INFLUENCE THE SITUATION AND THE OUTCOME OF THE INTERVENTION

The service recipient is engaged in a process of examining whether the worker is attempting to create a relationship with them, is hearing and understanding them, and can be trusted. This is especially true in child protection, where the power of the worker's role may cause distrust. The attitude of the worker, therefore, demonstrated in their questions and language, strongly influences outcomes.

STRENGTHS-BASED PRACTITIONERS MAINTAIN A FOCUS ON GOALS

The focus on goals indicates the hopefulness of the worker and their belief about the possibility of useful outcomes. It also provides direction and purposefulness for activity.

IN THEIR NEEDS, RESPONSES, HOPES, DREAMS AND ASPIRATIONS THE PEOPLE WE WORK WITH ARE MORE LIKE US THAN NOT LIKE US

Parents who have harmed or neglected their children have similar needs, hopes, aspirations and responses as other people, including the worker. Their angry responses and defensive position, for example, need to be seen more as normal behaviour in the circumstance, than as evidence of dysfunction. Their harmful or neglectful behaviour does not prevent them from having similar hopes for their children's future.

STRENGTHS-BASED PRACTITIONERS MUST BE RESPECTFULLY TRANSPARENT ABOUT THE POWER THEY HAVE AND USE IT AS A RESOURCE

There is power in the role of a child protection worker. This power cannot be surrendered. However, effective and respectful practice means workers, rather than taking a 'power over' position in people's lives, must acknowledge and address the power imbalance in the relationship, minimizing the difference as much as possible.

Practising the principles in the statutory setting

Following the principles described above, we examine five key factors that need to inform the processes and skills that emerge from a strengths approach and direct strengths-based child protection workers, enabling them to utilize these principles. The five factors are: the worker–service recipient relationship, strengths and safety, searching for strengths and exceptions beyond the obvious, the problem is the problem and handling issues of power.

The worker–service recipient relationship

In strengths-based work, relationships are characterized by collaboration and empowerment, based on an assumption that the service recipient has a contribution to make. The effectiveness of building such a relationship is borne out in research. The Darlington Social Research Unit (1995) found that effective collaboration between professionals is one of the two single most significant factors in increasing safety outcomes for children where there are care and protection concerns. The other is the relationship established between the worker and the child and family. These two go hand in hand.

The collaborative and empowering relationship is intentionally built by the worker, who must see the service recipient as someone 'worth doing business with' (Turnell and Edwards 1999). This worker position invites a relationship where the service recipient is valued as an active recipient of services, a contributor to outcomes. Their ideas are respected and their solution-finding attempts examined for possible clues to intervention strategies on which to build. For the care and protection worker, this will often involve demonstrating a genuine interest in the thoughts, experiences, ideas etc. of the service recipient. Their suspicion of the worker's intent and interest can only be eroded by careful work incorporating an understanding and articulation of the service recipient's views.

Thoburn and her colleagues (Thoburn, Lewis and Shemmings 1995) confirm this, finding a clear link between the involvement of parents and better outcomes for children in care and protection practices. They also found that the social worker's attitudes, skills and efforts were the key factors in establishing the parents' involvement in a collaborative relationship.

Believing that people are worth doing business with, however, is not the same as adopting the easiest way of doing business with them. The hope and belief that working together can make things better is entirely different from automatically or too quickly believing people where there are clear indications that their behaviour is unacceptable.

Building a collaborative relationship involves creating opportunities for service recipients to gain some control over their lives and the decisions affecting them, and to discover and use the resources within and around them. This process of empowerment invites the family to have as much control over the intervention process as possible within the constraints imposed by the legislative requirements.

For example, a worker who had made the decision that the children in a family were not safe enough to leave them in the home, talked through all of the possible options for how this might be done. The parent was clear that the children would be placed for a period somewhere outside the home for their safety, but was invited to participate in the decision about how that would happen and to whom they might go. There was no option to stay, but there were options for what action would be taken, and what resources would be engaged to ensure their safety.

Effective child protection work necessitates making professional judgements as in the above example. However, strengths-based practice invites the worker to reserve their judgement, coming to conclusions slowly and carefully. The worker needs to recognize that the details of harm or neglect are not, in themselves, conclusions about possibility, responsibility, intention or capacity for involvement. This is not to say that workers cannot make an assessment on an appropriate course of action in a timely manner, but that they may need to do it more slowly and carefully than they might otherwise. They need to give voice to the position that the client has, in order to hear it alongside their own and other professionals. Saleebey (1997) reminds us that the knowledge, information and perspectives of professionals are privileged and carry institutional and legal weight. The client's, however, does not. This is likely to need amplification to be heard amidst the perspectives of professionals.

We also need to consider the influence of our own behaviour on the nature of the relationship built. How we assert, or pursue, the 'truth' may aggravate service recipients. The conscious act of the worker, suspending their inherent disbelief or mistrust in the client's capacity and story, invites hearing the client prior to any judgement being made. It offers scope for collaboration even if decisions, like uplifting children, must be made. For example, one worker and her supervisor, when faced with clear evidence of intentional second degree burning as discipline to a child, asked themselves, prior to undertaking any action, 'How will we build a relationship with these parents in order to get safety for this child?' This question was pivotal and changed both their position towards the parents and the manner in which they engaged. They were able to demonstrate respect for the parents as people with whom they could work, and acted to keep the parents informed and involved. The children were initially removed under a warrant, but only after a conversation with the parents about the concerns, the reason for intervention, the process of resolution, and how the parents might be involved in creating a safe environment for their children. The workers acknowledged that they previously would have uplifted the child from school and informed the parents, rather than inviting them in with their children to discuss the concerns.

As demonstrated in the example above, the manner of engagement of the worker with the service recipient has a significant impact on the intervention outcomes. The interaction between the worker and the service recipients is a key vehicle for change. It is important, therefore, to view the initial interview as intervention, not just an investigation.

Strengths and safety

The simple act of initiating a conversation about the strengths, resources, capacities, and indications of safety with family members can open doors for collaboration rather than conflict, in a robust investigation of the concerns. For example, workers were called into a school to investigate significant bruising to the side of a child's face and head. The workers made a point of asking the principal about the strengths he and the teachers had observed with the parents and family. The workers went to meet with the parents and received a cold reception. They would not let the workers into the house to discuss the matter. One of the workers said 'Okay we will go, but just before we do, I would like you to know that the school are surprised by this event and have told us about how well your children are presented at school and behave.' The parents' response was to invite the workers in and to openly discuss the concerns. A full and useful investigation and intervention was possible.

The assessment of risk of danger and harm is often raised as incompatible with a strengths approach to practice. An inherent assumption is either that strengths practice cannot focus on risk, or that assessment of risk cannot incorporate an assessment of safety and strengths. It is clear that identifying strengths does not equate with identifying protective or safety factors, neither does identifying risk factors equate with an intervention strategy. In all situations, however, there are likely to be signs of actual and/or potential danger and harm, and signs of actual and/or potential wellbeing. It is not an either/or situation. It is a both/and situation. A robust assessment of risk of danger and harm is therefore not only possible within a strengths-based statutory approach, but a vital element. Similarly, a robust assessment of indications of strengths and capacities is a vital element of a robust assessment of risk of danger and harm.

The existence of strengths does not necessarily equate with adequate protection or care. To only highlight the strengths would not adequately attend to the issue of safety and wellbeing. This must be recognized, otherwise it blurs the real risk of danger and harm for children. The worker must be clear that they need to see the strengths that the family have operating over time, to ensure safety and adequate care before they can finish their involvement. They must actively observe how those strengths are being demonstrated as protective factors and provide feedback about their observations to the family.

Searching for strengths and exceptions beyond the obvious

Discovering the solution-finding efforts of clients is an active process. Madsen (1999) states that competence is quiet. Doing well needs to be listened carefully for, because it is not as noisy and obvious as doing poorly. The worker must find it amongst the often dominant story of problems and pathology.

The strengths, achievements, capacity and solution-finding of service recipients are only located by exploration. They may be missed by the expectations created by the generalized and negative descriptions of the client, which should not be accepted by strengths-based workers as the 'whole truth'. Instead they attempt to discover the concrete and specific details of the experience and struggles of the service recipient in order to explore both the exceptions and changes that support the development of a richer description of the client. For example, it is difficult to discover what a father who has been violent toward his child has done to reduce or prevent that violence, without asking about the times when he normally would have lashed out in violence but did not. What did he do to stop himself? What did he do differently? What did he have to tell himself to stop himself? What other support did he need? How successful was it? Did his child notice?

Child protection workers are taught to be clear about neglectful, harmful and dangerous behaviours, but they are not often taught to notice change and movement toward careful and safe behaviours. Professional doubt over a service recipient's change is more common than feedback that notices change. Strengths-based practice encourages workers to notice change and to offer positive feedback about changes. The changes are more likely to continue when they are noticed and reflected upon.

There are some cautions here. The first is that feedback about change can be received as paternalistic if it is not done genuinely and with care. Second, it has more impact if the service recipient is encouraged to notice and reflect on their own change. Furthermore, there must be a realistic acknowledgement of change in the context of where they have been and what must be achieved.

Additionally, social workers may have to overcome scepticism in other professionals. For example, workers in Child, Youth and Family Services (CYF) are finding that they have to strongly emphasize any changes they notice in the family when reporting to court-appointed counsel for children. The indicators of change will not always be those that professionals would normally look for. One family indicated that they knew they had made changes because they had had a food fight as a family at a fast food outlet. The children indicated that this was a sign of change because their father joined in instead of beating them, as he would have previously. He had been able to enjoy himself instead of controlling his children through threats and violence.

The problem is the problem

Working from a strengths perspective means speaking and behaving in a manner that indicates to the client that the problem is not the client, but rather the issue is the problem. In the example above, the father was asked by the worker what made the most difference in his ability to make changes to his violent behaviour. He stated that finally a worker believed that he could change and worked with him expecting change. In this situation he was not the problem, the violence was. The worker and father could both work together to reduce and eliminate the violence.

Where protective concerns are identified in a family, it is often assumed that there are deficits in the family that disable it from providing for the child's welfare, wellbeing and interests. In doing so, the problem is located within the family as part of the family. In this context, service recipients are reluctant to participate in intervention and are generally not invited into useful collaboration (Jack 2001). Saleebey (1997, p.5) indicates that much of our theory and practice is built on the 'supposition that clients become clients because they have deficits, problems, pathologies, and diseases, that they are, in some essential way, flawed or weak'. This perception invites the worker to try and fix the person, does not invite collaboration and does not encourage the worker to work differently with the family to facilitate change.

Addressing issues of power

Workers may, at some points in the investigation and assessment or provision of care, have to use a degree of coercion. They may have to exercise statutory power to address situations of risk or non-compliance. The social service relationship is not, and cannot, be an equal relationship with clients. There will be a power imbalance, with greater power vested in the professional. The strengths-based worker recognizes this and acts to reduce the imbalance as much as possible.

The workers ensure that the use of their power in the relationship is careful, and overt, privileges the client, affirms the client's aspirations, invites collaboration and works toward the identified goals. As one CYF worker stated: 'We do not need to go into families waving our power around. We can leave it at our feet' (personal conversation). Acting to address the power imbalance is facilitated by offering genuine choice and honouring the decision made. If the worker is unwilling or unable to go with the choice then it should not be offered.

Taking the time to understand the position of the service recipient towards the problem and the dangerous behaviours also contributes to addressing the power imbalance. Hearing and understanding the service recipient's position is neither excusing nor justifying unhelpful or unsafe behaviours. It is, however, the process of giving them voice and hearing their story.

This, as with other aspects of the approach, is worked out in the subtleties and nuances of practice. For example, if a worker arrives at the door of a family and says: 'I need to hear your side of the story', it is more likely to be received as a demonstration of power, than 'I need to discuss my concerns with you and understand what your perspective is.' The bottom line for both is that there are concerns that must be talked about, but the latter is more likely to address the power imbalance and invite collaboration, than the former. The worker needs to recognize that coercion and co-operation can exist simultaneously, and use skills that foster this.

In circumstances where safety issues are so serious that the worker needs to exercise the power of their role and their professional judgement in removing a child from their family/whanau, the emphasis remains on working respectfully and openly with the family/whanau to build and maintain a relationship which enables:

- an immediate engagement of the worker with the family

- open and timely exchange of information about the basis for and the nature of the statutory action taken

- awareness that while statutory action may be a necessary step now, the social worker(s) will continue to work with the family, family network, whanau, hapu and iwi to support them to develop the strengths needed to care for and/or manage their children safely in the future

- the development of a jointly designed and solution-focused plan that supports the family/whanau to achieve their 'future picture' within a timeframe that will be safe and meaningful for them and for the child

- active and regular involvement by the social worker with the family/whanau to support them to achieve their plan and work with them to review progress and notice achievements

- the contribution of relevant resources and services that complement the family/whanau strengths and resources and are designed to assist them to achieve their goals

- the affirmation of positive change and progress at each step in the plan.

Conclusion

Strengths-based work, in the arena of statutory child protection, needs to be done by workers who are thoughtful and reflective in their practice. Strengths-based social workers should be able to clearly articulate, at any given time, their current assessment of the risks, protective factors, strengths and resources within the family situation, and identify the factors that have informed their conscious choice of intervention and approach. These matters should be 'on the table' for family members who are aware of how they have contributed to those assessments and intervention decisions.

There will always be some situations where emergency statutory action is needed, and where families will not be in agreement with the action taken, but as much as possible all interventions should seek to engage the family.

Workers can build a collaborative relationship with people without condoning undesirable behaviour. This is not the easiest way to work initially, but it is necessary in order to generate change. Very few people will listen to, or allow themselves to be influenced by, someone who seems unresponsive to them, who indicates that they are the problem or is simply forcing them to conform – especially if they are being told that they are somehow flawed or their behaviour or views are unacceptable. The best opportunity to foster change is to build co-operative relationships based on respect for the person, focused on the issue and mobilized by the goal.

The processes and skills that contribute to effective strengths-based practice are relevant to statutory and non-statutory workers alike. Strengths-based child protection work involves working to manage and resolve child protection issues safely and effectively through a professional 'lens' that is informed by the principles and values of strengths-based approaches. It involves risk assessment and the identification and assessment of appropriate protective factors and strengths, as well as the facilitation of co-operative and mutually agreed change processes that wherever possible, are co-directed by the service recipients and the workers. The unique roles and functions of statutory social work are not exempt from strengths-based practice but, as it has been argued in this chapter, they are both challenged and enhanced by this perspective.

Questions for reflection

1. What are some of the tensions that care and protection social workers face when adopting the strengths-based approach in their work?

2. In what ways have the arguments in this chapter resolved these tensions?

3. What would you do differently in assessing the people you work with, having read this chapter?

Notes

1   The terms 'strengths-based practice' and 'strengths perspective' are used interchangeably by the author. The author uses the plural to indicate that there is more than one strengths-based approach within the wider description of strengths-based practice.

2   Service recipient is used in preference to 'client', because a notion central to the client relationship is the ability to choose to participate in that relationship. People receiving services from child protection services generally are unable to choose the relationship.

3   The information included in this section is largely drawn from internal unpublished material from Child, Youth and Family Services relating to the initiative to establish a project to develop a strengths-based approach in the department.

References

Adoption Act 1955. http://www.legislation.govt.nz/browse_vw.asp?content-set=pal_ statutes

Adoption (Inter-country) Act 1997. http://www.legislation.govt.nz/browse_vw.asp?content -set=pal_statutes

Adult Adoption Information Act 1986. http://www.legislation.govt.nz/browse_vw.asp? content-set=pal_statutes

Brown, M. (2001) *Care and Protection is about Adult Behaviour: The Ministerial Review of the Department of Child, Youth and Family Services.* http://www.cyf.govt.nz/ UploadLib/ images/BrownReport_20010620_172514.pdf

Cheyne, C., O'Brien, M. and Belgrave, M. (eds) (1997) *Social Policy in Aotearoa/New Zealand: A Critical Introduction.* Auckland: Oxford University Press.

Children and Young Persons Act 1974. http://www.legislation.govt.nz/browse_ vw.asp?content-set=pal_statutes

Children, Young Persons, and Their Families Act 1989. http://www.legislation.govt.nz/ browse_vw.asp?content-set=pal_statutes

Darlington Social Research Unit (1995) *Child Protection Messages from Research.* London: HMSO.

Department of Child, Youth and Family Services (2001) *New Directions in Action.* http://www.cyf.govt.nz/UploadLib/images/NewDirections1-Nov01.pdf

Employment Contracts Act 1991. http://www.legislation.govt.nz/browse_vw.asp? content-set=pal_statutes

Guardianship Act 1968. http://www.legislation.govt.nz/browse_vw.asp?content-set=pal_ statutes

Jack, R. (2001) 'After the telling – Intervention after the notification.' *Social Work Now 19,* August, 33–37.

Madsen, W. (1999) *Collaborative Therapy with Multi-Stressed Families: From Old Problems to New Futures.* New York: Guilford.

Public Finance Act 1989. http://www.legislation.govt.nz/browse_vw.asp?content-set= pal_statutes

Saleebey, D. (1997) *The Strengths-Perspective in Social Work Practice.* New York: Longman.

Staudt, M., Howard, M. and Drake, B. (2001) 'The operationalization, implementation, and effectiveness of the strengths perspective: A review of empirical studies.' *Journal of Social Service Research 27,* 2, 1–21.

State Sector Act 1988. http://www.legislation.govt.nz/browse_vw.asp?content-set= pal_statutes

Thoburn, J., Lewis, A. and Shemmings, D. (1995) *Paternalism or Partnership? Family Involvement in the Child Protection Process.* London: HMSO.

Turnell, A. and Edwards, S. (1999) *Signs of Safety.* New York: Norton.

Chapter 11

Bicultural Strengths-based Supervision

Introducing Strengths-based Social Work Supervision
Chris Thomas

He Taonga Tuku Iho – A Gift Handed Down
Sharlene Davis

Introduction

This chapter will begin with a discussion of the literature of strengths-based supervision and then consider the key principles and focus of strengths-based supervision with references to current research about strengths-based supervision being undertaken by the author (Thomas 2004). The second part of the chapter presents an example indigenous to Aotearoa/New Zealand and illustrates strengths-based supervision in action.

INTRODUCING STRENGTHS-BASED SOCIAL WORK SUPERVISION

When the literature around strengths-based practice is considered some key principles and concepts emerge; these are at the heart of strengths-based practice and have been clearly articulated by Saleebey (1997):

1. A belief that all people and environments possess strengths that can be mobilized.

2. People are experts on themselves.

3. Workers need to suspend their beliefs and assumptions in order to truly hear clients and enable their strengths to be present in the work.

The key to strengths-based approaches is in respectful, hopeful and solution-focused as opposed to deficit-focused, problem-solving processes. Blundo (2001) considers strengths-based practice as requiring a paradigm shift to avoid remaining a rhetorical language of strengths in our practice. Early and GlenMaye (2000) also support this view, conceptualizing strengths-based practice as much more than reframing and the identification of client strengths.

Supervision becomes a central ingredient in this paradigmatic shift to redefine the client–worker relationship. Wolin and Wolin (1997) recommend supervision and training as particular areas that can influence the development of a systematic vocabulary of strengths. This paradigm can stand up to the risk paradigm that reinforces the role of the expert supervisor directing the expert social worker to be the expert on the lives of the people we call clients.

Strengths-based supervision has arisen out of a view that supervision needs to support this paradigmatic shift in relationships between workers and clients by offering a parallel process in supervision. If strengths-based practice is to develop and thrive in working with clients, it must be experienced and modelled within supervision relationships and within the broader agency contexts in which practice is located. It offers supervisors and supervisees a clear framework for the development of supervisee-focused and directed supervision and provides a process for supporting supervisors and supervisees to continuously identify and make concrete links between their attitudes, values and positions.

If supervision and the relationship between supervisors and supervisees are mirroring these values, attitudes, and positions, then there can be greater congruence in the worker–client relationship. Strengths-based supervision is a way of being with supervisees and calls for relationships based in 'power with' not 'power over' principles. As well, it necessitates the redefining of relationships by supervisors and supervisees so that each is contributing their expertise. Lowe and Guy (2002, pp.144–5) discuss the positioning of strengths-based supervisors as being beside the supervisee supporting them to look beyond the horizon of their current perceptions to an appreciation of change, competencies and possibilities. The aim of strengths-based supervision is a supervisee focused and directed process thereby creating an environment and process that models, supports and facilitates the approach being used with clients.

There is a considerable body of literature discussing the principles and means to working in a strengths-based practice. The literature regarding strengths-based supervision is sparse in comparison. The majority of supervision literature is directed toward supervisors, with very little writing that speaks directly to supervisees. This reinforces a supervisor directed process and encourages supervisee passivity. This is paralleled in strengths-based supervision literature. Davys (2002, p.29) argues that much of the supervision literature reinforces the 'expert' role of the supervisor in supervision and a process that is done to rather than with supervisees.

Cohen (1999) contends that traditional supervision requires a major transformation, if it is to be based on strengths-based practice. He argues that strength-based supervision is a bridge between the academic writers around strength-based practice and the ownership of these principles by the profession: a place where the practice of strengths-based practice can be supported and nourished.

Principles of strengths-based supervision

In considering the principles of strengths-based supervision it is helpful to revisit Saleebey's (1997) three defining principles and explore how they relate to the supervision context.

1. A belief that all people and environments possess strengths that can be mobilized (focus on competence and strengths). Cohen (1999) redefines the strengths-based supervisory environment as one that is focused upon the joint evaluation of the worker's successes rather than a joint struggle with questions, problems and frustrations. Strengths-based supervision focuses on competence and provides a place to discover the 'hints of possibility' and times of exception where the problem is not present as a framework for the way the worker then works with the client. The focus in strengths-based supervision is thus on times of exception to the problem (Bucknell 2000; Cohen 1999; Juhnke 1996; Mainstone 1998; Rita 1998) or, in narrative terms, times of unique outcome or sparkling moments (Epston and White 1992) rather than being enmeshed in problem saturated talk (deShazer 1991). The emphasis is on creating opportunities for problem free talk (deShazer 1991) where the supervisees' strengths and competencies are encouraged to support the building of further competencies and times of exception. Supervision is a place that notices change and celebrates success as well as focusing on issues and problems. Strengths-based supervision is not a crisis-oriented process. Sometimes supervisees (and supervisors) are concerned that they do not have issues or problems to bring to supervision. This is something to be recognized, celebrated and encouraged in supervision and not construed as a problem or a reason for not having supervision.

2. People are experts on themselves – bringing who you are to supervision. A respectful relationship based on collaboration is at the heart of a strengths-based supervision relationship. It is a place where supervisees experience supervisors as offering their expertise, in a way that avoids reinforcing the status of the supervisor's knowledge and expertise over that of the supervisee. Supervisors need to understand the concept of not knowing and not presuming that they can know what to prescribe for supervisees, just as supervisees need to understand the importance of not knowing around client's needs. Lowe and Guy (2002) conceptualize this as 'expertise without "the expert"'. Saleebey describes workers as facilitators and collaborators with clients 'in mutually crafted projects' and this is the same process in strengths-based supervision. Supervision becomes a place where the supervisor is encouraging and modelling a belief in uncertainty and possibilities and the many ways that people's experience can be constructed. Anderson and Swim (1995) concretize this as a process that occurs slowly and is experienced as a journey from the need to understand (diagnose) to an acceptance of multiple meanings and constructions of the 'truth':

> The shift from a need for certainty and predictability through general psychological language to an acceptance and comfort with the uncertainty and randomness of human experience occurs slowly. It evolves as supervisees experience a collaborative and connected with way of constructing meaning, and thus learning with others. As they experience and recognize their own voice, 'power' and 'authority' to generate knowledge, certainty becomes a non-issue and the need for it dissolves. Supervisees often experience this shift and an acceptance of uncertainty long before they have the words to make sense of it. (Anderson and Swim 1995, p.6)

Mainstone (1998) describes this as a non-normative approach where the supervisor works with what the supervisee brings but not in a way that requires the supervisor to construct or interpret the material brought to supervision. The supervisor is not trying to fit the supervisee's world into their understanding or framework and vice versa. Within a strengths-based supervision framework supervisees are encouraged to bring themselves as whole people and to see their work in supervision as not focused on what to do next with a client, but to reflect on what they notice about how they are working with clients.

3. Supervisors need to suspend their beliefs and assumptions in order to truly hear supervisees and enable their strengths to be present in the work. Supervisors in the current climate of accountability and a culture that is focused upon risk assessment (Beddoe 2001; O'Donoghue 2003) need to be able to suspend their judgements and assumptions about their supervisees and the work that they are doing.

Strengths-based supervision incorporates and encourages conversations about challenging issues in a safe and *mana*-enhancing manner (one that enables the personal power and spirit of the supervisee to remain intact). This is linked to a competency-focused approach that enables supervisees and supervisors to address challenging issues. There is a clear expectation within a strengths-based approach that supervisors will offer alternative views and challenges in supervision. Challenges need to be offered safely within a process that has been negotiated at the outset of the supervision contract and is reviewed continuously within supervision. Strengths-based supervision is particularly relevant in challenging situations. It provides transparency, parameters for the relationship and a way of being that aids the challenging times.

The author's current research (Thomas 2004) suggests strong participant support for the view that there are no circumstances in which the principles of strengths-based supervision are not relevant, because the values and attitudes that flow from the approach provide a framework and structure for dealing with challenging situations and issues.

The key idea coming through from the research participants is that when the supervisee has control over this process, it then paradoxically encourages them to invite challenge within supervision as opposed to being defensive about revealing or exposing deficits and feeling judged by their supervisor about these. The author's research explores contracting in supervision and provides useful insights for the following section.

A strengths-based supervision contract – the key ingredients

The current research highlighted the significance of the supervision contract and the contracting process in achieving strengths-based supervision. Focus group discussions in the research identified that the initial contract developed between the supervisor and the supervisee became a foundation for the way in which 'hard' issues were dealt with. One participant saw this contract as the place to be clear about what issues she might want to be challenged about and this had led to a discussion with the supervisor about how this could occur.

The research under discussion has illustrated a clear set of ideas around contracting within a strengths-based supervision framework. The major consideration for the contract and the contracting process was that this would be overt, providing clarity about roles and expectations. Participants felt that there needed to be transparency about bottom lines in terms of the accountability and expectations of the supervision relationship. The group also considered that clarity and transparency about things such as reporting and recording should be in the contract. One key aspect that came out of the discussion was a focus on clarifying supervisor and supervisee understandings of what strengths-based practice is and developing a shared definition of this for use in supervision. Participants also saw the need for supervisors to not only define strengths-based practice but also have a commitment to this way of being.

The participants saw contracting as a collaborative and individualized activity that must include processes for dealing with 'bottom lines' and what happens if there is conflict in the relationship. This was considered essential to ensure that concerns or reservations on both sides were discussed explicitly and identified early, rather than remaining covert or submerged in the supervision relationship. Participants also reiterated the importance of seeing issues as issues rather than deficits, which could suggest an externalizing approach to problems. Transparency and clarity were regarded as guiding principles for the contracting process. Participants felt that being aware of change was an important means to focusing on competency and what was working rather than what was not working in supervision. Participants also considered that the contract should not be negatively focused around issues and concerns as this could perpetuate a deficits approach, hence the preferred focus on competency. The focus group noted that the key assumption that people can change and grow needed to be the focus of the contract and thus of the supervision process. Ideas generated by participants around contracting are summarized below:

- a commitment to strengths-based practice must be articulated and its implications for practice clarified. Includes identifying a shared definition of strengths-based practice in particular contexts

- confidentiality

- line management roles

- tea and cookies

- overt about what happens if there are issues/concerns, not about conflict – focuses you negatively

- process is named

- should there be individualized contracts?

- expectations for accountability within the contract – agency expectations need to be clear and supervisor expectations of the agency, reporting.

One participant in the current research identified a contracting process that began with workers having an opportunity to develop a framework around strengths-based practice and a clear idea about what they are wanting from supervision before engaging with an external supervisor. In considering what strengths-based supervision is and how this can be evaluated against the principles of strengths-based practice, the following checklists are offered for supervisors and supervisees to consider:

Checklist for supervisors

- How do I notice and celebrate success with the people to whom I offer supervision?

- How do I respond to work with clients? How do we talk about clients in supervision? How do I see the problems people bring to supervision? What am I modelling about the change process? How am I encouraging supervisees to construct problems?

- How does supervision model strengths-based practice with the people we call clients?

- What is the balance between focusing on strategies about working with clients and the implications of this work for the person coming to supervision?

- How does supervision focus on competence? How do we notice what is working and times of exception to problems?

- What power do I have in the relationship and what impact does this have? How important is it for me to be an expert? How do I offer what I know? Whose views predominate in supervision? How do I invite feedback from supervisees and respond to it?

- What is my process for contracting in supervision? How do we review this in supervision? What does a collaborative relationship look like? How do we talk about 'challenging issues' in supervision?

- How do I reflect on my supervision process?

Checklist for supervisees

- How do I understand supervision and who or what has contributed to the way that I construct supervision?

- How does my supervisor offer their expertise in supervision? How does my supervisor offer challenge in the sessions?

- What would a collaborative, successful supervision relationship look like?

- What do I understand by the term 'strengths-based practice'? How do I define strengths-based supervision? How does this fit with my experience of supervision? What does my supervisor understand by this concept?

- How does supervision focus on my competence and how/when is success celebrated in supervision? What do I notice about 'problem-free' talk – when/how does this occur?

- How and when do I give my supervisor feedback? How do I feel at the end of a session if we have talked about something I feel that I have not done well?

- How are clients talked about in supervision? How would they feel if they were in the room with us? How do we reflect on the nature of 'problems' in supervision?

- What does supervision tend to focus on – strategies for working with clients or how I am working with clients and what is happening for me?

This chapter has considered the key principles within the literature on strengths-based supervision, current research findings that describe one approach to translating these principles into action and supervisor and supervisee experiences around strengths-based supervision. The next section of the chapter locates the principles and experience of strength-based supervision within the Aotearoa/New Zealand context.

HE TAONGA TUKU IHO – A GIFT HANDED DOWN

The previous section illustrated one approach to strengths-based supervision. Unique to Aotearoa/New Zealand are tangata whenua[1] approaches to supervisory practice. The aim of this section of the chapter is to promote the positive place of Maori[2] models within the global village of supervisory practice. This piece has been especially written to encourage indigenous practitioners to develop and uphold the rightful place of taonga tuku iho - precious gifts such as knowledge, skill and experience handed down to successive generations, as a legitimate basis for best practice supervision.

Whether it be written, sung, carved, danced, drawn or chanted, it is hoped that globally, indigenous peoples are encouraged to celebrate their traditional beliefs, knowledge and approaches as the unique gift they have to offer the world.

Te whai matauranga – in the pursuit of knowledge

The concept of supervision has been long established in traditional Maori society as its foundations are deeply seated in the theories of creation – the knowledge base from which all practice and behaviour is derived. Tangata whenua creation stories identify how all elements living and non-living within our universe are linked together, from atua (gods) to us as tangata (people) and extended to include our wider taiao (environment). The maintenance of this link provided the core value base of traditional society, and in turn sought to guide human activity and behaviour.

When korero purakau (creation stories) are narrated, a pattern emerges that reveals the many layers and teachings on offer from the central characters. The act of retelling these stories transports the characters to the fore with validity and currency.

> Properly understood, Mäori mythology and traditions provide myth-messages to which Mäori people can and will respond today. All that is needed is that these myth-messages be more clearly sign-posted...they provide pre-scriptions for practical behaviour in given situations...even today Mäori will respond to the myth-messages and cultural imperatives embedded in their mythology...the erosion of Mäori culture by that of the European has made the thread of binding it to its mythology more tenuous... Myths reflect the philosophy, ideals and norms of the people who adhere to them as legitimiz-ing charters [tikanga]...the outward projection of an ideal against which human performance can be measured and perfected. (Walker 1978, p.19)

The relationships that have been identified within the creation of the universe through to the world as we know it, promote a series of significant events that form the basis of how Maori ancestors viewed the world. It was from this per-spective that societal philosophies, values and belief systems were established and developed into ethical behaviours otherwise known as tikanga. This process is best described by Cleve Barlow:

> Whakapapa is commonly known as the genealogical descent from the creation of the universe by Io, to the present time. The meaning of whakapapa is 'to lay one thing upon another'... Whakapapa is a basis for the organisation of knowledge in respect of the creation and generation of all things... Whakapapa is one of the most prized forms of knowledge and great efforts are made to preserve it. All the people in a community are expected to know who their immediate ancestors are, and to pass this information on to their children so that they too may develop pride and a sense of belonging through understanding the roots of their heritage. (Barlow 1991, pp. 173–4)

Hence, the sacredness of whakapapa and the origin of tikanga Maori are evi-denced in traditional stories that continue to bind tangata whenua to the central creation figures. Whakapapa knowledge seeks to assert membership and offers a basis on which to establish and maintain connection. This espouses a sense of obligation, responsibility and regard to protect and care for those with whom you have established a relationship.

> Whakapapa enable whanau members to establish linkages with each other... Whakapapa give whanau [family] members the knowledge needed to manage relations with other groups, especially at hui [meetings] and with strangers. (Metge 1995, p.91)

Relevance to supervision

Traditional Maori knowledge and practice has been central to continuity and survival. This knowledge centre has been refined and orally transmitted for thousands of years, offering new ways of understanding the obligatory relationships we formed not only with one another, but also with our wider environment. This provides a solid foundation as it legitimates the establishment and maintenance of human relationships while extending further to include environmental considerations.

As Maori, we see Maori creation and the practice that has evolved since providing a basis for developing tangata whenua models of practice today. This knowledge centre promotes the principles, skills, talents and attributes necessary for excellence in supervisory practice. The identification of a Maori knowledge centre forms the basis of all good practice as it supports both the frameworks and ethical behaviours expected of both the supervisor and supervisee.

Te whai pukenga – in the pursuit of a skill base

Individual strengths were seen as gifts from the atua (gods), handed down inter-generationally to tupuna (ancestors). Natural talent and traits were harnessed and individuals encouraged to develop those skills with knowledge founded in the beliefs and values of the people. This was evident in the tohi ceremonies performed at birth, whereby babies were observed and dedicated to particular atua from which they displayed similar traits. The realization of their birthright carried collective responsibilities and obligations.

> Children were observed, it was a pursuit of parents and teachers to study their children. When creative potential first expresses itself, this is said to be an ätua drawing that child in a particular direction...children were then dedicated to that particular deity...and taught knowledge pertaining to that ätua. The whole process works if the parents/teachers are accurate in their study of the child. This is the study of character. (Royal 2003)

Roles and responsibilities were earned and as easily removed if one was not upholding the agreed level of competency. Role selection and fulfillment was testimony to the strength of whanau and hapu continuity. Hence, leadership positions were afforded to those who were either born into or selected, trained and tested by venerated authorities otherwise known as tohunga. The ultimate consequence of failure meant either the demise of the people or of the individual.

Relevance to supervision

The reason for identifying this is that it was important within traditional society to observe and draw out the natural talents of individuals found within its collective membership. To some extent, sustainability was maintained in this manner. This is especially important to Maori practice as it validates the need for supervisors to be highly skilled and attuned to the art of observation and analysis. Mastery enables the supervisor to reveal a supervisee's strengths or talents, and the context and skill required to unfurl this. Thus, professional development is important. Failure of a Maori supervisor to practice in this way ensures almost certain removal of such responsibilities. This identifies a unique difference between legislative and traditional views of law.

Employment law may require a number of steps to be accounted for before a person is removed from their responsibilities, whereas Maori law only entitled you to a position provided you earned the right to retain it. Hence, accountability was measured by a person's ability to execute their skill and knowledge and was regulated by those they served.

Although supervisors are encouraged to use their own technical expertise, the following list offers a broad range of ideal skills and knowledge to be modelled:

- actively encouraging the validity and legitimacy of a Maori worldview

- negotiating an agreed set of ethical standards to be mutually upheld and followed in each session

- enabling the positive use of Maori customary practice and language

- providing a shared learning and professional development experience

- providing opportunities for the supervisee to demonstrate their own ability to meet the needs of whanau (extended kinship base), hapu (extended whanau base) and iwi (collective formation of hapu)

- negotiating and transforming supervisee limitations into learning opportunities

- promoting and developing identifiable tangata whenua models of practice that link kaimahi learning to all of the above

- attending to mutually agreeable, accountability requirements.

These ideals can be used as topics for further discussion when either employing a Maori supervisor or entering into a relationship with new supervisees, thus forming the beginnings of a supervision contract.

Te whai rauemi – in the pursuit of tools/models

As identified previously, role modelling serves as a framework in which tangata whenua supervision is centred. Thus, the models that reflect these practices are two whanau constructs called tuakana and teina:

> The concept of tuakana [older sibling], teina [younger sibling] operates through the dual nature of ako. The word ako means to learn as well as to teach. In the Maori world it is an acceptable practice for the learner to shift roles and become the teacher, and for the teacher to become the learner...the idea of the learner taking on the responsibility of being the teacher or tuakana to her or his teina is acceptable and in fact encouraged from an early age. (Royal-Tanaere 1997, pp.50–1).

Generally speaking, the tuakana is an older sibling of the same gender, and a teina is the younger sibling of the same gender. These are descent line positions within the family that promote a set of reciprocal obligations and responsibilities. If functioning correctly, the role of older sibling is to model and guide the younger sibling, while also encouraging self-learning and improvement from the younger sibling.

> This is the essence of love and care for one another in the whanau. It reinforces the principles of whanaungatanga... The responsibility of the tuakana is to assist the teina in their learning and development. By acting as a support, the tuakana facilitates the process of learning. (Royal 1997, p.50–1)

This framework determines how the tuakana and teina are to behave towards one another. This natural order is based on descent and is best described by Arahi Mahuru recorded by Metge:

> Ko te tuakana te kai-pupiri i te mana, ko te teina te kaiwhakatinana – the tuakana is the one who holds the mana of the whanau, the teina is the one who gives it substance, this is, the doer. The teina must always respect his tuakana; whatever he does, he must seek his permission before or his approval afterwards if it is to have mana (divine power made manifest in the world of the human experience)... Inherited mana is only potential power until it is realized in action. Lacking the desire or personality for leadership, the eldest sibling may hand that role on to a better qualified sibling. (Metge 1995, p.89)

Accordingly, teina are expected to earn trust and respect as prerequisites to receiving opportunities to exercise tasks on behalf or instead of their tuakana. The respect afforded between a tuakana and teina aims to maintain the integrity and social fabric of whanau and hapu alike.

Relevance to supervision

The tuakana/teina framework refers to a system of relationships. It identifies the importance of establishing rapport, trust, respect and the enormous amount of work associated with keeping these relationships intact. In a work situation, individual expectations and agreed boundaries are best clarified in a contract between both supervisor – the tuakana, and the supervisee – the teina.

Once relationships have been well-established, becoming open and transparent, it remains important for the tuakana to reaffirm the basis from which the relationship has been formed. Opportunities for regular review and improvement should be offered. Both tuakana and teina play an important role in maintaining a professional, supportive partnership that encourages growth and development for the teina. The role of the supervisor is to guide and lead a process that explores both the strengths and limitations of the supervisee. Equally so, it must be delivered in an environment conducive to mutual learning.

The function of the supervisor, identified by the responsibilities already referred to is that of kaiarahi. A kaiarahi is someone who facilitates, guides, leads or shows the way. This highlights the role of a supervisor as being to facilitate an exchange of learning that draws out and extends an individual's strengths, talents and traits. Hence tuakana/teina becomes a model the kaiarahi adopts in the delivery of supervision.

In a work setting, tuakana/teina roles may be interchangeable because sometimes the teina may possess specialist knowledge, experience or skills, different from the tuakana. Where this occurs, it should be acknowledged by the tuakana as healthy and be encouraged. It is important that these situations be discussed in full when negotiating the contract.

This framework serves to identify a construct that is relevant and known experientially by Maori as it is an enduring institution still found in whanau today. The framework offers further opportunity to explore the ideal models as portrayed in Maori creation stories, traditional society and current adaptations. By doing this one can develop a framework for supervisory practice that has relevance to one's own whanau or hapu context. This is encouraged as each whanau, hapu and iwi has differing views of practice that are legitimate in their own right.

Supervision practitioners facilitating from within a Maori framework must possess recognizable skills, knowledge and experience in the models they employ. Their credentials are not often gained within a tertiary environment as they are founded within the institution known as whanau. The teachers are almost certainly the wider whanau network and regulators are kaumatua (kin-based elders). In this instance, the most valuable resource to a Maori supervisor and supervisee is their own whanau.

Conclusion

If we are to adopt tangata whenua and other indigenous frameworks within supervisory practice then we need to understand the worldview from which they derive. The basis of good supervisory practice is the sustainability of human relations. This means developing a depth and breadth of knowledge in traditional values and beliefs, which is verified through practice.

Founded in a Maori worldview and intricately woven together by whakapapa, tangata whenua supervision identifies the importance of establishing, developing and maintaining complex systems of human relationships. Whakapapa supports the belief that one's future is connected to the past and places the individual within the context of his or her own ancestral heritage. Whakapapa lies at the heart of Maori spirituality as it embraces the esoteric and exoteric realms of past, present and future generations. It serves to chronicle the interconnectedness between the spiritual, environmental and human domains. The principles observed in caring for this taonga (precious treasure) serve to greatly enhance individual identity and collective wellness.

In essence, a framework that promotes supportive, professional supervision is founded within the whanau construct known as tuakana/teina. This framework encourages a respectful exchange of learning, personal growth and development. Maori supervisory practice is guided by a set of holistic ethical standards, which support and direct both the supervisor and supervisee. Standards are agreed to in a supervision contract that is reviewed regularly.

It is important for tangata whenua to reclaim the legitimate use of cultural models of practice as an essential foundation that seeks to reclaim the rightful place of our traditions as enduring models of practice in the pursuit of toiora – absolute wellbeing.

Strengths-based supervision, as with strengths-based practice, has many constructions and ways of being operationalized within the local context of the practice under consideration. In this chapter the authors have explored the application within an indigenous framework and from research that reinforces the importance and value of the strengths-based approach in the context of Aotearoa/New Zealand. This approach has relevance in all parts of the world where we work with people we call clients and the people we call supervisees. The authors encourage social workers around the world to interpret the constructions of strengths-based supervision from their own cultural and value framework. As supervisors and supervisees we must look within ourselves and our practice for the areas of commonality that bring us together and that support us to name, notice and own strengths-based supervision in all its forms as one of the keys to transformative social work.

Questions for reflection

1. What are the key elements of a strengths approach to supervision?

2. Identify some of the links between generic and indigenous strengths approaches and principles for strengths-based supervision.

3. How could you incorporate a strengths approach into your current approach to supervision?

Notes

1   Tangata whenua – people belonging to any particular place, natives [of New Zealand] used interchangeably with Maori; Williams, H.W. (1992) *Dictionary of the Maori Language.* Wellington: GP Publications.

2   Maori – Normal, usual, ordinary; native, or belonging to New Zealand, person of the native race, New Zealander; Williams, H.W. (1992) *Dictionary of the Maori Language.* Wellington: GP Publications.

References

Anderson, H. and Swim, S. (1995) 'Supervision as collaborative conversation: Connecting the voices of supervisor and supervisee.' *Journal of Systemic Therapies 14,* 2, 1–13

Barlow, C. (1991) *Tikanga Whakaaro: Key Concepts in Maori Culture.* Auckland: Oxford University Press.

Beddoe, L. (2001) 'Learning for supervision in contemporary social work practice in Aotearoa.' In L. Beddoe and J. Worrall (eds) *Rhetoric to Reality, Supervision Conference Proceedings 7–8 July 2000,* Auckland: Auckland College of Education.

Blundo, R. (2001) 'Learning strengths-based practice: Challenging our personal professional frames.' *Families In Society 82,* 3, 296–304.

Bucknell, D. (2000) 'Practice teaching: Problem to solution.' *Social Work Education 29,* 125–144.

Cohen, B.Z. (1999) 'Intervention and supervision in strengths-based social work practice.' *Families in Society 80,* 5, 468.

deShazer, S. (1991) *Putting Difference to Work.* New York: Norton.

Davys, A. (2002) *Perceptions Through a Prism. Three Accounts of 'Good' Social Work Supervision.* Palmerston North: Massey University. Unpublished MSW thesis.

Early, T. and GlenMaye, L. (2000) 'Valuing families: Social work practice with families from a strength perspective.' *Social Work 45,* 2, 118–129.

Epston, D. and White, M. (1992) *Experience, Contradiction, Narrative and Imagination. Selected Papers of David Epston and Michael White 1989–1990.* South Australia: Dulwich Centre Publications.

Juhnke, G. (1996) 'Solution-focused supervision: Promoting supervisee skills and confidence through successful solutions.' *Counselor Education and Supervision 36,* September, 48–57.

Lowe, R. and Guy, G. (2002) 'Solution-oriented inquiry for ongoing supervision: Expanding the horizon of change.' In M. McMahon and W. Patton (eds) *Supervision in the Helping Professions: A Practical Approach.* New South Wales: Pearson Education.

Mainstone, F. (1998) 'Practice teaching, A solutions focused approach.' In H. Lawson (ed) *Practice Teaching – Changing Social Work*. London: Jessica Kingsley Publishers.

Metge, J. (1995) *New Growth from Old*. Wellington: Victoria University Press.

New Zealand Ministry of Justice (2001) *Maori Social Structures : Te Hinatore ki te Ao Maori*. Wellington: Government Print.

O'Donoghue, K. (2003) *Restorying Social Work Supervision*. Palmerston North: Dunmore Press.

Rita, E. (1998) 'Solution focused supervision.' *The Clinical Supervisor 17*, 2, 127–139.

Royal-Tanaere, A. (1997) 'Maori human development learning theory' In P. Te Whaiti, P. M. McCarthy and A. Durie (eds). Mai I Rangiatea. Auckland: Auckland University Press.

Royal, T. (2003) 'Whanau: Giving birth to our potential.' Symposium given at Whanau Development Conference, *Te Wananga O Raukawa*. Otaki, New Zealand.

Saleebey, D. (ed) (1997) 'The strengths perspective in social work practice: Extensions and cautions.' *Social Work 41*, 3, 296–305.

Thomas, C. (2004) 'An analysis of supervision in an organisation with a vision of strengths-based practice.' MSW thesis work in progress. Palmerston North: Massey University.

Walker, R. (1978) 'The relevance of Maori myth and tradition.' In M. King (ed) *Tihe Mauri Ora: Aspects of Maoritanga*. Wellington: Methuen New Zealand.

Wolin, S. and Wolin, S. (1997) 'Resiliency in practice. Shifting paradigms: Taking a paradoxical approach.' *Resiliency in Action 2*, 4, Fall, 23–28.

Part IV

Attachment: Reworking Relationships

Introduction

This final section completes the integrated framework with its macro, meso to micro perspectives, fixing our attention on attachment work with individuals and their families. Following on from the strengths-based perspective, it continues with the theme of hope. People are resilient and social workers can work with them to achieve their clients' goals in reworking relationships.

The chapters in this section explore some key aspects of attachment theory, developing them with examples taken from work with adults, adolescents and children. The opening chapter presents key concepts, arguing that how parents and children relate in the early months and years is crucial for the development of trust and the ability to relate successfully to people. The following two chapters discuss attachment issues and practices drawing on research and practical experience.

In 'Working with Adults who are Parenting' Nicola Atwool takes the reader into the world of social work with families where children's difficult behaviour has brought them to the attention of social workers. She shows how parents can be helped with opportunity to heal and strengthen their own and their children's internal working models. A key theme in this chapter is the significance of thorough assessment for successful intervention. Nicola provides excellent ideas for intervention with parents and caregivers.

In the next chapter, Nikki Evans and Marie Connolly explore issues of attachment specifically in the context of adolescent work. Drawing on their research, they discuss the formation of internal models of attachment. They show the relevance of attachment theory to practice within the residential placement setting, including family work following transition from residential care. Issues for practice are considered, with particular reference to cross-cultural issues.

Chapter 12

Attachment Theory and Social Work

Sue Watson

Introduction

International concern about the transmission of family violence across the generations means we need to discover how to break this cycle. Attachment theory has led the field in explaining and testing hypotheses about the link between early experiences and later development. There is growing recognition that the intellectual and emotional development of children is strongly conditioned by the care an infant experiences (Schore 2003; Siegel 2001). Social workers need to be increasingly alert to the key features of family interaction that are being revealed by attachment research so that new ways of making sense of client behaviour may lead to effective interventions (Howe 1995).

There is widespread acceptance that what parents do has long-term consequences for children. Theoretical approaches offer explanations as to how and why some child-rearing practices produce adults who are healthy and productive citizens while others lead to problem behaviours and emotional difficulties (Fonagy *et al.* 1994). Social workers, teachers and others depend on these theories to inform and guide their interventions. The influences of nature and nurture are both acknowledged in recent theories such as attachment theory. In addition, individuals' interpretations of their own environments can shape their development, as do events which occur in an individual's life that can alter the course that their social environment or their personality type might otherwise have predicted (Oppenheim and Waters 1995). Attachment theory is particularly important for social workers, who are often working with troubled people, to have an understanding of the different ways that the caregiving received by infants influences their subsequent beliefs about themselves and the world they live in.

This chapter discusses how attachment theory focuses on the human need for belonging, for membership of social groups regardless of culture or ethnicity, and in particular, the need for intimacy. Throughout life, people need to matter to those who matter to them. It is this that binds social groups through reciprocal caregiving (Simpson 1999). Secure attachment results in greater flexibility when dealing with life's problems and promotes resiliency.

Experience-dependent brain development

The period from birth to three years is considered critical for infants' learning and development. The foundations for cognitive development, language, social and emotional development are established during this time (Silva and Stanton 1996). Recent research into neurology, and especially the development of the brain in the early years (Schore 2003), provides striking evidence that the infant brain develops through interaction with its environment. Experiences in infancy produce differences in the physiology of the brain. A wide array of different cultural provisions for infants – a 'good-enough' environment – produces normal development of the infant brain. Research indicates that there is no advantage in attempting to provide a 'rich' environment for infants (that can be overstimulating) while at the other extreme, a neglectful environment may not provide the conditions necessary for normal brain development to occur. An abusive environment distorts the pattern of connections in an infant's brain, which may be difficult to correct in later life. Thus Schore (2003, p.219) argues:

> the period from 7 to 15 months (roughly Bowlby's period for the establishment of attachment patterns) has been shown to be critical for the myelination and therefore the maturation of particular rapidly developing limbic and cortical association areas (Kinney *et al.* 1988; Yakovlev and Lecours 1967).

A brief history of attachment theory

Attachment theory originated in the work of John Bowlby and Mary Ainsworth in the 1940s and 1950s. It has had a major impact on efforts to provide a framework for understanding 'the making and breaking of affectional bonds' (Bowlby 1979) and to find evidence-based interventions to assist practitioners working with people with relationship difficulties. John Bowlby was a child psychiatrist who proposed that relationships formed between children and their parents were the result of real life experiences rather than infantile fantasies as argued by Freud. From his study of 'forty-five thieves', he became aware of family deprivation and early loss or separation from their mothers that had featured in the lives of these boys.

Bowlby worked with the Robertsons (childcare case workers), who filmed normal children being separated from their mothers under ordinary conditions. He became convinced that children go through protesting and mourning phases with separation from their mothers that parallel grief and mourning of loss in adulthood. This work has influenced procedures in the hospitalization of children across the world. At one time nurses and doctors complained about how the visiting of parents upset their patients and they kept parents away from children in hospital. Now parents are expected to stay with their young child if the child is hospitalized.

> Just as children are absolutely dependent on their parents for sustenance, so in all but the most primitive communities, are parents, especially their mothers, dependent on a greater society for economic provision. If a community values its children it must cherish their parents. (Bowlby 1951, p.84)

Bowlby has been vilified as stating that mothers must be constantly available to their infants who would otherwise suffer from maternal deprivation (Meade 1988). It is true that Bowlby considered maternal care the ideal for infants, but he recognized the difficulties mothers face in balancing the demands of home and work. Hence his call for communities to cherish parents, especially mothers. Bowlby was saying that for most infants, mothers were (and still are) their primary caregivers and therefore probably their principal attachment figures (see Figure 12.1).

Figure 12.1 Falling in love

Mary Ainsworth was Bowlby's research assistant before going to Uganda in 1954 where she observed how infants expressed their expectation of care in a society very different from that of the children she had studied in London. She subsequently conducted a year long series of structured observations in Baltimore of infants and their mothers at home. At the end of that year she brought them into the laboratory for the 'strange situation' procedure, which has proved to be pivotal in the study of attachment. This is a videotaped structured observation of a caregiver, usually the mother but also the father, the *metapelet* in Israel, the nanny or other child caregiver in childcare facilities, with a child about 12 to 18 months old. This procedure has been used and shown to be an effective assessment tool in many cultures, originally English-speaking Western cultures, but then in other European cultures, Japan, Israel and Puerto Rico.

Ainsworth derived three clusters of behaviours called attachment patterns that provide a robust set of criteria for assessing infant attachment: *secure, insecure avoidant,* and *insecure resistant.* Ainsworth's students later described a fourth attachment category, *disorganized* (Main and Solomon 1990). In addition, the group devised an interview for mothers to discover whether there were explanations for the different sorts of mothering they offered their infants (George, Kaplan and Main 1996).

The adult attachment interview revealed differences in the 'state of mind regarding attachment' signalled by the different ways that mothers spoke about their attachment experiences as children. This instrument can predict the strange situation category of a child whether the mothers were interviewed before the infant was born or at the same time as the strange situation procedure (van IJzendoorn 1995). The adult category 'autonomous' is associated with secure infants. Dismissing adults tend to have avoidant infants. Preoccupied adults are likely to have ambivalent/resistant children. Adults whose discourse becomes incoherent in talking about experiences of loss or abuse in childhood are given the extra classification of 'unresolved/disoriented' and tend to have disorganized infants.

These tools have enabled researchers to explore transmission of expectations about attachment, self-esteem and caregiving through the generations. Attachment issues in adults influence not only how they care for their children but also how they relate to intimate partners, other family members and people in general (Edelstein *et al.* 2004). Social workers will find that attachment theory can explain the patterns of responses of clients to their efforts to help them. Dismissing adults tend not to seek help and resent interference. Preoccupied adults are constantly seeking help and never satisfied with the help offered. Autonomous adults in trouble generally accept the help offered. Unresolved/disoriented adults are very difficult to assist and require long-term commitment and effective interventions before any change is noticeable (Howe 1995).

Some key definitions

Attachment and bonding

In the popular press there is confusion between the terms 'attachment' and 'bonding'. These should refer to different concepts. 'Bonding' is the term given to the emotional connection a parent feels for a particular child. This powerful emotion facilitates caregiving and protection for a defenceless infant. It can happen almost like magic, the turning on of a switch in the parent. In other cases it develops slowly, especially when the child is adopted or has a physical abnormality. Bonding may be interrupted by traumatic experiences occurring around the time of the birth.

'Attachment' is the term given to the mutual affectionate relationship that develops between a caregiver and an infant, child or other intimate partner. Attachment grows and evolves between two people in a continuous caring relationship. The most powerful attachment is that established between a child and the principal caregiver in the first year of life. This will form a framework of expectations about relationships that will continue throughout life unless there are major life events that cause change in the types of attachment experiences.

Bonding happens in the mind of a caregiver and directs attention to the need to care for a child (see Figure 12.2). Attachment is a two-way special relationship created by the ongoing interactions of caregiver and child, or affec-

tionate partners. The development of attachment relationships does not relate to the quality of care received because infants become attached to insensitive and abusive figures as well as to supportive ones. Social workers have long been puzzled by this phenomenon. Attachment research seeks to understand why a child will form an attachment bond to a maltreating parent (Lyons-Ruth and Block 1996).

Figure 12.2 Fathers matter too

Multiple attachments

Research has shown that infants may have different types of attachment with each of their parents and with other long-term early childhood caregivers as observed in strange situation procedures (Sagi *et al.* 1995) or with Attachment Q-sort (Howes and Hamilton 1992). No experiment has been devised that can answer the question whether there is a hierarchy of attachment figures with one primary attachment figure, the relationship with whom colours expectations about future relationships, as Bowlby argued. The observations of Ainsworth in Uganda and Tronick, Morelli and Ivey (1991) with the Efe in Zaire show that in these cultures where there are several sensitive caregivers living with infants and an expectation that all the adults in the group care for all the children, it is still the mother to whom the children go when alarmed and with whom they seek most contact.

Evidence suggests that children need one person as a principal caregiver (Colin 1996), that the person who spends the most time caring for the child in the first year is the one with whom the child will be most attached - even if that person is not the most sensitive and responsive person. Social workers concerned about care and protection issues have to carefully consider cases individually to work out the best solution for infants and children who are securely or insecurely attached to a caregiver and recognize the primal instincts operating with a child pining even for an abusive mother (Hesse and Main 2000).

Non-attachment

Non-attachment is the term given to the situation in which there is no evidence that a child has a preferred caregiver, and is either withdrawn or indiscriminately friendly (Zeanah 1996). It is seen in infants who do not experience care from a single consistent caregiver, or have suffered the disengagement that Bowlby described as the result of a lengthy period of separation from the principal caregiver. This may happen when a child is placed in an orphanage or a series of foster homes, and is seen today in children who have had many caregivers (O'Connor *et al.* 1999). Non-attachment may also occur where children have a succession of nannies, which can inhibit attachment formation.

Types of behaviour exhibited by children of different attachment classifications

Research shows that once the attachment system has been activated the following behaviours (secure, insecure avoidant, insecure/ambivalent/resistant, insecure/disorganized) are identifiable when using assessment procedures such as the strange situation.

Secure

A secure child is happy to see his/her parent upon reunion and, if upset, can be comforted by that parent's presence. This child easily returns to some form of joyful exploration and uses the parent as a secure base from which to explore. Secure children usually cope well with childcare. They enjoy being around other children and their social skills are advanced, which brings them positive responses from peers and adults. They are likely to be resourceful in solving problems but turn to adults for help if necessary. These are foundational skills for school entry and adaptation. Because these children are secure in their attachment they can devote their attention to play and exploration and are more likely to have good self-esteem. When older, they are co-operative, have good self-control and confidence, care about friendships and can manage well when away from parents (Sroufe, Egeland and Carlson 1999).

Insecure avoidant

An insecure avoidant child typically offers no sign of pleasure on his/her parent's return and keeps at a distance, showing little distress at separation. He/she explores toys with no reference to their parents. They appear to manage well when seperated from the caregiver and can learn in childcare and in school. They do not seek help when it is needed. They can misunderstand the feelings of others and try to hide their own. They tend to be noncompliant and to disobey rules. Some are distant but competent, others become aggressive and diruptive (Sroufe, Egeland and Carlson 1999).

Insecure ambivalent/resistant

These children display extreme distress at separation and both seek and reject contact. They may be inconsolable, either passively whining or angrily crying and unable to settle upon reunion or play effectively. They become upset when left in childcare and take a long while to settle. Because they tend to keep close to caregiving adults, and whine and cling, they elicit irritated responses from adults and peers, thus confirming their insecurity. They have high levels of attention-seeking behaviours and instead of dealing with problems themselves, they can be impulsive, dependent or helpless. They mix their strategies to gain acceptance, being sometimes coy and seductive, and at other times angry, or even switching between the two. These children neither play nor learn well. They have poor social skills, lack confidence and have a low tolerance for frustration at home, in childcare and at school (Landy 2002).

Insecure Disorganized

Insecure/disorganized children have no apparent strategy for handling distress, which may be extreme at separation. Their attachment behaviour may be directed at strangers and they may seem dazed, confused or frightened at reunion. They may 'freeze', show repetitive, stereotyped gestures and display depressed, emotionless facial expressions. Because they have no organized way of managing the competing needs to be cared for and to play, their behaviour often appears bizarre. They usually have behaviour difficulties, poor self-control and poor social skills. They can be both bully and victim. They can seem frightened with parents and when away from parents, yet exhibit sudden outbursts of aggressive behaviour. Sometimes they seem spaced out and disso-ciated, often sad and anxious. Many adults find them difficult to cope with, which adds to their environment of negativity.

In their work with disorganized children, Solomon and George (1999) have taken a particular interest in the group of pre-schoolers they call disorga-nized/controlling who can be extremely solicitous of an apparently helpless mother, or extremely bossy and punitive. No research has yet been done on how this behaviour with the mother might carry over into peer and school rela-tionships.

Conditions that create different attachment patterns

Autonomous parents → Secure children

'Autonomous' is the attachment term for adults whose discourse shows that they have a mature appreciation of the responsibility of adults for their own actions and who value attachment relationships, whether or not they had loving parents themselves. Autonomous parents are likely to be competent and protective of their children. Secure children are more likely to have at least one autonomous parent, to be protected by caregivers and to have their nutrition and health well provided for. Secure children do not necessarily come from better-off families, but such families have more choices available for providing adequate food, shelter, safe environs, health care and other opportunities. The chief characteristic of secure children is that they have learned early that their caregivers are reliable and can be trusted, and that the world is a stable and benign place. This gives them the opportunity to explore their world, to be curious and yet protected against their own lack of judgement. Because others care for them, they learn to care for others and to care for themselves. They learn to take other people's feelings into consideration – an intellectual accomplishment that facilitates the parenting that these children will eventually provide for their own offspring. Their flexibility and resilience is likely to make their life course more positive, and although secure attachment does not prevent life difficulties, it is a protective factor when they occur (see Figure 12.3).

Figure 12.3 Confident of care, open to learn

Dismissing parents → Insecure avoidant children

Parents who as infants learned to be insecure avoidant are not inevitably at a disadvantage, although they are likely to be dismissing of the importance of close relationships. There are four major directions they can take.

1. Some feel angry if they feel disadvantaged and will determine to secure a place for themselves even at the expense of others. They can be active, aggressive, enterprising, cold and calculating, and successful.

2. Others are more likely to be involved in anti-social or criminal activities and can be dangerous since they will have a feeling of thwarted entitlement. Their sexual relationships are likely to be unsympathetic, even violent.

3. Where they have grown up with no real understanding of warm, loving relationships they become competitive and appearances will be important to them. They can work hard and may be manipulative and unconcerned about damage to people caused by their pursuit of success.

4. On the other hand, some will not satisfy their achievement needs and so feel themselves to be failures. They cannot find compensations in warm family relationships so may become loners, eccentrics and/or substance abusers.

As parents, people who are dismissing of attachment do not enjoy the physicality of caring for infants and young children and may resent the demands made of them. Busy, achievement-oriented parents may allow little time to get to know their infants, and children learn that making demands does not get them closer to their parents. They learn that their parents want them to become independent, that getting upset only annoys their parents resulting in further withdrawal from them, and consequently they fail to develop an emotional repertoire that would enable them to express and manage their feelings. Dismissive adults become parents who fail to read the needs of their infants, who can be proud of their children but find it hard to be forgiving, who perceive they are doing well as parents if they supply material goods, but really do not enjoy their children's company. It is only the extremely disengaged parents who will be perceived as problematic for social workers.

Preoccupied parents → Insecure ambivalent children

Parents who learned as toddlers to be uncertain about attachment become insecure ambivalent or resistant. 'Ambivalent' indicates the swinging between two perceptions of themselves and their caregivers. Sometimes their caregivers were loving and showed it and sometimes they were cold and ignoring, yet pretending they were loving. It is the inability to trust the expressed affection of caregivers and to read their inconsistent behaviours that leads to uncertainty about whether they deserve care. As adults these people can be seen to be seeking affection but not satisfied by what they get. They repeat for their own children the conditions that have made them preoccupied with relationships.

In assessing the behaviour of toddlers in the strange situation procedure, ambivalent toddlers could also be described as resistant, because when their caregivers appeared to be offering them comfort the children were not calmed but squirmed and cried and often hit out at the caregiver. As they grew older, these were the children that saw ill-intention in the actions of others and often invited it. They are the children who hang around the teacher seeking caregiving and whining about the misdeeds of others. As they grow older peers and adults find them harder to like so their sense that they are not cared for is reinforced. They can become compulsive care-seekers or attempt to become indispensable by becoming compulsive caregivers. Either way their attempts to gain closeness to others are experienced as intrusive. As parents, preoccupied with attachment, they seek caregiving from their children ('You love your Mummy, don't you?') and resent the care they need to give their children. This uncertainty about their lovability is thought to be what passes on this attachment pattern to the next generation. It also interferes with their adult relationships, including that with social workers, from whom they seek constant reassurance that they are being attended to.

Attachment researchers have recently argued that these three infant patterns, secure, avoidant and ambivalent, and the adult equivalent patterns, autonomous, dismissing and preoccupied, are all adaptive, because they arise in a particular ecological niche – a family where that pattern best copes with the child's need for proximity (Solomon and George 1999). In adulthood, following a childhood and adolescence where there has been no intervening circumstance to show the child another way of relating, adults make partner choices which may or may not fit their attachment expectations. Research is attempting to investigate the partner choices of adults of different attachment types, how that affects the stability of marriages and the nature of the attachment of their children. Early research indicated that autonomous people tend to select autonomous partners (Collins and Read 1990), while dismissing individuals tend to be paired with preoccupied individuals, and thus each partner's expectations about attachment is confirmed (Kirkpatrick and Davis 1994).

Disorganized and unresolved

This discussion has so far been mainly about the *organized* patterns of attachment in children and in adults. It has become increasingly apparent that people who are in clinical populations, and those who become the clients of social workers, have not established workable strategies for conducting interpersonal relationships. Instead, their behaviour prevents the establishment of stable relationships. Relationship issues are almost certain to underpin whatever difficulties have brought them to the attention of social workers.

In 'at risk' populations, high numbers of disorganized attachment behaviours are found. These sad and alarming cases will occur often for social workers. In some cases there will be little information that can point to the origin of the disorganization but there is enough research done now to lead to some suggestions. Main and Hesse (1990) have suggested that disorganized infants were cared for by someone who has abused them or was abused him/herself. If a child has been abused in infancy this can explain odd behaviour in the strange situation procedure. On the other hand, research conducted by clinicians who describe the effect on a baby when a mother dissociates shows that as the mother becomes 'spaced out' the infant becomes alarmed and tries different ways to cope with the peculiar presence yet absence of the mother (Schuengel et al. 1999). Other mothers who themselves have been abused have been observed to behave in ways that can be very alarming to babies. The mothers usually perceive such behaviours as amusing, such as 'looming' – coming down too close to a baby's face too fast from above, or making loud 'surprise' noises that startle a child, and laugh when the child cries (Reder and Duncan 2001).

Social workers may see examples of behavioural interactions between children and caregivers that seem to make no sense. Research using the strange situation procedure can occasionally capture bizarre behaviour. In the strange situation, when a mother leaves the room, the toddler usually responds with protest, and the cries are more alarmed after she leaves the second time. When the mother returns the usual behaviour is for mother and child to at least acknowledge one another, even if the child does not seek to be picked up. In one research case, when the mother was out of the room, the toddler did not cry but stood with his back to the wall in a frozen position for a full three minutes. When his mother entered the room she did not go to him but went to the chair and sat down. She put out her arms to him. He took a step forward and put his arms out towards her. Neither moved. They were both frozen in this position. In this research situation there was also access to the mother's adult attachment interview (AAI).

Although this is not direct evidence of the caregiving environment in which that child was raised, the AAI gives a strong indication that it was indeed a disturbed one. The mother had grown up in a household connected to gangs. Both she and her mother suffered physical violence within the family and as a young teenager she witnessed her father's murder. Her discourse throughout the interview was vague and difficult to follow, and she showed no signs of emotion (Pederson 1997). While this example sounds extreme, it is apparent that extreme events have happened in the lives of women and children needing care and protection – and probably also in the lives of the abusive men with whom they are associated. Social workers will find that clients with organized attachment strategies will be more likely to accept help, even if underlying expectations about themselves and others remain unchanged. The ones who are most difficult to help, and who will need long-term support, are those who would be classified as disorganized as children, unresolved/disoriented regarding abuse or loss as adults.

Attachment research in Australia and New Zealand

Attachment assessment methods that have been developed have allowed the principles of the theory to be tested, and this has led to more and more research questions that need to be investigated. In Australia there have been several projects using attachment instruments and attachment as a variable (e.g. Radojevic 1994). In New Zealand, the only research with attachment instruments have been small-scale projects (e.g. Watson and Sweney 2003). So far it seems that attachment research is robust cross-culturally; all attachment patterns are found in any society although different behaviours may be interpreted differently. In any society it is the disorganized patterns that signal cause for concern.

Attachment theory is valuable for social workers because of the absolute importance of interpersonal relationships in human lives. As humans, infants need complete care for many years. Attachment theory helps us understand why children who have been kept clean and fed in orphanages fail to thrive without the experience of attachment to a caregiver and why, when adopted into caring families, they exhibit extreme difficulty in responding to the care offered. Attachment theory provides an explanation for why children who have been abused by their mothers continue to pine for them and seek to be reunited when removed to the care of more nurturing families. Attachment theory provides an explanation for battered wives staying with their violent partners and for violence in intimate relationships, especially when abandonment is threatened. It is not just a theory that is concerned about babies.

Caregivers too need the support of a community while rearing the children of the tribe. Modern societies are causing major changes in many cultures to the ways that children can be cared for: changes in the structures of families, the way families fit into the wider community and the methods by which communities feed, house and clothe their members and the activities that occupy their days and nights. Attachment theory helps us understand why it is so important that parents are supported so that they can care for their children, not in many cases as their unhappy parents parented them, but in a way where the cycle of neglect and abuse is broken and children can grow emotionally healthy and into strong and competent parents themselves.

Questions for reflection

1. What is the difference between bonding and attachment?

2. Describe some aspects of the environment that lead to secure or insecure attachments.

3. Which aspects of attachment are likely to be universal?

4. What does attachment theory indicate to be key factors in the placement of children for adoption?

References

Bowlby, J. (1951) *Maternal Care and Mental Health.* Geneva: World Health Organisation.
Bowlby, J. (1979) *The Making and Breaking of Affectional Bonds.* London: Tavistock.
Colin, V.L. (1996) *Human Attachment.* New York: McGraw-Hill.
Collins, N.L. and Read, S.J. (1990) 'Adult attachment, working models and relationship quality in dating couples.' *Journal of Personality and Social Psychology 58,* 4, 644–663.
Edelstein, R.S., Alexander, K.W., Shaver, P.R., Schaaf, J.M., Quas, J.A., Lovas, G.S. and Goodman, G.S. (2004) 'Adult attachment style and parental responsiveness during a stressful event.' *Attachment and Human Development 6(1),* 31–52.
Fonagy, P., Steele, M., Steele, H., Higgitt, A. and Target, M. (1994) 'The Emmanuel Miller Memorial Lecture 1992: The theory and practice of resilience.' *Journal of Child Psychology and Allied Disciplines, 35,* 2, 231–257.

George, C., Kaplan, N. and Main, M. (1996) *Adult Attachment Interview,* 3rd edn. University of California: Unpublished manuscript.

Hesse, E. and Main, M. (2000) 'Disorganized infant, child, and adult attachment: Collapse in behavioral and attentional strategies.' *Journal of the American Psychoanalytic Association 48,* 4, 1097–1127.

Howe, D. (1995) *Attachment Theory for Social Work Practice.* London: Macmillan.

Howes, C. and Hamilton, C.E. (1992) 'Children's relationships with caregivers: Mothers and child care teachers.' *Child Development 63,* 856–859.

Kirkpatrick, L.A. and Davis, K.E. (1994) 'Attachment style, gender, and relationship stability: A longitudinal analysis.' *Journal of Personality and Social Psychology 66,* 502–512.

Landy, S. (2002) *Pathways to Competence: Encouraging Healthy Social and Emotional Development in Young Children.* Baltimore: Brookes.

Lyons-Ruth, K. and Block, D. (1996) 'The disturbed caregiving system: Relations among childhood trauma, maternal caregiving and infant affect and attachment.' *Infant Mental Health Journal 17,* 3, 257–275.

Main, M. and Hesse, E. (1990) 'Parents' unresolved traumatic experiences are related to infant disorganized attachment status.' In M.T. Greenberg, D. Cicchetti and E.M. Cummings (eds) *Attachment in the Preschool Years: Theory, Research and Intervention.* Chicago: University of Chicago Press.

Main, M. and Solomon, J. (1990) 'Procedures for identifying infants as disorganized/disoriented during the Ainsworth Strange Situation.' In M.T. Greenberg, D. Cicchetti and E. M. Cummings (eds) *Attachment in the Preschool Years.* Chicago: University of Chicago Press.

Meade, A. (1988) 'Education to be more: Report of the Early Childhood Care and Education Working Group.' Cited in S. Kedgeley (1996) *Mum's the Word: The Untold Story of Motherhood in New Zealand.* Auckland, NZ: Random House.

O'Connor, T.G., Bredenkamp, D., Rutter, M. and the English and Romanian Adoptees (ERA) Study Team (1999) 'Attachment disturbances and disorders in children exposed to early severe deprivation.' *Infant Mental Health Journal 20,* 1, 10–29.

Oppenheim, D. and Waters, H.S. (1995) 'Narrative processes and attachment representations: Issues of development and assessment.' In E. Waters, B.E. Vaughn, G. Posada and K. Kondo-Ikemura (eds) *Caregiving, Cultural and Cognitive Perspectives on Secure-base Behavior and Working Models: New Growing Points of Attachment Theory and Research.* Monographs of the Society for Research in Child Development, 60, 197–215.

Pederson, D.R. (1997) Personal communication, training video.

Radojevic, M. (1994) 'Mental representations of attachment among prospective Australian fathers.' *Australian and New Zealand Journal of Psychiatry 28,* 505–511.

Reder, P. and Duncan, S. (2001) 'Abusive relationships, care and control conflicts and insecure attachments.' *Child Abuse Review 10,* 411–427.

Sagi, A., Lamb, M.E., Lewkowicz, K.S., Shoham, R., Dvir, R. and Estes, D. (1995) 'Security of infant-mother, -father, and -metapelet attachments among kibbutz-reared Israeli children.' In I. Bretherton and E. Waters (eds) *Growing Points of Attachment Theory and Research.* Monographs of the Society for Research in Child Development *50,* 257–275.

Schore, A.N. (2003) *Affect regulation and the repair of the self.* New York: W.W. Norton.

Schuengel, C., Bakermans-Kranenburg, M.J., van IJzendoorn, M.H. and Blom, M. (1999) 'Unresolved loss and infant disorganization: Links to frightening maternal behavior.' In J. Solomon and C. George (eds) *Attachment Disorganization.* New York: Guilford Press.

Siegel, D.J. (2001) 'Towards an interpersonal neurobiology of the developing mind: Attachment relationships, "mindsight", and neural integration.' *Infant Mental Health Journal, 22(1-2)*, 67–94

Silva, P.A. and Stanton, W.R. (1996) *From Child to Adult – the Dunedin Multidisciplinary Health and Development Study.* Auckland: Oxford University Press.

Simpson, J.A. (1999) 'Attachment theory in modern evolutionary perspective.' In J. Cassidy and P.R. Shaver (eds) *Handbook of Attachment: Theory, Research and Clinical Applications.* New York: Guilford Press.

Solomon, J. and George, C.E. (1999) *Attachment Disorganization.* New York: Guilford Press.

Sroufe, L.A., Egeland, B. and Carlson, E.A. (1999) 'One social world: The integrated development of parent–child and peer relationships.' In W.A. Collins and B. Laursen (eds) *Relationships as Developmental Contexts: The Minnesota Symposia on Child Psychology V.* Mahwah, NJ: Lawrence Erlbaum.

Tronick, E.Z., Morelli, G.A. and Ivey, P.K. (1992) 'The Efe forager infant and toddler's pattern of social relationships: Multiple and simultaneous.' *Developmental Psychology 28*, 568–577.

van IJzendoorn, M.H. (1995) 'Adult attachment representations, parental responsiveness, and infant attachment: A meta-analysis on the predictive validity of the Adult Attachment Interview.' *Psychological Bulletin 117*, 3, 387–403.

Watson, S. and Sweney, S. (2003) ' "Earned security": Can the Adult Attachment Interview distinguish between parents who have suffered abuse as children who will and will not abuse their own children?' *New Zealand Journal of Counselling 24*, 2, 25–39.

Zeanah, C.H. (1996) 'Beyond insecurity: A reconceptualization of attachment disorders in infancy.' *Journal of Consulting and Clinical Psychology 64*, 42–52.

Chapter 13

Working with Adults who are Parenting

Nicola Atwool

Families are the focus for considerable social work time and energy. Increasing concern is expressed about levels of neglect and abuse and how best to intervene in these situations. Children's difficult behaviour leads to their referral to social service agencies. Children in out of home care also present particularly difficult challenges. In such cases attachment theory is an invaluable resource for social workers. In this chapter I address the significance of early attachment experience for the developing child, outline the relevance of attachment in these common social work scenarios and conclude with guidelines for assessment and intervention.

Bowlby's (1969, 1973, 1980) concept of inner working models explains the long-term impact of early attachment experiences. Internal working models form the basis for the organization and understanding of affective experience (Bretherton 1985, 1990; Crittenden 1990; Main, Kaplan and Cassidy 1985), as well as helping to make sense of new experiences and shaping subjective reality (Howe 1995), as explained in the introductory chapter to this section. They are constructed from the infant's experience of interaction and Sroufe (1988, p.18) argues that 'Such models concerning the availability of others and in turn, the self as worthy or unworthy of care, provide a basic context for subsequent transactions with the environment, most particularly social relationships.' Although internal working models tend to be self-perpetuating, they are also flexible and can be modified as the result of experience and increasing cognitive capacity (Main *et al.* 1985). Ainsworth's (1979) original three categories of attachment represent three distinct internal working models. The secure pattern provides the context for optimal development. The two insecure categories represent the infant's capacity to adapt to a less than optimal environment.

Attachment and behaviour in the developing child

Attachment continues to shape behaviour as the child develops and Ainsworth's 'strange situation' (as described in the preceding chapter) provides researchers with a paradigm for studying the way attachment relationships develop over time and a way to link attachment patterns with subsequent behaviour. Findings include:

- A link between attachment quality and competence at two years (Matas, Arend and Sroufe 1978).

- Significant differences in a group of 40 pre-school children including their confidence, relationships with peers and teachers, and both the content and process of fantasy play (Sroufe 1988).

- In a high risk sample, the quality of attachment at 12 and 18 months was found to be a strong predictor of behaviour in pre-school at ages four-and-a-half to five (Erickson, Sroufe and Egeland 1985).

- A link between attachment and the later development of conduct problems. 'In many cases, the behaviors commonly labeled as "conduct problems" can be viewed as strategies for gaining the attention or proximity of caregivers who are unresponsive to the child's other signals' (Greenberg and Speltz 1988, p.206).

- A link between negative elementary school behaviour and attachment history. Insecure attachment and poor adjustment, inadequate or hostile parental care, and stressful or chaotic life circumstances were three predictors for elementary school aggression and passive withdrawal (Renken et al. 1989).

- A link between neglect and abuse and attachment patterns. Researchers have found that children who experience abuse may either show an extreme avoidant response (Main and Goldwyn 1984) or an avoidant/ambivalent pattern or a disorganized one (Crittenden 1988; Main et al. 1985), as discussed in Chapter 12.

Fahlberg (1988, p.13) addresses issues of attachment for children in care, succinctly summarizing the function of attachment for the child. Attachment helps the child:

- attain full intellectual potential

- sort out what he or she perceives

- think logically

- develop a conscience

- become self-reliant
- cope with stress and frustration
- handle fear and worry
- develop future relationships
- reduce jealousy.

Attachment provides the context within which development takes place. Rather than being one aspect of the child's total experience, relationships with significant others provide the framework within which children learn about themselves, other people and the world around them. Despite a clear demonstration of the long-term consequences of early attachment experiences, three features of attachment give cause for optimism. First, the brain remains 'plastic' or open to change throughout the life span and especially during childhood (Perry 1997; Siegel 2001). Second, children strive to form attachments in the face of rejection, abuse and other adverse experiences, becoming more 'clingy' when needs are not met (Rutter and Rutter 1993) and only withdrawing completely in the most extreme situations (Crittenden 1988). Third, by age two or three children are able to understand social rules beyond the family and their close relationships are coloured by their understanding (Dunn 1993), thus contributing to and enriching the development of internal working models. Considerable potential clearly exists for different experiences of relationships to influence the internal working models that children are in the process of developing. Despite negative experiences, children remain open to modifying existing working models through new relationship experiences, which may serve as a buffer against or modifying factor upon, established models. To realize such potential, social work intervention must take account of the quality of children's relationships with their primary attachment figure(s). Understanding attachment dynamics provides a valuable resource for assessment and intervention when working with parents and caregivers. It assists the social worker's decision-making by providing insight into the child's existing and potential significant relationships and helps to explain a child's behaviours.

Relevance of attachment to social work with families

Social work with families encompasses a range of activities and issues. Three common scenarios are considered – care and protection concerns, behaviour problems, and children in care. The relevance of attachment theory to each of these aspects of practice is discussed.

Attachment and children for whom there are care and protection concerns

Children's obvious efforts to maintain contact with their primary caregiver(s) can lead social workers to make naïve assumptions about attachment. Although most children will exhibit attachment behaviour, the quality of the relationship and in particular the adult's response, should be the paramount concern. Sometimes those working with families fail to recognize the detrimental effects of long-term exposure to a situation in which the child strives for recognition and signs of affection despite repeated experiences of neglect, rejection, abuse or abandonment. Children become the scapegoats, in extreme cases losing their lives and in other situations sustaining significant emotional damage that may lead to their being labelled the problem.

The timing of intervention is an important consideration. Although early intervention may maximize the potential for change, pragmatic and philosophical reasons dictate a more cautious approach. Part of the ambivalence results from inadequate resources to undertake intensive intervention with families. Some social workers argue that the philosophy of family preservation precludes the possibility of permanent placement away from family of origin. In the New Zealand context, the 1989 Children, Young Persons and their Families Act has been interpreted by some social workers as meaning that the option to return home always remains open (Atwool 1999). Although the increase in child deaths is calling this assumption into question, there is still a tendency to 'wait and see'. Multiple notifications may therefore occur before the option of removing children is considered.

Attachment in children who exhibit 'problem' behaviour

Despite evidence that supports the opinion that temperament and behaviour are genetically influenced, behaviour does not occur in isolation and children are not born bad or disturbed. Interaction with the environment remains critically important when determining the outcome for an individual child (Fonagy 2003). *Securely attached* children are likely to have confident internal working models enabling them to form positive relationships and increasing their ability to cope with new challenges. Good attachment experiences generate confidence that adults, such as teachers, will respond to them positively. Should such children encounter difficulties they are likely to have both internal and external resources to draw on. By adolescence, those with secure internal working models present as confident and outgoing young people who have the ability to negotiate challenges (Allen and Land 1999).

Within the home environment, *ambivalently attached* children continue to struggle with inconsistent and unreliable attachment figures. Their desperation for attention generates difficult and demanding behaviours, reinforcing their worst fears when the attachment figure cannot respond sensitively. These children are intolerant of separation, difficult to comfort and demonstrate 'poverty of exploration' (Matas *et al.* 1978). By adolescence, those in the ambivalent category are often engaged in intense and explosive relationships with parents, continuing the pattern that began in infancy (Allen and Land 1999). This is likely to carry over into peer relationships which may be characterized by 'come here/go away' messages.

Within the home environment, *avoidantly attached* children continue to manage difficult relationships with unavailable and, possibly, actively rejecting parent(s). These children focus their attention on toys, are not upset by separation and do not initiate contact following this (Matas *et al.* 1978). Such children have not formed positive expectations of others, and may display feelings of low self-worth, isolation and angry rejection, placing them at risk for the development of learning difficulties. Avoidant adolescents present as sullen and withdrawn with intermittent outbursts of rage (Allen and Land 1999). Peer relationships tend to be superficial and aggressive behaviour may be triggered in close relationships because past experience has taught them that you cannot trust others, especially those close to you.

Children with *disorganized attachment* are unlikely to trust adults. Their probable failure to internalize rules governing daily existence ensures that their behaviour is determined by reaction to external cues. Lacking secure attachment and trust in adults, these children have no incentive to comply with requests or instructions. They may resent and resist attempts by adults to control them. Their behaviour may fluctuate and they may be labelled ADHD (Perry 1997). Without intervention most, if not all, of this group are in serious difficulty by adolescence. They are likely to gravitate to peers with similar problems and engage in activities that reinforce their internal model of the world as a chaotic and confusing place where people (including themselves) have no intrinsic value.

Attachment categories do not always present in such clear-cut ways. Within each group, there is a continuum of behaviour with those at the more extreme end of the spectrum attracting the most attention. For example, in some cases children with disorganized attachment patterns in infancy appear to have reversed roles with the parent by the age of six, resulting in the 'parentification' of the maltreated child (Carlson *et al.* 1989). Such children may present in similar ways to securely attached children. Close observation shows, however, that they differ by being hyper-alert, strongly attuned to non-verbal cues and that they repress negative emotional displays even in situations that warrant such a reaction (Crittenden 1988). Despite possible difficulties with concentration, these children are anxious to please, making great efforts to 'get it right', creating the opportunity to do well in the school environment. Because they become so attuned to other's needs, however, such children fail to develop a sense of themselves as autonomous individuals with needs and rights.

CHILDREN IN CARE

The material in the preceding section applies to children in care as well as children living at home. One crucial difference is that children in care are separated from their attachment figure(s) and any attachment difficulties they have will be exacerbated. In rare cases when a child with secure attachment experiences disruption, they fare better because they are more open to forming new relationships. When a child has never experienced secure attachment, their ability to trust is severely limited and they may be wary of adults, expecting rejection. At best, they have been let down by adults, and at worst they have suffered emotional, physical and/or sexual abuse. Most children coming into care have experienced the world as a chaotic and dangerous place. Their experiences cause them to develop internal working models and protective strategies based on dysfunctional attachment patterns. They will have difficulty regulating emotion. Some may be extremely withdrawn, silent, watchful and/or anxious and retreat into themselves months and years later when stressed or insecure. Such behaviour is very stressful and I have been told by experienced caregivers that a disruptive child is preferable because there is interaction. The withdrawn child invokes feelings of helplessness and rejection that may be intolerable for the caregiver. At the opposite end of the continuum are children who test every limit and need to be constantly on the move. Often volatile and loud, they create chaos wherever they go. Although they rely on external cues, their co-operation with directions is by no means guaranteed because secure attachment is a necessary prerequisite to co-operation. While a child remains insecure in their attachments to adults, there is no good reason to comply with requests or instructions.

Perhaps the most difficult are the children described by Rene Hoksberger (1997) as suffering 'bottomless pit syndrome'. These children have very low self-esteem, a phenomenal memory for negative events and cannot store and recall positive experiences. These children have no core. The first step is to begin to develop this. A significant relationship is crucial to this process. As many highly motivated caregivers will testify, however, it is not that easy! Research on the implications of attachment disruption is limited but does suggest that caregivers require greater sensitivity than is the case in more typical parenting situations (Howes 1999). This has implications for the selection of caregivers and the level of post-placement support necessary to maintain placements. In the next section the implications for social work assessment and intervention are discussed.

Assessment

Assessment is the key to good social work practice. Attention to attachment provides crucial information that increases the possibility of accurate assessment and effective intervention (Howe 1995; Howe *et al.* 1999). In this section

I outline the relevance in common scenarios and describe some strategies that social workers can introduce to parents and caregivers wishing to increase the security of their children's attachment to them.

Assessment: attachment where there are care and protection concerns

Recent focus in care and protection assessment has been on assessing risk (Parton 1996). Although attachment is mentioned as just one of many factors in such assessments, it is important to recognize that other factors symptomatize or exacerbate underlying attachment difficulties. Attachment is centrally important when assessing safety and wellbeing because it provides the context for the child's development and the absence of secure attachment significantly increases the risk of abuse. Assessment of attachment should precede any decision about whether or not the goal is to maintain the child within the family. During the assessment, the pattern of interaction and the way in which the adult describes the child should be a particular focus. For example, the attribution of persecutory intent to the child is a significant danger sign. The parent(s) should recognize the child as a separate person in his or her own right and should feel empathy for the child, especially when s/he is distressed. Much can be learned from careful observation and useful guidelines for children of different ages are available (Fahlberg 1988; Howe et al. 1999). The pattern of interaction will change as the child develops. For example, some parents cope very well with a dependent infant but not with a more active and assertive toddler. Social workers should explore the parent's experience of being a child and the beliefs about parenting that have developed from this because such information provides insight into the parent's own internal working model. Knowing how many adults are involved in the child's life allows assessments with all the adults who have a significant caring role.

If the child is placed outside the family while the assessment is completed, access with the birth family can provide further opportunities to observe attachment behaviour (Ansay and Perkins 2001). Careful observation of the reaction of the child and the parents during reunion and separation will yield important information. A key factor in the assessment is to determine whether the possibility for secure attachment exists within the family. If so, the appropriate goal is return home in the foreseeable future and placement needs to be with caregivers willing to facilitate that goal. If the child cannot return home in the foreseeable future then s/he should have the opportunity to establish a primary attachment in another family. The appropriate goal is permanent placement. It is important that parents are given realistic timeframes within which to achieve goals and if unable to make satisfactory progress, the goal needs to change from return home, to permanent placement.

Assessing parent and child when there are behaviour problems

Whenever a child presents with difficult behaviour a full assessment is needed. Attention must be paid to the family history, the child's early experience and the patterns of interaction within the family. Questions must be asked about significant separations from attachment figures, possible exposure to trauma such as abuse or violence within the family, and the discipline measures used by the parent(s). A timeline is a useful strategy to track significant events. In using this technique with families, I have found not only that it provides invaluable information for the social worker but that it also provides parents with a different appreciation of their child's behaviour and may offer possible solutions. Parents may be so self-absorbed that they have never reflected on the child's experience or the impact that events may have had on them. Parents who cannot engage in this type of exploration will be unlikely to support their child in changing his/her behaviour. A key aspect of the assessment is whether parents can accept responsibility for their role in the difficulties and are willing to actively participate in change efforts. Change will not be possible unless they can reflect on their part in the problem and be prepared to modify their response to the child.

Children in care

An attachment focus raises important issues about how we assess caregivers and select placements. Secure attachment in a caregiving situation is elusive because both the caregivers and the child have internal working models based on their own unique experience of relationships. The caregiver's response to a particular child will largely be influenced by how their experience, and the expectations they have, enables them to respond to the child's behaviour and especially the child's reaction to them. For example, there will be limited possibility of an avoidant child forming a secure attachment with a caregiver who copes with disappointment in relationships by withdrawing. The caregiver is likely to feel punished by the child's lack of response and may cease to initiate contact with the child, thus intensifying the child's avoidant behaviour. The same caregiver may be much better able to cope with a child who acts out.

Such complexities are further deepened when placement is sought for siblings. In my experience, children from the same family may develop different patterns of attachment. It is not uncommon for one child to have developed an avoidant pattern and another child to have an anxious pattern characterized by attention-seeking behaviours. Coping with such different children is extremely demanding and is probably only manageable for caregivers with secure attachment experiences in the past and the present.

Given the shortage of people offering to foster children and their voluntary status, it can be difficult to obtain the information necessary to assess their particular strengths and weaknesses in relation to attachment. If we do not, however, we increase the risk of placement breakdown. Mary Main's adult attachment interview facilitates an in-depth exploration of adult attachment (Hesse 1999). Analysis of the interview narrative enables the identification of adult attachment categories that correspond to childhood patterns. The categories are autonomous (secure), dismissive (avoidant), preoccupied (ambivalent) and disorganized/unresolved (disorganized). Considerable expertise and training are necessary and it would not be appropriate for social workers to routinely use this as part of assessment. Caregiver training should include attachment information and social workers should address these issues during their assessments. It is not a matter of finding 'perfect' people. Adults who have resolved difficulties associated with early attachment problems may have a lot to offer children in need of care.

Children's enduring loyalty to their families of origin and their desperate need for their parent(s) to demonstrate love for them should not be forgotten. Children in care continue to grapple with the complexities of their families of origin at the same time that caregivers are attempting to establish meaningful relationships with them. Caregivers need to tolerate this and support children in resolving these issues. In my experience, many caregivers struggle to do so, feeling that their job would be simpler and that the child would be happier if there was no contact with the family of origin. Social workers should consider such attitudes when assessing caregivers and when making placement decisions.

It is important that an assessment of the child is completed at the time of placement. Any learning difficulties or health problems should be appropriately assessed and the information shared with caregivers. Caregivers must be given a realistic assessment of the child's potential. In my experience, many caregivers respond positively to attachment information because it helps make sense of children's behaviour. It also helps them develop different strategies for dealing with difficult behaviour.

Intervention

Placement decision-making

Once a decision to intervene has been made, attachment considerations are crucial for families. Whether the focus is the child's behaviour or care and protection concerns, the most important initial decision is whether there is potential to work with the family to improve the quality of relationships or whether the child is in need of alternative care. The decision must be achieved within a child-centred timeframe. Timeframes appear to be dictated by adult concerns rather than child concerns and sometimes the potential for conflict is not recognized (Atwool 1999). Parents and social workers do not always understand that children's lives cannot remain on hold for indefinite periods. When a placement outside the home is made, for example, there is often a lengthy period in which the goal remains 'return home' without significant progress toward this goal. Working with an attachment perspective highlights the importance of parents having the opportunity to address their own past and factors that may be impacting on their ability to foster secure attachment in their children. In New Zealand, since the introduction of the 1989 Children, Young Persons and their Families Act, children are more likely to remain in limbo for long periods while unsuccessful attempts at return to birth parents are made. Although contact with the child may be maintained through access visits, there may be no support or intervention focusing on the quality of the relationship.

An attachment perspective also alerts us to the importance of relationships at all levels, both within the family and among the workers implementing the intervention plan. Caregivers who will actively support the goal of 'return home' are needed. Attention to matching caregiver, child(ren) and family of origin will increase the likelihood of successful reunification. Additionally, all the professionals involved must be willing to work co-operatively towards this goal.

The child's situation may change significantly when the time taken to achieve specific requirements extends beyond the initial plan. Parents need accurate information about the impact of the circumstances leading to intervention on their children and the effect of separation from the family. They also need clear information about the timeframes within which goals must be achieved if the child's best interests are to be attended to. Such information should be shared in a manner that increases the likelihood that it serves as a motivating factor rather than a punitive measure. Social workers must remain clear about the focus of the work. Is alternative care a temporary arrangement with a planned return home, or is care designed to be long term with no immediate plan for return home? It is important that the passage of time does not simply erase the distinction (Cooper and Webb 1999; Katz 1990).

When permanent placement is considered necessary, the significance of the child's early attachment experiences must be recognized and incorporated in the plan. This includes attention to the challenges they are likely to present and matching with caregivers able to cope with this. No matter what the child has experienced, social workers cannot indulge in rescue fantasies that exclude the family of origin. The child's first attachment figure(s) will remain important people whose love the child will continue to seek. We have to think in terms of managing the total situation, including the family of origin, rather than simply finding the child a new home (Kates et al. 1991). The child's needs must remain the focus of access arrangements and the impact of access should continue to be monitored. Emotional reactions are to be expected and are not necessarily a reason to stop access.

SUPPORTING PARENTS AND CAREGIVERS TO ACHIEVE BEHAVIOURAL
CHANGE

It is important to address underlying issues rather than targeting symptoms.
Behavioural management strategies and individual counselling are largely ineffective when unmet emotional needs and conflicted relationships continue to
characterize the child's environment. The key to building secure attachment is
the sensitive responsiveness that is so important in infancy. The basic needs of
the baby are still unmet in the child who is not securely attached. These include
the need to be understood and responded to, held, enjoyed and admired. The
following strategies may assist parents and caregivers wishing to build a more
secure attachment with a child.

Insecure children may have no expectation that adults will respond to
them. If they cope by withdrawing, they may need help to move out of this
state. Eye contact is crucial in this process because without it, the child does not
see the positive reflection of themselves that is the first step to feeling understood and having a sense of being enjoyed and admired. Demanding eye
contact when trying to discipline a child, will only result in avoidance. Eye
contact needs to be built up at times when positive interactions are taking place.
There are cultural issues in relation to eye contact, for some children direct eye
contact with an adult is disrespectful and the child may have been punished for
this in the past. Other alternatives include parallel play, shared activities such as
baking or fishing, reading to the child, and having conversations while driving
in the car.

In even the busiest household, five minutes can be set aside each day that is
the child's special one-to-one time (Donovan and McIntyre 1990). Persistence
and patience are essential requirements in implementing this strategy, as it may
be a long time before the child responds. The purpose is to demonstrate to the
child that they are important enough to receive an adult's undivided attention
and interest. The more difficult the child, the longer it will take for a positive
response. Withdrawal and anger may co-exist and a child may alternate
between them, which means that finding a middle road may take time and
patience. Finding safe ground such as activities that the child enjoys doing is
very important in this process. Children may have missed out on opportunities
that we take for granted, such as the chance to engage in messy play or water
play. Such activities have therapeutic potential and should be encouraged.

Counselling or therapy is often seen as a last resort, but with attachment
related issues early intervention is most important. Some counsellors and therapists have expertise in working with attachment issues. Strategies that focus
intervention on the attachment relationship may include joint sessions for the
parent or caregiver and child, providing an opportunity for one-to-one interaction in a supportive environment. This type of intervention early in a new
placement may greatly reduce the risk of breakdown. Counselling or therapy
on their own cannot 'fix' children. Healing is a lifelong process for children

who have experienced trauma. Because the most significant contribution to healing comes from everyday experience and interaction, it is vital that therapy involves parents and caregivers and that they support therapeutic intervention and are willing to be involved in the process. Social workers have an important role in facilitating appropriate referrals and ensuring that resources are available to support the therapy. A teamwork approach can be most effective.

Many of the children who come to the attention of social workers have complex and confusing life stories. They may lack any clear idea of the sequence of events, let alone the reasons for these events. A life story-book in which the child is the central character helps the attachment process by making sense of the child's life. We cannot protect children from their own lives. No matter how painful their experiences we cannot take them away. We can help children to live with them, however. Putting together a life story-book can be a therapeutic experience that provides an opportunity to talk about significant people and events. Social workers can play a key role as they have access to relevant information, and engaging in this task can facilitate a positive relationship with the child. In some agencies there may not be time to undertake this task but with information and support from social workers, parents and caregivers may undertake this work with a child. In long-term placements, for example, this task can be a valuable way to facilitate the attachment process.

Parenting requires more than meeting the child's immediate needs for physical care. Many children in difficulty have given up any hope of being listened to, or responded to with care and concern. Children value the experience of caring relationships with adults who listen and who are consistent in their response (Butler and Williamson 1994). Paying attention to a child allows adults to make a far greater contribution than they realize. Fulfilling this role is more likely when there is a good match between adult and child, especially in relation to patterns of attachment. Many children do not clearly understand why they are in care or how decisions are made (Smith *et al.* 1999). But we must not disempower children by underestimating their ability to participate in planning. Children's security of attachment is likely to be increased when they are actively involved in decision-making (Curtis 1986). This can be achieved by facilitating children's participation in decision-making forums such as family group conferences and planning meetings. If the child is very young or reluctant to participate, it is important that time is spent with them prior to any meetings, their view is presented to the meeting and they are informed of the outcome.

When working with children with attachment difficulties parents' and caregivers' needs should be met by others in their environment. Adults have internal working models of attachment and differing capacities to cope with the challenges of parenting. Children are not always rewarding and it is important that adults are able to meet their emotional needs from within their network rather than placing this expectation on the child. Considerable support is required to care for these children in a way that creates the opportunity for secure attachment to begin to develop. Some children's needs are so great that it may be unrealistic to expect one family to meet them. In such situations, it is much wiser to put in place a network of support rather than risk burning out parents and caregivers.

When there is limited potential for change, but it is deemed safe for the child to remain in his/her current environment, the goal should be to provide the child with relationships that might serve as a buffer and modify internal working models. These relationships are most influential if they can be found within the child's existing network, for example, aunts, uncles or grandparents. Other possibilities include neighbours and leaders of community groups, or recreational activities. When no possibilities exist within the established network, a buddy or mentor can make an important contribution. Respite care may also serve this purpose and is more effective when implemented with a focus on the child's need for positive relationship experiences. It is important that social workers do not underestimate the importance of their role in a child's life. The social work relationship is another opportunity for the child to have a positive relationship experience.

Many people are involved when working with families in difficulty. Working relationships must be established and maintained between all parties, including the family of origin, caregivers, lawyers, teachers, health professionals and counsellors. Previous caregivers may also exist. Clarity about the goal for the child is vital in such working relationships. All too often conflict and confusion cut across these relationships. Adult issues may get in the way and when this happens, the child becomes invisible (Atwool 1999). Continuity of relationships is important. If the child moves to another placement or returns home, attention should be paid to maintaining contact with people who are significant for the child such as other children, siblings and friends as well as adults. Secure attachment relationships depend on these remaining the focus of decision-making (Pilowsky and Kates 1995). The social worker has a crucial and unique role in managing these processes.

Conclusion

Society undervalues the challenging task of parenting. Caring for children who have experienced disruption and abuse is even more challenging. Attachment provides the key to success for parents, caregivers and children, providing the glue that holds families together and makes them safe. Frustration and a sense of failure often result when energy is poured into working for behavioural change. Such energy is better directed to developing secure attachment. Children (and adults) are more accepting of guidance and direction once they have begun to develop trust and confidence, and there is nothing more rewarding for a parent or caregiver than the smiles and the cuddles that come from children once they have begun this process. Attachment theory is pivotal to social work practice, offering a framework that assists with assessment and intervention in a range of family situations. Attachment theory is compatible with other key theoretical perspectives such as the ecological, strengths, narrative, advocacy and empowerment models, providing an essential focus for effective social work practice.

Questions for reflection

1. Why does understanding attachment dynamics provide a valuable resource for assessment and intervention when working with parents and caregivers?

2. What are the key contributions that attachment theory can make that help caregivers accommodate to the needs of children in their care?

3. How can the practitioner encourage the development of secure attachment in troubled children?

References

Ainsworth, M. (1979) 'Infant–mother attachment.' *American Psychologist 34*, 932–937.

Allen, J.P. and Land, D. (1999) 'Attachment in adolescence.' In J. Cassidy and P. Shaver (eds) *Handbook of Attachment.* New York: Guilford Press.

Ansay, S.J. and Perkins, P.F. (2001) 'Integrating family visitation and risk evaluation: A practical bonding model for decision makers.' *Family Relations 50*, 220–229.

Atwool, N.R. (1998) 'Making connections: attachment and resilience.' In A. Smith and N. Taylor (eds) *Enhancing Children's Potential.* Dunedin: Children's Issues Centre.

Atwool, N.R. (1999) 'Attachment and post-intervention decision-making for children in care.' *Journal of Child Centred Practice 6*, 1, 39–55.

Bowlby, J. (1969) *Attachment and Loss: Vol. 1. Attachment.* New York: Basic Books.

Bowlby, J. (1973) *Attachment and Loss: Vol. 2. Separation.* New York: Basic Books.

Bowlby, J. (1980) *Attachment and Loss: Vol. 3. Loss, Sadness and Depression.* New York: Basic Books.

Bretherton, I. (1985) 'Attachment theory: Retrospect and prospect.' In I. Bretherton and E. Waters (eds) *Growing Points of Attachment Theory and Research.* Monograph of the Society for Research in Child Development 50, 1 & 2, Serial No. 209, 3–35.

Bretherton, I. (1990) 'Communication patterns, internal working models, and the intergenerational transmission of attachment relationships.' *Infant Mental Health Journal 11*, 237–251.

Butler, I. and Williamson, H. (1994) *Children Speak.* Harlow: Longman.

Carlson, V., Cicchetti, D., Barnett, D. and Braunwald, K. (1989) 'Disorganised/disoriented attachment relationships in maltreated infants.' *Developmental Psychology 25*, 525–531.

Cohn, D.A. (1990) 'Child–mother attachment of six-year-olds and social competence at school.' *Child Development 61*, 152–162.

Cooper, A. and Webb, L. (1999) 'Out of the maze: Permanency planning in a postmodern world.' *Journal of Social Work Practice 13*, 2,119–134.

Crittenden, P. (1988) 'Relationships at risk.' In J. Belsky and T. Nezworski (eds) *Clinical Implications of Attachment.* Hillsdale, NJ: Lawrence Erlbaum.

Crittenden, P. (1990) 'Internal representational models of attachment relationships.' *Infant Mental Health Journal 11*, 259–277.

Curtis, P. (1986) 'Involving children in the placement process.' *Adoption and Fostering 7*, 45–47.

Donovan, D.M. and McIntyre, D. (1990) *Healing the Hurt Child.* New York: Norton.

Dunn, J. (1993) *Young Children's Close Relationships.* Newbury Park, CA: Sage.

Erickson, M., Sroufe, L.A. and Egeland, B. (1985) 'The relationship between quality of attachment and behaviour problems in preschool in a high risk sample.' In I. Bretherton and E. Waters (eds) *Growing Points of Attachment Theory and Research.* Monograph of the Society for Research in Child Development 50, 1 & 2, Serial No. 209, 147–166.

Fahlberg, V. (1988) *Fitting the Pieces Together.* London: British Agencies for Adoption and Fostering.

Fonagy, P. (2003) 'The development of psychopathology from infancy to adulthood: The mysterious unfolding of disturbance in time.' *Infant Mental Health Journal 24*, 3, 212–239.

Garmezy, N. (1994) 'Reflections and commentary on risk, resilience, and development.' In R.J. Haggerty, L.R. Sherrod, N. Garmezy and M. Rutter (eds) *Stress, Risk and Resilience in Children and Adolescents. Processes, Mechanisms and Interventions.* Cambridge: Cambridge University Press.

Greenberg, M. and Speltz, M. (1988) 'Attachment and the ontogeny of conduct problems.' In J. Belsky and T. Nezworski (eds) *Clinical Implications of Attachment.* Hillsdale, NJ: Lawrence Erlbaum.

Hesse, E. (1999) 'The Adult Attachment Interview: Historical and current perspectives.' In J. Cassidy and P.R. Shaver (eds) *Handbook of Attachment.* New York: Guilford Press.

Hoksberger, R. (1997) *Uncertainties and Doubts for Adoption Professionals.* Presentation at the International Conference on Adoption and Healing. Wellington.

Howe, D. (1995) *Attachment Theory for Social Work Practice.* London: Macmillan Press.

Howe, D., Brandon, M., Hinings, D. and Schofield, G. (1999) *Attachment Theory, Child Maltreatment and Family Support.* London: Macmillan.

Howes, C. (1999) 'Attachment relationships in the context of multiple caregivers.' In J. Cassidy and P. Shaver (eds) *Handbook of Attachment.* New York: Guilford Press.

Kates, W.G., Johnson, R.L., Rader, M.W. and Streider, F.H. (1991) 'Whose child is this? Assessment and treatment of children in foster care.' *American Journal of Orthopsychiatry 6*, 4, 554–591.

Katz, L. (1990) 'Effective permanency planning for children in foster care.' *Social Work 35*, 220–226.

Main, M. and Goldwyn, R. (1984) 'Predicting rejection of her infant from mother's representation of her own experience: Implications for the abused–abusing intergenerational cycle.' *Child Abuse and Neglect 8*, 203–217.

Main, M., Kaplan, N. and Cassidy, J. (1985) 'Security in infancy, childhood and adulthood: A move to the level of representation.' In I. Bretherton and E. Waters (eds) *Growing Points of Attachment Theory and Research.* Monograph of the Society for Research in Child Development 50, 1 & 2, Serial No. 209, 66–104.

Matas, L., Arend, R.A. and Sroufe, L.A. (1978) 'Continuity of adaptation in the second year: The relationship between quality of attachment and later competence.' *Child Development 47*, 547–556.

Parton, N. (1996). 'Social work, risk, and "the blaming system".' In N. Parton (ed) *Social Theory, Social Change and Social Work.* London: Routledge.

Perry, B. (1997). 'Incubated in terror: Neurodevelopmental factors in the "cycle of violence".' In J.D. Osofsky (ed) *Children in a Violent Society.* New York: Guilford Press.

Pilowsky, D.J. and Kates, W.G. (1995) 'Foster children in acute crisis. Assessing critical aspects of attachment.' *Journal of the American Academy of Child and Adolescent Psychiatry 35*, 8, 1095–1097.

Renken, B., Egeland, B., Marvinney, D., Mangelsdorf, S. and Sroufe, L.A. (1989) 'Early childhood antecedents of aggression and passive-withdrawal in early elementary school.' *Journal of Personality 57*, 259–281.

Rubin, K. and Lollis, S. (1988) 'Origins and consequences of social withdrawal.' In J. Belsky and T. Nezworski (eds) *Clinical Implications of Attachment.* Hillsdale, NJ: Lawrence Erlbaum.

Rutter, M. (1994) 'Stress research: Accomplishments and tasks ahead.' In R.J. Haggerty, L.R. Sherrod, N. Garmezy and M. Rutter (eds) *Stress, Risk and Resilience in Children and Adolescents. Processes, Mechanisms and Intervention.* Cambridge: Cambridge University Press.

Rutter, M. and Rutter, M. (1993) *Developing Minds. Challenge and Continuity Across the Life Span.* New York: Basic Books.

Siegel, D. (2001). 'Toward an interpersonal neurobiology of the developing mind: Attachment relationships, "mindsight", and neural integration.' *Infant Mental Health Journal 22*, 1–2, 67–94.

Smith, A., Gollop, M., Taylor, N. and Atwool, N. (1999) 'Children's voices in foster or kinship care: Knowledge, understanding and participation.' *Journal of Child Centred Practice 6*, 1, 9–37

Sroufe, L.A. (1988) 'The role of infant–caregiver attachment in development.' In J. Belsky and T. Nezworski (eds) *Clinical Implications of Attachment.* Hillsdale, NJ: Lawrence Erlbaum.

Sroufe, L.A. (1989a) 'Relationship, self and individual adaptation.' In A. Sameroff and R. Emde (eds) *Relationship Disturbances in Early Childhood: A Developmental Approach.* New York: Basic Books.

Chapter 14

Attachment Issues and Work
with Adolescents

Nikki Evans and Marie Connolly

Introduction

Literature and research focusing on the nature, prevalence and stability of attachment patterns often implicitly convey secure attachment patterns as an ideal or a goal. As such, theorists have viewed secure attachment as a 'prototype' (Fletcher 2002). However, insecure attachment patterns cannot be considered rare when they are displayed by a significant percentage of young children (Fletcher 2002). For example, Howe (1995) reports that 40 per cent of children display insecure attachment patterns, of which 25 per cent are assessed as avoidant, 10 per cent ambivalent, and 5 per cent as disorganized attachment styles. Significantly, longitudinal research has generally demonstrated the endurance of attachment patterns (Daniel and Taylor 2001), highlighting the importance of attachment style stability over time and across the lifespan. Given the potentially widespread significance of insecure attachment styles and their enduring nature, adolescent attachment issues are likely to be of concern to practice. This chapter, in this section, builds on the previous ones by exploring issues of attachment specifically in the context of adolescent work. It discusses the formation of internal models of attachment, and considers the relevance of attachment theory to practice within the residential placement setting, and family work following transition from residential care. Issues for practice are explored, with particular reference to cross-cultural issues.

Internal models of attachment

By definition, attachment is relational – it concerns the nature of relationships between people. Neglect, maltreatment and abuse always occur in the context of *relationships* (George 1996). Young people who are raised in difficult and adversive social and emotional environments are likely to experience interpersonal relationships as stressful, unfulfilling and frustrating. This in turn can lead to the development of insecure attachment patterns and problem behaviours (Howe *et al.* 1999).

Grossman (1995) suggests that it is within attachment relationships that infants and children begin to organize and regulate their expression of emotion and behaviour. As children grow older and move towards adolescence, the internal organization of emotion and behaviour extends to taking note of the affective states of others and the social and cultural environments in which these occur (Grossman 1995).

Adolescents therefore develop ways of thinking about and representing the world around them (Howe *et al.* 1999). As children, they acquired internal working models of their own worthiness based upon the attachment figure's availability, ability and willingness to provide care and protection (Ainsworth *et al.* 1978). The internal working models are argued to contain expectations and beliefs about:

1. the self

2. other people

3. the relationship that develops between the self and others.

The adolescent continually learns about the self, others and the interactive relationship as they experience relationships (Howe *et al.* 1999). Having developed an internal working model of their own behaviour and that of the attachment figures in childhood, the adolescent then habitually uses the internal working models to organize expectations and guide behaviours in all other significant relationships. These include peer relationships, dating relationships, relationships with those in authority, teachers and coaches, relationships with social workers, counsellors and group facilitators.

The internal models employed by the adolescent tend to become self-fulfilling as parents, caregivers, peers, social workers and others react or behave congruently with their expectations. The critical aspect here is that experiences in the adolescent's life are organized and understood according to the model, rather than the working model being modified by new experiences (Howe *et al.* 1999). New relationships formed by the adolescent are created in accordance with their internal model, which is based on their previous relationship experiences (Howe *et al.* 1999). Young people who have experienced disrupted attachments, for example, those experiencing transitions within formalized care systems, or those involved with social workers in agencies where there are high staff turnovers, generally have ample opportunity to maintain their insecure attachment beliefs about others. Hence, their new care experiences can serve to reinforce their insecure attachment-based internal model.

The development of the internal working model, then, involves a complex interplay of the young person's sense of self in relation to the attachment figure and their positive or negative evaluation of the attachment figure. In this model, the adolescent's sense of self is appraised in relation to the attachment figure's responses to them. The self is evaluated as either deserving of care or not, worthy of protection or not, loveable/likeable or not, valued or not, worthy of interest and attention or not, socially effective or not, competent or not. This process evokes an evaluation of self that is either positive or negative (Howe *et al.* 1999).

The quality of the interaction between the child and their attachment figure(s) is argued to serve a critical function in the development of the internal working model (Howe *et al.* 1999). For example, a caregiver who is able to demonstrate sensitivity, co-operation, consistency, accessibility, availability, and acceptance can create an environment within which the young person can learn to regulate and when necessary reduce their feelings of intense emotion. This generally enables them to better manage their affective responses. This coping capacity can then be incorporated into their internal model. Alternatively, if a caregiver is insensitive, emotionally or physically unavailable, rejecting or interfering, the young person, while still experiencing high affective arousal, is less likely to be able to regulate or reduce the intensity of their feelings. In addition, the familial backgrounds of adolescents who engage in offending or anti-social behaviour are often characterized by instability, poor boundaries, and criminal or anti-social role-modelling. Such backgrounds are more likely to result in the young person having a limited ability to regulate their emotions. In response to these experiences being repeated over time and contexts, the adolescent may develop maladaptive behaviours such as engaging in emotional abuse, violence or aggression, self-harming and/or risk-taking behaviours.

Why explore issues of attachment when working with adolescents?

Without privileging parent–child relationships as the sole determinant of children's behaviour Howe *et al.* (1999) advocate strongly for consideration of the nature of close relationships or attachment experiences in assessment and practice interventions with adolescents and their families. Drawing attention to the importance of a developmental perspective that encompasses an individual's historical and current socio-emotional experiences, they argue that this perspective provides important insight into personality factors, styles of caregiving and the nature of interpersonal relationships.

In working with adolescents individually, within family contexts, and in groups, social work practitioners endeavour to assess and understand behaviour, and the interrelated patterns of thinking and affective responses. Understanding internal models of attachment and how they impact on the young person's capacity to adjust to their environment increases the potential for more effective work with both the young person and the family system more broadly. For example, a worker who is knowledgeable about internal models of attachment and their impact on a young person's behaviour can help a new foster family work through their confusion and bewilderment caused by a young person's rejection of their offers of love and support. The worker can assist the family in developing routines, consistent strategies and clear limits with an ambivalently attached youth in their care. Likewise, the worker can assist a family in understanding the need to provide care and support and keep the avoidant adolescent close, despite the family members' urge to push them away in frustration.

Equally, within the group-work setting, these understandings can help exasperated workers better understand an adolescent's dismissal of care, support and ideas offered by the facilitators. The workers can then employ attachment focused responses within the group setting that might include: increased structure and routine, reciprocity, caring, consistent and positive affect as well as empathy (Levy and Orlans 2003). Hence, an understanding of a young person's internal model of attachment can help the worker to better understand and work with the consequential adaptive or maladaptive attachment behaviour.

Attachment behaviour is considered to be any behaviour designed to evoke a close, protective relationship with attachment figures when the adolescent experiences anxiety/distress. Attachment behaviour is frequently described as a way for infants to have their basic needs met (for instance, food, shelter, protection from danger, comfort, security). Later, within an adolescent's developmental trajectory, attachment behaviour is a habitual or automatic response to feeling insecure or distressed and is designed to bring that young person into close proximity to and elicit particular responses from attachment figures. Attachment behaviour can be adaptive or maladaptive, depending on the nature of their internal model. Secure attachment requires a perception that the attachment figure is psychologically *and* physically available to them (Howe *et al.* 1999). The adolescent is then able to explore the world, and the new experiences often associated with this developmental or life stage, from a secure base (Moretti and Holland 2003). It is also suggested that the peer relationships formed in adolescence in time replace the attachment to parents (Freeman and Bradford Brown 2001). Understanding the nature of peer attachments then becomes important to practice. Because of the greater significance of peer relationships to the adolescent, it is imperative that assessments undertaken access relationships with peers as well as familial and extra-familial attachment figures.

Adolescents with a history of multiple care placements are likely to experience attachment figures as physically and emotionally unavailable. Social workers working with adolescents in these circumstances need to be aware that they are not likely to perceive the new caregiver as an attachment figure in the first instance and that this may not change within the time span of the placement. It is noted by Howe (1995, p.110) that '(C)hildren who are placed for adoption or with foster parents are expected to relate to these caregivers as securely attached children... children's previous attachment experiences will initially affect the way they relate to new caregivers.' In these situations the worker has a clear role in advocating for financial and time resources to assist in the processes of skill acquisition and relationship building between the young person and the caregiver(s). Additionally, the worker has an educative role, providing encouragement, support and promoting skill acquisition as well as a role in normalizing caregivers responses when they 'don't like' the adolescent in their care.

Attachment-focused practice requires that a worker pay attention to all attachment relationships, and assess the nature of those relationships. Daniel and Taylor (2001) note that when a father is absent it is important for the worker to consider the nature of the separation in their assessment. There may be unresolved guilt toward the father that may impact on the young person's future attachment relationships. Within an assessment process, Daniel and Taylor also argue that it is critical to consider whether other father figures have been present and the reasons for their absence. In these situations, dealing with consequential grief and loss may be critical to the work. This assessment is likely to involve the collation of information from a variety of sources and enables the worker to also consider whether absent family have the potential to continue to act as an attachment figure (Daniel and Taylor 2001).

Despite the insights gained from interventions and research with children and adults in the attachment field, comparatively little research and clinical investigation has been undertaken with adolescents (Moretti and Holland 2003). One of the problems in assessing attachment style and attachment behaviour in adolescents is the lack of empirically validated assessment tools available. Adult attachment interviews and inventories comprise of items that are developmentally inappropriate for adolescents, and the assessment measures used for children are equally inappropriate, leaving the social worker to rely primarily on the attachment interview.

Current knowledge and research into the area of attachment is more exploratory and descriptive rather than explanatory in nature, which limits the ways that this information can be used in informing assessments, making recommendations and treatment planning. The application and utility of attachment theory in clinical and research contexts across a variety of practice areas has been widely documented (see Bretherton 1992; Rutter 1995). For example, a relationship between insecure attachment patterns and anti-social behaviour in late childhood and adolescence has been documented in research in this area (Greenberg *et al.* 1997; Rosenstein and Horowitz 1996). However, like all correlational research findings, research pertaining to the relationship between attachment style and anti-social or offending behaviour is likely to be affected by a range of other factors, including gender, temperament and the number of out-of-home placements. Therefore, the attachment style of the adolescent who has offended, or quality of the attachment relationship, cannot be utilized as predictive tool regarding treatment outcomes or likely reoccurrence of the problematic behaviours. It is not yet clear whether attachment styles can be seen as predictive of severity of anti-social behaviour (current or future) and future research in this area is clearly warranted (Speltz, DeKleyn and Greenberg 1999).

Despite difficulties in measuring attachment for adolescents, social work assessments need to include consideration of the individual's attachment style, as well as implications of this in terms of interventions and recommendations. Being able to demonstrate how attachment impacts on a young person's developmental trajectory and future life chances may be critical in strengthening a case for securing treatment and/or service resources.

Issues of attachment in alternative care

Social workers are involved in placing young people with a range of personal and interpersonal issues in care situations for a variety of reasons. Alternative care placements are frequently described on a continuum. This includes low intervention options such as placement with extended family or foster situations through to group homes or specialist residential facilities.

In New Zealand, recent press releases from the Department of Child, Youth and Family (CYF) indicate that the numbers of children in care has risen significantly, from 3,265 in 1999 to 4,480 in 2002 (Department of Child, Youth and Family press release, 2003). Accommodating adolescents in state care has been and continues to be a significant challenge for the service.

In Great Britain there has also been a movement away from residential care facilities with an increased emphasis on foster care placements for children and young people. For specific groups of young people, such as those who have sexually abused, this poses a multitude of problems (Bankes, Daniels and Quartly 1999). Adequate resourcing is a fundamental issue in relation to care of children and young people. However, intensive resourcing alone does not produce good outcomes for young people in care. Political, financial and professional restraints all impact on appropriate placement outcomes (Bankes *et al.* 1999). Family factors, and how workers respond to them, are equally critical to good outcomes for children and young people.

Removal from home will inevitably have an impact on the family system and needs to be a part of a carefully planned and integrated process. It is imperative that placements are sourced according to the needs of the adolescent and that corrective attachment experiences are engaged in. Unfortunately, placement is often dictated by availability rather than what is best suited to the adolescent's needs and level of risk, or others placed there (Bankes *et al.* 1999). For example, Araji (1997) reported that around 50 per cent of sexually aggressive children and/or young people were placed in the only placement available.

A paucity of resources surrounding placement options for young people and the professionals working with them can be linked to indiscriminate placement and lack of planning (Bankes *et al.* 1999; Green and Masson 2002). Farmer and Pollock (1998) highlight that a lack of planning is characterized by inadequate preparation, training, supervision and support of carers, and low engagement of child protection services. It is indicated that this pattern results in placement difficulties, which include difficulties maintaining young person in treatment, high stress for caregivers and difficulty in managing move-on or family re-integration. Therefore, factors that reflect insecure attachment lead to reinforcement of these patterns in a systemic way – placement breakdown – frequent moves with sometimes as little as an hour's notice. Furthermore, the ability to implement attachment-focused interventions depends upon the relationship between caregivers and the professionals they are working with, as well as the caregiver's passion or interest in the attachment ideas (Golding 2003). When caregivers are stressed and poorly resourced enthusiasm for intensive attachment-focused interventions is less likely.

Often based on social learning and behavioural perspectives, traditional models for residential care are primarily grounded in the assumption that difficult or problematic behaviour needs to be contained and controlled (Moore, Moretti and Holland 1998). Green and Masson (2002) highlight that regimentation and rigidity are often evident in reduced spontaneity and individuality. From an attachment perspective this type of residential environment contributes to maintenance of insecure attachment styles via staff turnover, inconsistent approaches, lack of warmth and connection in the residence. A control and containment approach may well further damage fragile attachment bonds formed by the adolescent (Moore *et al.* 1998). Furthermore, the efficacy of behavioural interventions in the residential context can be questioned when staff are working with adolescents who have developed internal working models of adults as unreliable, untrustworthy, rejecting and punitive (Moore *et al.* 1998). It is possible to advance the argument that the function of the aggressive behaviour needs to be considered from an attachment perspective and guide interventions with the adolescent alongside other intervention approaches.

Young people who have experienced disrupted care histories or distant parent or caregiver figures are likely to have developed insecure attachment styles. Many have also had disrupted school histories with associated changes in adult figures (teachers, social workers, health care professionals, and so on).

The young person's behaviour maintains the attachment style. The systems that they are part of also maintain the attachment style. The system can reinforce the young person's beliefs, through ongoing exposure, that adults are not reliable and will not be around. There is a clear onus on statutory and community based services to provide the stability and resourcing required for planned transitions and positive outcomes for young people in care.

Returning to the family: attachment issues following alternative care

Periods of residential care for adolescents can be extensive, particularly for those adolescents who have taken part in residential treatment services for sexually abusive behaviour and offending. The following transcript from a clinical interview with an adolescent who has had extended time away from family illustrates some of these transitional issues:

Interviewer: I'm interested in that idea of learning to do things again in a different way and I am wondering how that fits with your relationship with your family?

Adam: Pretty huge. Yeah, um, I'm totally different to before I came to [the programme]. I used to take them for granted. Just do whatever I wanted and expect them to listen to me and obey what I say. And now it's really…well, I really fucked up, and trying to…become part of my family again and they have moved on, and I haven't and so I have to learn to move on, move up almost.

Interviewer: Say some more about that.

Adam: Well, they have gone past me and it's like I have been here for two and…about three years and it's really a long time. And sort of life has slipped me by… I mean, my family has slipped me by, so I have to learn to come back.

Understanding a young person's attachment style and internal model of attachment can help to work through issues of transition, and the complexities of reconnecting family relationships following such periods of separation. Secure attachment with key adults can be seen as promoting closeness and connection as well as shared values and identification with relevant societal norms. In viewing the attachment figure(s) positively, the adolescent is likely to have an investment in conformity and refrain from engaging in anti-social behaviour. Alternatively, those with juvenile offending problems may have little regard for parental or societal values. It is possible to understand this pattern as a function of insecure attachment styles, leading to conformity only in the presence of supervision and threats of consequences. Additionally, poor attachment to key adults is likely to contribute to poor pro-social skills and may be related to association with delinquent peers leading to involvement in offending behaviours, and in some cases the development of deviant behaviours and substance use by young people (Elliot, Huizinga and Menard 1989).

In the clinical example above, Adam suggests that the onus is upon him to make the necessary adjustments to life back in the family. However, inevitably, whole family system adjustments are more likely to result in successful transitions. Sometimes young people returning home can be confronted with an unchanged family system, and the benefits of new learning within the residential environment can be endangered. Marshall *et al.* (1993), highlight the relationship between parenting skill deficiencies (that is, inappropriate supervision, rejection) and adolescent problem behaviour. These authors note, like Bowlby, that attachment is only one of the behavioural systems operating in the parent–child relationship. Parents model appropriate and inappropriate behaviours in the home and when this is considered alongside the attachment patterns, the family can be seem as a powerful vehicle for maintaining or disrupting the abusive patterns.

Inclusion of family therapy work with adolescents enables attachment-focused therapeutic work to explore the nature of attachments within family relationships and the development of new, shared understandings and patterns of communication.

Issues for practice

For many children and adolescents the primary attachment figure is their mother or main caregiver, and this has certainly been the focus of early research and theorizing in cultures where the role of female as caregiver has been valued. However, the notion of 'family' is not static – indeed, contemporary family systems are increasingly diverse, as are the roles and expectations within family groups. In addition, while a small number of cross-cultural studies have been undertaken, most empirical work has been with white nuclear families (Daniel and Taylor 2001).

Cultural understandings of attachment are likely to vary, and the utility of the assessment of attachment across ethnic groups raises a number of important questions for practice. While it is commonly accepted in the literature that children may have a small number of attachment figures, this may not be relevant for families cross-culturally where there is a greater emphasis on collective family care. It is likely that extended family constructions did not inform the development of attachment theory, and as such diverse cultural configurations are unlikely to be well represented in the development of established theoretical frameworks. These cultural considerations lead to challenges both with respect to the universality of attachment categorizations and the universal relevancy of attachment measurement. Attachment theory needs to be tested not only in terms of ethnicity but also in relation to other diverse family situations. For example, the development of attachment patterns and family relationships for children of gay and lesbian parents is a relatively unexplored area (Josephson 2003). When social workers employ attachment approaches within their practice, they need to do so alongside a developed understanding of the cultural context of the families with whom they work. In other words, any model that attempts to explain the nature and dynamics of family needs to be carefully critiqued and scrutinized for cultural relevance and fit within culturally-responsive practice.

With the provision of an attachment focused intervention, young people have the opportunity to experience a therapeutic relationship that is stable, supportive and consistent. In experiencing group work with co-gender facilitation there is an opportunity for young people to observe and develop new patterns with male and female adults that can be used to deconstruct the gendered understandings that they might have previously developed.

There is a multiplicity of implications for attachment focused practice. There are implications for workers, programmes, agencies and, critically, for clients. Workers require adequate training and knowledge of attachment theory in order to integrate this approach with others that inform practice interventions. Workers need time to build relationships and to undertake more in-depth work with families. This raises issues for the agency. Importantly, the agency or programme needs to foster an environment within which staff are able to model attachment focused approaches. It is intensive work that requires resources. Staff retention rates need to be high, workloads manageable and resourcing and training appropriate.

Ultimately, attachment focused work has the potential to respond to some of the deeply significant issues confronting young people. Indeed, we would argue that a failure to address issues of attachment in adolescent work may impact on a young person's ability to maintain positive, enduring attachments in later life. In the long term, resources dedicated to attachment focused work may well prove to be resources well spent.

Questions for reflection

1. Do internal models of attachment relationships help explain interpersonal dynamics and processes?

2. What are the limitations around assessment of attachment in adolescence?

3. What are the cultural and contextual factors that need to be considered in relation to attachment theory and attachment focused assessment?

4. What are the particular attachment issues in the residential context?

5. What are the resourcing implications of working from an attachment approach?

6. What might be the implications of not doing attachment focused work?

References

Ainsworth, M.D.S., Blehar, M., Walters, E. and Walls, S. (1978) *Patterns of Attachment.* Hillsdale, NJ: Erlbaum.

Araji, S. (1997) *Sexually Aggressive Children: Coming to Understand Them.* Thousand Oaks, CA: Sage.

Bankes, N., Daniels, K. and Quartly, C. (1999) 'Placement provisions and decisions.' In M. Erooga and H. Masson (eds) *Children and Young People who Sexually Abuse Others: Challenges And Responses.* London: Routledge.

Bretherton, I. (1992) 'The origins of attachment theory: John Bowlby and Mary Ainsworth.' *Developmental Psychology 28*, 5, 729–775.

Child, Youth and Family Press Release, November, 2003. Wellington: New Zealand.

Daniel, B. and Taylor, J. (2001) *Engaging with Fathers. Practice Issues for Health and Social Care.* London: Jessica Kingsley Publishers.

Elliot, D.S., Huizinga, D. and Menard, S. (1989) *Multiple Problem Youth: Delinquency, Substance Use and Mental Health Problems.* New York: Springer-Verlag.

Farmer, E. and Pollock, S. (1998) *Sexually Abused and Abusing Children in Substitute Care.* Chichester: Wiley.

Fletcher, G. (2002) *The New Science Of Intimate Relationships.* Oxford: Blackwell.

Freemen, H. and Bradford Brown, B. (2001) 'Primary attachment to parents and peers during adolescence: Differences by attachment style.' *Journal of Youth and Adolescence 30*, 6, 653–674.

George, C. (1996) 'A representational perspective of child abuse and prevention: Internal working models of attachment and caregiving.' *Child Abuse and Neglect 20*, 5, 411–24.

Green, L. and Masson, H. (2002) 'Adolescents who sexually abuse and residential accommodation: Issues of risk and vulnerability.' *British Journal of Social Work 32*, 149–168.

Greenberg, M.T., DeKleyn, M., Speltz, M.L. and Endrign, M.C. (1997) 'The role of attachment processes in externalising psychopathology in young children.' In L. Aitkinson and K.J. Zucker (eds) *Attachment and Psychopathology.* New York: Guilford Press.

Golding, K. (2003) 'Helping foster carers, helping children: Using attachment theory to guide practice.' *Adoption and Fostering 27*, 2, 64.

Grossmann, K.E. (1995) 'Evolution and history of attachment research.' In S. Goldberg, R. Muir and J. Kerr (eds). *Attachment Theory: Social Development And Clinical Perspectives.* Hillsdale, NJ: Analytic Press.

Howe, D. (1995) *Attachment Theory for Social Work Practice.* Houndmills: Palgrave.

Howe, D., Brandon, M., Hinings, D. and Schofield, G. (1999) *Attachment Theory, Child Maltreatment and Family Support. A Practice and Assessment Model.* Houndmills: Palgrave.

Josephson, G.J. (2003) 'Using an attachment-based intervention with same-sex couples.' In S.M. Johnson and V.E Whiffen (eds) *Attachment Processes in Couple and Family Therapy.* London: Guilford Press.

Levy, T.M., and Orlans, M. (2003) In S.M. Johnson and V.E Whiffen (eds) *Attachment Processes in Couple and Family Therapy*. London: Guilford Press.

Marshall, W.L., Hudson, S.M. and Hodkinson, S. (1993) 'The importance of attachment bonds in the development of juvenile sexual offending.' In H.E. Barbaree, W.L. Marshall and S.M. Hudson (eds) *Assessment and Treatment of the Juvenile Sexual Offender*. Guilford Press.

Moore, K., Moretti, M.M. and Holland, R. (1998) 'A new perspective on youth care programmes: Using attachment theory to guide interventions for troubled youth.' *Residential Treatment for Children and Youth 15*, 3, 1–24.

Moretti, M.M and Holland, R. (2003) 'The journey of adolescence: Transitions in self within the context of attachment relationships.' In S.M. Johnson and V.E Whiffen (eds) *Attachment Processes in Couple and Family Therapy*. London: Guilford Press.

Rosenstein, D.S. and Horowitz, H.A. (1996). 'Adolescent attachment and psychopathology.' *Journal of Consulting and Clinical Psychology 64*, 2, 244–253.

Rutter, M. (1995) 'Clinical implications of attachment concepts: Retrospect and prospect.' *Journal of Child Psychiatry and Allied Discpilines 36*, 4, 549–571.

Rutter, M., Giller, H. and Hagell, A. (1998) *Antisocial Behaviour by Young People*. Cambridge: Cambridge University Press.

Speltz, M.L., DeKleyn, M. and Greenberg, M.T. (1999) 'Attachment in boys with early onset conduct problems.' *Development and Psychopathology 11*, 269–285.

Further reading

Heinz Brisch, K. (2002) *Treating Attachment Disorders: From Theory to Therapy*. New York: Guilford Press.

Howe, D., Brandon, M., Hinings, D. and Schofield, G. (1999) *Attachment Theory, Child Maltreatment and Family Support. A Practice and Assessment Model*. Houndmills: Palgrave.

Johnson, S.M. and Whiffen, V.E. (eds) (2003) *Attachment Processes in Couple and Family Therapy*. London: Guilford Press.

Levy, T.M. and Orlans, M. (1998) *Attachment, Trauma and Healing: Understanding and Treating Attachment Disorder in Children and Families*. Washington, DC: Child Welfare League of America.

Conclusion: Integrated Theory in Action

Kieran O'Donoghue, Mary Nash and Robyn Munford

This final chapter brings together the principles of the integrated practice framework through an illustrative case study. Integrated practice takes into account several contexts, namely:

- client world
- practitioner world
- social service agency
- wider social and community environment (see Figure 15.1).

The authors in the book have shown effective practice by illustrating in their chapters how these four contexts provide the foundation for effective integrated practice. This includes:

- the practitioner's personal and professional worldview
- specialist knowledge concerning issues, client group and community
- theoretical lenses and concepts
- prescriptive models and methods
- skills and strategies (see Figure 15.2).

Best practice includes all of these elements as illustrated in the chapters. Central to this practice is ongoing critical reflection.

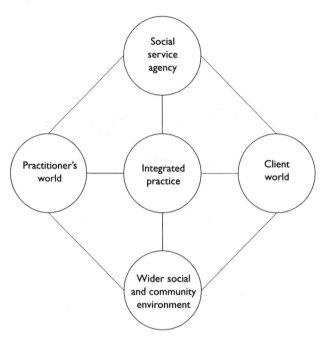

Figure 15.1 Locating integrated practice

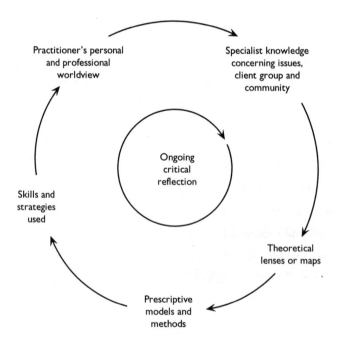

Figure 15.2 Integrated practice framework

Case study

The following case study is an illustration of integrated practice in action. The case study is presented in a narrative format with reflection moments woven throughout.

Introductory narrative

David is an 80-year-old man who has been married to Mae for 54 years. Mae is 75 years old. David and Mae have five adult children. The children's names are Frank, Rachel, Barry, Adelaide and Brigid. The children and their families either live close to or within an hour's travel from David and Mae's home. Recently, David's health has been declining and he was admitted to hospital with pneumonia. Following an intensive battery of medical investigations, it was discovered that David had an advanced and aggressive form of cancer. The oncologist has told David the news and explained that they cannot cure the cancer and that the only thing that they can do is to help him be comfortable. The oncologist advised that he would contact the palliative care co-ordinator and the ward social worker who would help plan his discharge from hospital.

Charlotte, the social worker, has received David's referral from the palliative care co-ordinator. She starts to reflect on it and her initial thoughts concern her worldview and feelings in relation to older people, terminal illness, death and loss. She starts to imagine who her client is and what their outlook on the world might be and how can she locate herself in relation to this. Upon re-reading the referral, Charlotte starts to tentatively identify for herself the specialist knowledge she might draw from in relation to possible issues, the illness, the discharge planning process, older people in general, as well as people and their families who are facing death. She also starts to consider what possible community supports and resources may be available or needed.

REFLECTIVE MOMENT 1

If you were the social worker:

- Where would you locate yourself in relation to the client(s) and their outlook on the world?

- What cultural frameworks would influence your thinking? Other worldviews?

- What would be your preliminary and tentative thoughts about this referral?

- What aspects of ecological systems perspective, community development, strengths-based practice and attachment theory might help you prepare to work with the client(s)? What other theoretical approaches are relevant?

- How would you plan to engage David and Mae? And their family?

Engagement narrative

Shortly after reading the referral, Charlotte goes to see David. She introduces herself and checks out with David whether he is up to talking with her at this time. When he says 'yes' she explains to him what her job involves. David tells Charlotte that he is worried about Mae and asks that someone carefully explains the situation to her. He is also unclear about what a discharge from hospital will mean for Mae, who is not in the best health herself, since she suffers from arthritis and high-blood pressure. He also tells Charlotte that he is not sure how Mae will take the news and he wonders whether Charlotte could be present when Mae is told. David states that the doctor will be telling Mae this afternoon when he does his rounds. He also tells Charlotte that Mae comes in every day at visiting time and stays with him until visiting time ends. Charlotte asks David about how he would prefer that Mae is told the news. David says he wants to tell her himself, and asks if Charlotte could come back to see him just prior to visiting time and be there when he tells Mae. Charlotte agrees and then briefly asks David whether he had thought about where he would go once he was discharged from hospital. David indicates that he has not thought about this yet. Charlotte says, 'Perhaps we could talk with Mae and your family about that later?' David replies, 'Yes, later'. Charlotte leaves David, who rests till visiting time.

Mae arrives at the ward at 2pm precisely and goes straight down to see David. When she gets down to David's room, she is surprised to see this young woman with David. Charlotte greets Mae respectfully and introduces herself as a social worker. She then asks David and Mae if they would like a drink. They both say 'That would be lovely, dear' and Charlotte goes and gets them a cup of tea each. When she returns with the cups of tea, David tells Mae that they have found cancer and that he has got about a month to live. He also mentions that the doctor will be coming in to see them later and that she can ask questions then. After Mae and David's tears subside. Charlotte asks Mae and David if she can check in with them later in the day, perhaps at 4pm after the doctor has seen them.

REFLECTIVE MOMENT 2

If you were the social worker:

- What would be your initial reaction to this engagement narrative?

- How would you engage these client(s) respectfully if they were Maori or another cultural group, different from you own? Or if they were migrants and refugees?

- What ideas from the various chapters in this book could you use to inform you in engaging with these client(s)?

- What things would you want to know from the client(s) to help you in your work with them?

- What questions would you be taking to supervision?

- Which other professionals and networks would be involved at this stage, other than those already mentioned?

Information gathering narrative

Charlotte returns to see David and Mae just after 4pm. She exchanges greetings with them again and then asks them about whether they have seen the doctor this afternoon and what has happened at that meeting? David and Mae report that Dr Warner has seen them and explained everything, and said that David can go home in a couple of days. Charlotte asks if they can recall whether Dr Warner mentioned about hospice and nursing care for David? They answer that he did say something about that, and then said that the palliative care co-ordinator and Charlotte would arrange everything. Charlotte then explains that her role is to work with David, Mae and their family to ensure that when David leaves the hospital he has the best care possible. For this to occur, she she will need help both from them and their family so that a decision can be made about where the best place might be for David to go upon leaving hospital, who will be caring for him and what is needed to make sure that he is well cared for. Charlotte then spends some time listening to David and Mae talk about their concerns. After about half an hour, Charlotte leaves after arranging a further meeting with them both at 10am the next day. She signals that at this meeting she would like to discuss with them their wishes and needs. Upon leaving, Charlotte tells David and Mae that other family members will be most welcome to come to the meeting the next day.

The next day Charlotte meets with David, Mae, Frank and Rachel. She greets each person respectfully and introduces herself and briefly describes her role. She then discusses with them their wishes, their home, family, Mae's health, people or groups that David and Mae belong to that might be able to help them at this time. After this general conversation, the focus turns to exploring the options for discharge. This involved imagining what it would be like if David went home, or to a hospice and how his needs would be met. This discussion includes the practicalities of the activities of daily living such as toileting and bathing. As they discuss the various issues, Charlotte offers information concerning resources that the DHB will provide for David if he goes home. These include a hospital bed, linen, bedpans, commode, hospice respite or day stay services and access to nursing and other supports. She also outlines what will happen if David enters the hospice and gives them brochures on the hospice's services.

REFLECTIVE MOMENT 3

If you were the social worker:

- How would you go about gathering information?

- What ideas from the theories outlined in previous chapters would guide you in your information gathering?

- How would your information gathering process be different if these client(s) were Maori or another cultural group (and a group different from you own) or migrants and refugees?

- What would be your assessment at this stage and how would you share this with the client(s)?

Assessment and planning / contracting narrative

After about three quarters of an hour and in a pause in the conversation, Charlotte says: 'We have been talking for nearly an hour and I am wondering from your point of view what things are important for us to be working on now?' The family members present state that:

1. They want to spend as much time as is left with David and prefer that he comes home.

2. They want to know that should David come home for the remainder of his days that: a) he has everything he needs to be as comfortable as possible and b) that Mae is not left on her own caring for David and that there is help at hand and support for her too.

David then indicates that he needs to rest, so Charlotte asks him if it is alright if they go out for a little while, get another drink and develop an initial plan that they can start putting into action. David is happy with this.

They all go down to the hospital cafeteria and work out the following plan:

Goal

- For David to come home on Friday.

Tasks

- Charlotte to send a community referral through to the hospice by 5pm this afternoon.

- Charlotte also to send an urgent request through to the palliative care co-ordinator to arrange for the delivery of a hospital bed, linen, pillows, bedpans, commode, catheter bags etc. by 5pm this afternoon.

- Frank to develop the roster of support for Mae and send it to Charlotte and everyone else by Wednesday.

- Mae to contact the caring community she belongs to and ask if they could help her with the housework and occasional meal, by Wednesday.

- Charlotte to arrange for the family support co-ordinator at the hospice to meet David, Mae and any other family members prior to his discharge on Friday.

- Charlotte to advise and liaise with medical and nursing staff to ensure that David is discharged on Friday with an adequate supply of medication.

- Charlotte to arrange with St John's Ambulance to take David home on Friday. This booking to be made on Thursday once the doctor approves the discharge.

REFLECTIVE MOMENT 4

If you were the social worker:

- What would be your assessment and plan? And how might that assessment and plan be different if the client(s) were Maori or another cultural group (and a group different from your own), migrants and refugees?

- How would your assessment and plan be informed by the elements of the integrated practice framework described in Figure 15.2?

- How would you record this information and how would you share it with the family?

- How would you engage other professionals and informal networks? Which other networks might Charlotte have identified?

- Which aspects of ecological systems theory, community development, strengths-based practice and attachment theory could contribute to the assessment and planning process? And other theoretical approaches?

- Which intervention model would you use in the next stage and how would this be informed by theory?

- How will you engage in critical reflection? What would you take to the supervision meeting?

Intervention, monitoring and review narrative

Over the next few days, Charlotte and the family work on the tasks they have developed in the plan. Charlotte sends the referral through and the urgent request for delivery of the bed and other equipment to the palliative care co-ordinator, who subsequently contacts her about the orderlies only being able to deliver this equipment on Thursday and in the afternoon. Charlotte talks with Mae and other family members about this, and helps them work out a solution whereby Adelaide's eldest son, Tipene, will spend Thursday at Mae's house so that some one is home and so that Mae can visit David as usual.

On Wednesday, morning Frank contacts Charlotte and advises her that he has had some challenges with developing the roster because people keep ringing him to make changes. Also a roster for the month seems to be too unwieldy. Charlotte arranges to meet with Frank at the hospital during his lunch break. At this meeting, Charlotte and Frank rework the roster by changing it to a fortnightly one that is continuous, by including adult grand-children and developing a list of reserves for each day. Frank, drawing on his staff management experience from Telecom, also writes some guidelines for the roster that include: if people need to change times they are responsible for finding their own replacement, and if someone does not turn up, Mae could call the reserve who would either come or follow up with the person listed.

Also on Wednesday, Charlotte sees Mae when she, Adelaide and Barry are visiting David. On this occasion, Charlotte introduces herself to Adelaide and Barry and updates the family on progress with the plan. Mae tells Charlotte that she has been unable to bring herself to ring the caring community about help with the housework and the occasional meal. Charlotte hears from Mae that she is finding it hard to come to terms with David's diagnosis and has not been sleeping that well. Charlotte asks Mae what would help. Mae answers that she would like some company in the evenings after she comes back from the hospital. Adelaide says, 'Tipene is currently on a study break from university and he was going to stay at your house tomorrow afternoon anyway. What about I call him and arrange for him to come over tonight and stay through till Saturday?' Mae is happy with this suggestion. Adelaide says 'How about I ring

Janice at the caring community for you as well?' Mae replies, 'Oh, that would a great help, dear. I wasn't looking forward to talking to Janice about it – you know how she makes a fuss.'

Charlotte then tells the family that she has spoken with Sarah, the family support co-ordinator at the hospice and that she will be coming over to meet David and any other family members who will be here at 2.30pm the next day. Charlotte also suggests that after that meeting it would be good if she could briefly catch up with the family and check that everything is in place for David to go home on Friday.

REFLECTIVE MOMENT 5

You are the social worker and you are presenting this work to your supervisor:

- How would you tell the story of your practice with the client(s) to date?

- What model of practice and skills would you say you are using?

- What concepts from ecological systems theory, community development, strengths-based practice and attachment theory (and other theories) would you use to explain your practice?

- How would you outline the resources you were using (including formal and informal networks)?

- How would you describe the cultural frameworks you are using and their integration into your practice?

- What plans will you outline to your supervisor in terms of your future work with this family?

Evaluation, review and closure narrative

On Thursday the equipment arrives and is set up in Mae and David's house. Dr Warner and the palliative care team approve David's discharge and the ambulance is booked to take him home at 10am on Friday. Adelaide has spoken to Janice who has arranged for Flora and Jim to do some housework and bring an evening meal for Mae. Tipene is now staying at Mae and David's house and Frank has distributed the roster to everyone. At 2.30pm David, Mae, Frank, Adelaide, Brigid and Barry all meet with Sarah from the hospice and become clear about what services are available to David and to them. They also arrange with Sarah to have a family meeting with her at home early next week. Once Sarah leaves Charlotte reviews with the family what will be happening the next day and checks out with them that everything is in place and whether there is anything else she can do. She then says goodbye to them individually and wishes them all the best for their time together.

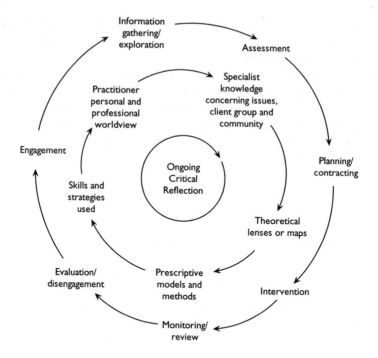

Figure 15.3 Integrated framework in practice

Charlotte does not see the family again in person, because on Friday morning she is involved in working with another family. On Friday afternoon, before finishing work, Charlotte makes a brief telephone call to Mae and David and checks that everything has gone to plan, which it has. Upon putting down the phone, Charlotte finishes the cup of tea on her desk, gets her things together and goes home to her family (see Figure 15.3).

Questions for reflection

1. Referring to Figure 15.3, how did Charlotte use the differing lenses as she worked through the phases of practice with family?

2. Which lenses would you use if you were in Charlotte's position?

3. How might your work with the family be different if the client(s) were:

   a) Maori or another cultural group (a group other than your own), migrants and refugees?

   b) At a different stage in their lifespan?

   c) A family with few informal supports and without a supportive family living close by?

Glossary of Maori and Pacific Words

ako	teach and learn
Aotearoa	name used by Maori for New Zealand, literally, Land of the White Cloud
atua	God
faikava	kava drinking ceremony
faka'apa'apa	to show deference or respect
fakatokilalo	to be humble
fano, fono	workshops/meetings
fetokoni'aki	helping eacho other; mutual assistance
ha'a tu'i	royalty
hapu	sub-tribe, made up of extended families
hapu whakapapa	subtribal geneology
Hokio	name of a stream in the Horowhenua
hou'eiki	chiefs
hui	gathering, meeting
iwi	tribe, tribal group
kaikaranga	woman who welcomes visitors with a call
kaiarahi	leader, guide
kaimahi	worker
karakia	prayer, incantation
kau tu'a	commoners
kaumatua	elder
koka'anga	women's groups for staining bark cloth (tapa)
koloa	riches
korero	talk, speak
mahi tahi	working together, working as one

mana	prestige
mana motuhake maori	Maori independence
mano	thousand
Maori	native, indigenous New Zealander
marae	place, courtyard
matapule	chief's attendant and spokesperson
moemoea	dream
nga matatini Maori	Maori diverse realities
nga moemoea a te hapu	dreams of the subtribe
ngati	descendant of
Ngati Pareraukawa	descendants of Pareraukawa
Ngatokowaru	the name of an ancestor
'ofa	love or compassion
Pakeha	non-Maori European New Zealander
palangi	Western or "white"
puao-te-ata-tu	day break
Raukawa	the name of an eponymous ancestor
taiao	environment, world
takanga 'enau fohe	proverb translated as 'mates at their oars; perhaps their oars are mates'
tangata whaiora	mental health clinics
tangata whenua	people of the land
taonga	taonga, gift, treasure
Tararua	mountain range in the North Island
tauiwi	foreigner
tautau	stewardship (Samoa)
te ao Maori	the Maori world
Te Kohanga Reo	Language Nest – Maori Pre-school
Te Komako	title in Maori of Maori issues of *Social Work Review* – key social work journal in Aotearoa/New Zealand

te taha hinengaro	emotional, mental side
te taha tinana	physical side
te taha wairua	spiritual side
te taha whanau	family side
Te Ukaipo	maternal, mother
Te Tiriti o Waitangi	the Treaty of Waitangi
te whai matauranga	seeking knowledge
te whai rauemi	seeking resources
te whare tapa wha	the four sides of a house
teina	younger person, younger brother or sister
tikanga	customs
tino rangatiratanga	self-determination
tipuna, tapuna (pl.)	ancestor
tohi	ceremony which celebrates a rite of passage
tokoni	help
totara	a species of native tree
toulalanga	to work for one another in turn in weaving
toutu'u	plantation divided into strips (one for each person)
tu mau	stand strong (Tokelau)
tuakana	older person
waiata	song, composition
wairua	spirituality
whakapakari whanau	strengthening family
Whakakotahi	to bring together, to make one
Whakatupuranga Rua Mano	Generation 2000
whanau	family
whanaungatanga	promoting family values

Contributors

Carole Adamson is a Senior Lecturer in social work in the School of Sociology, Social Policy and Social Work, Massey University in New Zealand. She has had extensive experience as a social worker in a range of contexts in mental health. She researches on trauma and critical incidents in the workplace.

Nicola Attwool in the Department of Community and Family Studies, University of Otago. She has researched and published extensively in the area of attachment theory and its relevance in a number of social work contexts.

Marie Connolly is Senior Lecturer and Director of the Te Awatea Violence Research Centre at the Department of Social Work, University of Canterbury, Christchurch, New Zealand. She teaches social work theory and research methodology. Her research interests include sexual offending, reflexive practice, and child and family welfare.

Sharlene Davis is from Ngati Raukawa, Ngati Toa Rangatira, Taranaki and Te Atiawa iwi. Her background is in the health, education and social service sectors, specializing in Maori provider development. With her partner she has recently started her own business, MokoPuna Solutions Limited specializing in workforce development, management and organizational development solutions for Maori and Pacific businesses in the private and not for profit sectors. Her supervision experience spans all three sectors with personnel at varying levels including managers, supervisors, practice/field workers and administration staff in both paid and unpaid professions. She is committed to developing and utilizing cultural models of practice and is currently developing leadership and supervision packages to meet the specific needs of whanau, hapu and tangata whenua in Aotearoa/New Zealand. Sharlene completed her Bachelor of Sociology and Maori in 1995 and is currently studying towards her Masters in Maori Laws and Philosophies at Te Wananga O Raukawa, Otaki.

Nikki Evans lectures in the Department of Social Work at the University of Canterbury, Christchurch, New Zealand. She teaches in the areas of group work, mental health, policy, practice and research. She is currently undertaking a doctoral research project into attachment styles and social supports of adolescents who have sexually abused, and is also a Senior Clinical Worker for the STOP adolescent programme in Christchurch, New Zealand.

Christa Fouché has a passion for research, assessment and making life easier for children in distress. She spent many years as a consultant in private practice and as a lecturer and academic administrator in different programmes at other universities, before joining Massey University. She had been involved in research, development and evaluation of training materials for the assessment of abused and traumatized children as well as people with HIV/AIDS.

Rodger Jack has worked in the statutory and non-government sectors as a social worker, family therapist, supervisor, trainer, counsellor and social service manager. He is accredited as a trainer in strengths-based practice and has written and lectured on strengths-based approaches to practice. He is the project manager of the strengths-based project in the Department of Child, Youth and Family Aotearoa/New Zealand.

Matthew Keen is a psychiatric social worker in acute inpatient mental health services in Palmerston North. Since graduating from Massey University with a BSW Hons, he has primarily worked in a comprehensive range of mental health settings. He reluctantly describes himself as a 'closet' academic who balances his passions for clinical practice and the street-level application of theory with a love of policy and professional discourse, enhanced with a wicked sense of humour.

Tracie Mafile'o is a New Zealand born Tongan and is a lecturer in social work in the School of Sociology, Social Policy and Social Work, Massey University. She is researching Tongan frameworks for social work practice. Tracie has extensive experience in youth work in Australia and New Zealand.

Jane Maidment is currently Head of School of Social Work and Welfare Studies at Central Queensland University, Rockhampton, Australia. During her career in social work she has had an abiding interest in investigating the relationship between theory and practice. Her most recent publication is a co-edited book, *Practice Skills for Social Work in Welfare*.

Robyn Munford has published widely in social and community work and disability studies and research. She is Head of School in the School of Sociology, Social Policy and Social Work at Massey University in New Zealand and Professor of Social Work. Her research on families has gained international recognition.

Mary Nash is a Senior Lecturer in the School of Sociology, Social Policy and Social Work at Massey University in New Zealand. She has researched and published in a variety of social work settings, including social work fields of practice, social work history, spirituality and social work and most recently, migrants and refugees.

266 / SOCIAL WORK THEORIES IN ACTION

Kieran O'Donoghue has worked in probation, community mental health services and was Programme Coordinator for the Diploma of Social Work, Waikato Institute of Technology, New Zealand. He is now the lecturer in the School of Sociology, Social Policy and Social Work at Massey university in New Zealand, where his focus is social work theory and practice together with supervision and fieldwork practice.

Jackie Sanders is a Senior Lecturer in the School of Sociology, Social Policy and Social Work, Massey University. She is currently involved in a number of research and evaluation programmes that focus on family and community wellbeing. Her work makes extensive use of action research methodologies.

Rachael Selby is a New Zealand Maori woman who is a teacher and oral historian. She works within her tribal area of Ngati Raukawa promoting hapu development, economic and social development and higher educational attainment. She is a writer and editor, passionate about recording the stories of Maori people from within her tribal area. She lectures in New Zealand history, social policy and Maori development at Massey University and Te Wananga-o-Raukawa.

Chris Thomas completed a Bachelor of Social Work in 1983 and a Certificate in Social Service Supervision in 1986. Her MSW research is focused on the area of strengths-based supervision. She has worked in a variety of practice contexts including community development, fostering and adoption services and health social work. She has been in private practice as a supervisor for a number of years and has valued working with a diverse range of social service providers predominantly from the non-governmental sector. Chris teaches in the BSW at Massey University and is the Programme Co-ordinator for Clinical Supervision Training offered to supervisors employed by the Department of Child, Youth and Family Services.

Wheturangi Walsh-Tapiata is Maori and currently researching with Maori youth on health and wellbeing and also lectures in social work in the School of Sociology, Social Policy and Social Work, Massey University. Her areas of interest are in teaching and research, community development and indigenous development.

Sue Watson has been a secondary school teacher of English, a literacy/special needs teacher, an adult educator in a prison and is now a lecturer at Massey University College of Education in the Department of Health and Human Development. In 1997 she trained to code the adult attachment interview (AAI) and has since been working with attachment researchers in the USA and Australia and using the AAI with New Zealand populations.

Subject index

Author Index